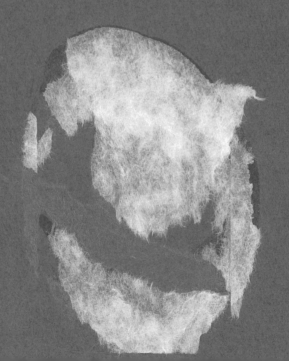

EFFECTIVE SPEECH
FOR THE TEACHER

McGRAW-HILL SERIES IN SPEECH

Glenn E. Mills, *Consulting Editor*

Armstrong and Brandes • The Oral Interpretation of Literature
Baird • American Public Addresses
Baird • Argumentation, Discussion, and Debate
Baird and Knower • Essentials of General Speech
Baird and Knower • General Speech
Black and Moore • Speech: Code, Meaning, and Communication
Carrell and Tiffany • Phonetics
Hahn, Lomas, Hargis, and Vandraegen • Basic Voice Training for Speech
Henning • Improving Oral Communication
Kaplan • Anatomy and Physiology of Speech
Kruger • Modern Debate
Ogilvie • Speech in the Elementary School
Ogilvie and Rees • Communication Skills: Voice and Pronunciation
Powers • Fundamentals of Speech
Robinson and Becker • Effective Speech for the Teacher

EFFECTIVE SPEECH FOR THE TEACHER

KARL F. ROBINSON

ALBERT B. BECKER
Professor of Speech
Western Michigan University

McGRAW-HILL BOOK COMPANY
New York · St. Louis · San Francisco
London · Sydney · Toronto
Mexico · Panama

CARL A. RUDISILL LIBRARY
LENOIR RHYNE COLLEGE

EFFECTIVE SPEECH FOR THE TEACHER

Copyright © 1970 by McGraw-Hill, Inc. All rights reserved.
Printed in the United States of America. No part of this
publication may be reproduced, stored in a retrieval system,
or transmitted, in any form or by any means, electronic,
mechanical, photocopying, recording, or otherwise, without
the prior written permission of the publisher.

Library of Congress Catalog Card Number 74–77558

53184

1 2 3 4 5 6 7 8 9 0   MAMM   7 6 5 4 3 2 1 0 6 9

808.5024
R55e
74885
august, 1971

PREFACE

This book came about as a response to two needs in the area of communication. The first is the need for improved oral communication in the teaching process. Teaching, on whatever level or in whatever subject, is dependent upon sensitive interaction through talking and listening. Too often it is assumed that the interaction will take place if the teacher talks and the student listens—regardless of the manner in which each of these activities takes place. Teaching requires an application of knowledge and principles of speech in specialized ways; so, it will not do to approach speech improvement for teaching by conceiving of the teacher as just another public speaker, as another group leader, as a performer of the spoken word, or as a bright TV personality. In this book the choice of materials and the methods of handling them have been dictated largely by the unique roles of the teacher.

The second need to which this book responds is for a text which focuses on the *improvement* of speech. The user of this text may be a college student or a person who is already teaching. In either case, he needs to know how to go about improving his speech, as well as to have basic information and concepts about speech. The authors have combined their interest in improved teaching with their wide background in working with prospective teachers and teachers in service to offer stimulation and help toward the personal and professional growth of the reader.

To the college instructor who uses this as a text, let us make it clear that this book was written for your students. Many of the things we have said are not new—simply because there is much truth that is still functional that comes to us from the past. On the other hand, much of what we have said may be new to your students, and we are sure that you will wish to supplement with information or ideas of your own.

If the reader knew Karl Robinson, the co-author of this book, he may also know that Karl died before the final draft of the book was completed. All who worked with him came to have great respect and love for him, and such was the case in our relationship. It is my wish, therefore, that he be regarded as the senior author of this book. It was his wish that because of this book, "a higher quality of teacher will result, as well as more articulate leadership in education."

ALBERT B. BECKER

CONTENTS

PART ONE

EFFECTIVE TEACHING
AND SPEECH PROFICIENCY

CHAPTER ONE

SPEECH—AT THE CENTER OF EDUCATION

It is a fair question—if you should ask it—How can the study and practice of speech contribute to my education? You paid your tuition to an institution of higher education so that you might further your education. Now you are enrolled in a speech class. Why? You wanted to overcome your nervousness, your lack of confidence in yourself, your fear of a group? We don't blame you! You wanted to be able to express yourself fluently and have a better command of ideas and language? This is commendable. You wanted to improve your use of voice and diction? That, too, is desirable. But why should you want any or all of these? Will they contribute to what your education should be?

THE KIND OF EDUCATION YOU NEED

To answer the above questions, perhaps you will have to answer another question: What kind of education do I need? We hear much talk about "education for survival"; yes, that is what we need. If man cannot survive, nothing else matters. If life continues at a somewhat normal course, your next thought may be that you need education for success—to become some-body of importance. Many students think that success is having a high-paying job in which there is little work. But the stories of the lives of leaders in education, business, government, and the arts reveal that they worked not less, but more, than the mediocre person. Your years in college ought to teach you to work harder and to work more for a social purpose than you otherwise would. This is one of the assumptions in a democratic society.

PAST, PRESENT, FUTURE

Perhaps in struggling with this question, the idea has come to your mind that you are not considering your needs as being related to one particular time in your life. Actually, your need involves the past, the present, and the future. It involves the past because, in the minds of many educators, educa-tion is a process of passing on the culture of the past to the next generation. Of course, it is important that we have an understanding and appreciation of our heritage. If we know where we have been and how we received what we have, this can guide us to where we are going and what we shall do.

The present, also, figures in your education. While preparing for the future, you are—or should be—a living, active part of the time in which you live. Your achievements now in classes, your activity in campus affairs, your concern regarding social problems, your creativity of thought and talent—all these presage what you will be doing after graduation. College libraries have newspapers and hundreds of magazines and journals because the current scene and new thought are both history in the making and signposts to the future.

And what of that future? Its events are not easily foreseen; its needs are more readily discernible. We shall need manpower for the trades and the professions; we shall need a continued expansion of knowledge—knowledge in the area of living with more and more people, and knowledge of the kind that will not cause us to become enslaved to the technology we are creating; we shall need, therefore, minds that will be disciplined and, at the same time, flexible and free to cope with ever-new events, ideas, and situations.

SELF AND SOCIETY

In considering the kind of education you will need, you can approach it in a second way. How is your education related to yourself and to society? In a democratic society which postulates that human personality should be inviolate and that human beings are "endowed by their Creator with certain inalienable rights," the degree to which you can utilize your potential toward self-fulfillment and to which you can find a satisfying response to life should be an important concern of education. In achieving this, one of your goals will be self-knowledge. While professor of psychiatry at Wayne State University and president of the Highland Park Board of Education, John M. Dorsey wrote: "My belief in the use of the schools is that in them the student shall learn more to appreciate the power of the mind and to discover that he must find what truth is in terms of his own human being. . . . What we cannot acknowledge observing in ourselves we cannot identify with, and we are not ready to work with it."[1] The kind of education you will need, then, is a personal one; it requires that you try to know who you are and for what purpose you exist.

But the founders of our democracy did not envision education as existing for individual life processes; rather, they conceived of it as a necessity for

[1] By permission from John M. Dorsey, "Wisdom," *Michigan Education Journal*, September, 1951, p. 15.

the democratic process.   That is probably the chief reason that our representatives in local, state, and national government are willing to levy taxes and appropriate money for the support of education today.   As one writer has put it, "The purpose of public education in America is that men and women may be so prepared that *life and thought*—thoughtful life and living thought—may come together and play their parts in the common life of free men."

Education for society's purposes is not incompatible with education for the needs of the individual.   This has been well expressed by a United States Commissioner of Education as follows:

> *There is a sense in which American education seems destined to become a major testing ground for democracy, for it is a basic assumption of the democratic political ideal that there is a coincidence of what is good for the individual with what is good for society as a whole.   It is the faith of a free democratic society that when the good of the individual is intelligently pursued, the well-being of the total social order is in some way enhanced.*[2]

Thus, there need be no inconsistency in the concept that the kind of education you need lies both in the development of self as well as in the contribution you can make to society.   For, said John Ruskin, "The training that makes men happiest in themselves makes them of most service to others."

KNOWLEDGE AND BEHAVIOR

Consider now a third aspect of education.   How can education accomplish that two-fold objective?   Two points of view exist in regard to this question.   One is that the student should acquire knowledge; the other is that he should change his behavior.   Knowledge is important, partly because we as human beings enjoy knowing.   It gives us a feeling of being at one with our world; it gives us, also, a sense of power over our environment.   Yet, knowledge is more often sought because it is functional.   A person cannot build a house without knowledge of building materials and of principles of construction.   Neither can he build highways, write a state constitution, rear a family, or care for the health of a community without knowledge.   The premise on which universities are established is that not only should knowledge be

[2] By permission from Sterling M. McMurrin and the *Saturday Review*, "A Crisis of Conscience," *Saturday Review*, Sept. 16, 1961, p. 77.

disseminated, but new knowledge should be constantly sought; hence, the university's role in research.

But your need for education goes beyond the acquisition of knowledge. If, at the beginning of a course, your instructor were to say to you, "This course is meant to change you from what you are into something different," you might look at him with a feeling of resistance or even fear. But ask yourself this question, Why should I spend four years of my life and from $6,000 to $12,000 so that at the end I will be the same as I was before? You see, your need is to be changed. On this point President Arthur T. Hadley of Yale University said, "The purpose of education is to make something out of a man, not put something into him." In direct support of this view John Ruskin wrote, "Education does not mean teaching people; it means teaching them to behave as they do not behave."

This does not discard knowledge; it puts it to work. Instead of having a mind like a museum, where there is nothing but an interesting collection of information, the educated person uses the knowledge as a generating force to help him realize his potential; he uses it also to make a contribution to lives of those about him.

If you have been thinking as you read the above paragraphs, perhaps another idea has bothered you—that what you really came to college for was to improve your *mind*. You might well cling to that idea, especially if you will accept the concept that mind is not something that you are born with; rather, it is the result of your experiences and the cultural pattern in which you have lived. It is the organization of your whole nervous system, and it is expressed in all your behavior—verbal and physical. So improving your mind can be interpreted as meaning the improvement of your reactions to information, to problems, to people, to situations. This reaction will be expressed in what you do, what you write, and what you say.

Now, what is your goal in the process of improving your mind? In other words, what kind of a mind would you like to have? This could call for a lengthy discussion, but here are five characteristics for you to consider:

1 *Alertness:* a mind that is sensitive to perceptions and ideas; a mind that is ready to respond
2 *Useful habits:* a mind which habitually sees the whole; a mind that habitually sees things as neither all white nor all black; a mind that habitually looks for more than one cause for an effect; a mind that habitually seeks more evidence; a mind that habitually takes into account emotional involvement

3 *Desirable values:* a mind that puts a high premium on the truth; a mind that values people and personality above things; a mind that places the greater good ahead of the lesser; a mind that has the long view
4 *Flexibility:* a mind that can adapt to reality; a mind that can accept that which cannot be changed, that can deal effectively with that which can be changed, and that has the wisdom to know the difference
5 *Freedom:* a mind at liberty to use information available to it

SPEECH AND EDUCATION

Thus far we have been saying much about your educational needs, but little about speech; so now let us look at speech against the backdrop of education in general. As we did with education, we shall look at it in terms of: (1) past, present, and future; (2) self and society; (3) knowledge and behavior.

PAST, PRESENT, FUTURE

Speech, more than any other discipline, has its roots deep in the past. Education, as we know it, began in Egypt, Greece, and Rome through the study and practice of public discourse. It was *the* "core" subject. Teachers and writers on rhetoric (public address) urged their pupils to be informed in all branches of knowledge: history, literature, mathematics, and politics. Just as our physical makeup is a result of a "stream of heredity" and just as our concept of what America is includes what it has been from its beginnings, so our appreciation of what speech means in education must include the past. Nor should you overlook the fact that your own speech now is the product of your past.

Speech has a tremendous significance in your present life. The invention of the printing press has been a great aid to civilized man, but the value of speech has not declined. With the advent of talking pictures, radio, and television, we find ourselves flooded with a sea of spoken words. We can write letters and issue statements, publish books, circulate magazines, and distribute daily issues of newspapers; yet we still engage in conversation at all hours of the day, have committee meetings and staff meetings, go to conventions, and depend on legislative sessions and meetings of various bodies of the United Nations to carry on effectively the work of the world. It has always been true that when the needs are pressing and the issues of life are sharp, men meet in face-to-face situations and use speech for communication.

It is no less true in education. We need textbooks and libraries, but the classroom is still the heart of the instructional system. In that classroom speech is the only tool that is absolutely essential. It is the means of explaining, of questioning, of interaction of minds. There you have the opportunity, as a student, to formulate what you think and to test your ideas with your listeners. You will not become educated merely by being a sponge.

Can speech contribute to your educational needs for the future? Answer this question for yourself. How can it function in your making a vocational contribution to society—which has provided so much for you? How can speech and listening aid in your acquiring and passing on knowledge? How can speech—how must speech—be the agent by which people are able to live together in a family, in a community, and in one world? How can speech be involved in developing minds that are disciplined and flexible in order that we may be able to adapt to changing times in a changing world and to resolve satisfactorily the problems that arise from change? Mentor Graham, Lincoln's teacher, is said to have advised him, "The right words can change the world."

SELF AND SOCIETY

Turning now to view speech in terms of education for the self and for society, it is not difficult to note the implications. "Know thyself" is an important admonition to us today, just as it was to the ancient Greeks. Through speech we learn about ourselves in two ways: We have reflected back to us from others the image they have of us; by self-listening we can discover more clearly the quality of our thinking and the values we hold. Since, as was noted earlier, the kind of education is a personal one (we "must find what truth is in terms of our own human being"), and since speech is the surest way of revealing ourselves, then speech becomes central in our efforts toward self-fulfillment.

But speech is also central in education as it pertains to society. "Speech is the great medium through which human cooperation is brought about. It is the means by which the diverse activities of men are co-ordinated and correlated with each other for the attainment of common and reciprocal ends."[3] In a democratic society we counsel together, we conduct "hearings,"

[3] Grace de Laguna, *Speech: Its Function and Development*, Indiana University Press, Bloomington, Ind., 1963, p. 19.

we speak from the public platform or by radio and television in advocacy of or in opposition to proposals. There the knowledge possessed by the participants, their habits of mind, their ability to think—their rational powers—come to focus when they speak. An education, then, which omits the development of effective speech is like an automobile which has been well-designed, assembled out of quality parts, and then put on the market without wheels. Unless our self-development is going somewhere, society does not benefit.

KNOWLEDGE AND BEHAVIOR

Our third consideration is the role of speech in education for knowledge and education for behavior. A cynic might ask, How can speech development contribute to my knowledge? There are two answers. One is that speech has content within itself; there is considerable to know about such subjects as audience analysis, selection and arrangement of ideas, the oral use of language, the psychology of attention and listening, communication theory, the physics of sound, phonetics, the physiology of speech, and the meaning of gesture. The subject area widens when one includes the application of speech to acting and play production, radio and television, studies of rhetoric and public address, discussion and debate, interpretative reading, speech correction, and other fields.

The other answer is that when people intend to speak, they are motivated to acquire knowledge in other fields. A good actor studies more than the play in which he is acting; a public speaker does research on the subject of his speech; a debater studies the subject for debate more intensively than many lawmakers do; a clergyman draws upon wide reading and observation for his sermons. Speech, therefore, is the activating agent for the acquisition of knowledge.

Even though the study and use of speech contributes greatly to one's knowledge, there are even greater rewards in the area of changing behavior. After all, speech is behavior—a kind of behavior which makes us human. It takes but a little reflection to realize that the people whose behavior you understand best are those with whom you have talked a great deal. Ben Johnson once wrote, ". . . speak that I might see thee." Listening to a person speak is a highly useful way of learning how he sees himself and how he relates to others. Bonaro Overstreet shows this relationship by saying: "The fact is that our capacity to build a life which is whole and sound is closely tied up with our capacity to talk sense. . . . Our words . . . must be fitting—which is to say they must serve their basic purpose of building relationships between the otherwise isolated self and the world surrounding that self."[4]

Thus, we see in a person's speech his image of himself; we see his reactions to associates; we see his emotions; we see his mind at work.   In applying this truth to yourself, you are now faced with the hard reality that improving your speech means a change in your behavior.   However, this need not be frightening, for your instructor does not intend to take you all apart and put you together again.   It does mean some changed points of view, more sensitivity to your environment, some new habits to replace old ones, some better means of handling emotions, more skills in oral presentation of ideas, new or better skills in the use of language, greater ability to relate yourself to your listeners, and better listening for varied purposes.

Naturally, if all you want is a certain number of hours of credit, the above paragraph does not pertain to you.   On the other hand, if you wish to make something of yourself and take an educated person's role in our society, you will be glad for the opportunity to follow those suggestions.   This will require initiative on your part, coupled with self-discipline and effort.   If you are willing to give these, the kind of education you need will be yours in a large part through your study and development in speech.

[4] By permission from Bonaro Overstreet, "The Power to Verbalize," *National Parent-Teacher*, vol. 47, pp. 22–24, January, 1953.

FOR FURTHER READING

Braden, Waldo W., ed.: *Speech Methods and Resources*, Harper & Row, Publishers, Inc., New York, 1961, chap. 2.

Dance, Frank E. X., ed.: *Human Communication Theory*, Holt, Rinehart and Winston, Inc., New York, 1967, pp. 264–287.

Mead, Margaret: *The School in American Culture*, Harvard University Press, Cambridge, 1964.

Montagu, Ashley: *On Being Intelligent*, Abelard-Schuman, Ltd., New York, 1951, chap. 1.

Reid, Ronald F., ed.: *Introduction to the Field of Speech*, Scott, Foresman and Company, Chicago, 1965, chaps. 1, 14, 15.

Sarett, Alma Johnson, Lew Sarett, and William T. Foster: *Basic Principles of Speech,* 4th ed., Houghton Mifflin Company, Boston, 1966, chap. 1.

Whitehead, Alfred North: *The Aims of Education*, The Macmillan Company, New York 1927.

CHAPTER TWO

THE NATURE OF YOUR SPEECH

The purpose of this chapter is to explain the nature and function of speech and to help you evaluate your own speech in its present state. Perhaps you have already drawn some conclusions about your own speech proficiency from your experience and from the comments of former teachers, members of your family, and friends. A new look now might clarify your concept of speech, as well as produce a more accurate appraisal of your own speech needs. Then you will be ready to improve it—if you care to.

THE SPEECH ACT

SPEECH AS A MEANS OF COMMUNICATION

Speech belongs to the general class of activities known as *communication*. This word has its root in the Old French verb *communer*, which is translated, "to put in common." To communicate, therefore, means to make that which one knows common to others; in other words, it is sharing with others that which is primarily one's own. We can do this by means of pictures, numbers, special signs, words, etc.

Speech is one of the specific means of communication; it is made up of conventionalized sounds and visual cues. The sounds are called oral language; the visual cues are the movements of any part of the body or the whole body. This means that speech includes the language of visible actions as well as the language of the spoken word. In the individual, as well as in the race, man learned to speak before he learned to draw pictures, write, or use the typewriter. He learned to speak by using the air in his lungs, the valve at the top of his windpipe, and other organs and muscles that were originally intended for maintaining life.

Using his organs and muscles, early man discovered that he could share with other men his discomforts, his satisfactions, his information, and his attitudes. Doing so required a code that could be understood by his fellows. So he would *represent* his perceptions or the state of his mind by signs—verbal or nonverbal; thus began the use of symbols—those things created by human beings to represent or suggest other things. Then a man could signify that he caught two fish simply by showing two fingers; he would not have to produce the fish, unless his veracity was in question.

Then, too, a person could summon another person without going to him and pulling him to the place where he was wanted. One who had traveled for a day could symbolize to a listener where he had been and what he had seen, thus saving the other person a trip.

SPEECH AS BEHAVIOR

Speech, then, is a form of symbolic behavior. Behavior is usually thought of as the way in which a person reacts to various stimuli. Anything he does is a part of his behavior, and his speech is a highly significant way of behaving. It expresses through the symbols of words, voice changes, facial expression, and gesture such things as our perceptions of the world about us, our emotions, our desires, our intents, our beliefs. To see this in sharp relief, compare the actions of a dog in a fight with the behavior of an island dictator who is threatened. The dog engages the other dog with nail and fang. When the fight is over, he finds a comfortable place, lies down, licks his wounds, and takes a nap. The dictator, for his fight, orders a big rally, stands before some microphones, and for a period of two hours symbolizes many of the things the dog was doing in the fight.

Our ability to interpret the facts and events in our environment, as well as our ability to live in a satisfying way with others and with ourselves, depends a great deal upon our knowledge of and our proficiency in the use of symbols. Since this is done more through speaking and listening than in any other way, our speech attitudes, habits, and skills become of prime importance.

BASIC ELEMENTS

An analysis of the speech act reveals that there are four basic elements involved. They are sketched briefly below.

Thought: the speaker's motive, his purpose, his central idea, the arrangement of ideas, the support for statements, significance of ideas, deciding what should be said and what should not be said, etc.

Language: the range of vocabulary, word choice, acceptability of usage, the level of usage, the degree of abstraction, style, fluency, etc.

Voice: strength, quality, pitch level, inflection, intensity, tempo, use of variety, articulation, pronunciation, etc.

Action: general bodily tonus, posture, movement, gesture, facial expression, etc.

YOUR SPEECH DEVELOPMENT

Your speech is a part of your total development—physical, mental, emotional, social. As such, it is dependent, originally, upon the body you inherited. Nature provided you with certain characteristics in your lungs, breathing muscles, trachea, cartilages, and muscles—to say nothing of your whole nervous system, your glands, etc. It is with these that you will express yourself with oral and visual language.

LEARNING TO SPEAK

All the above came into play when you uttered your birth cry—regarded by some speech authorities as the baby's first speech effort. Later you discovered that the sounds made by forcing air through the aperture between your vocal bands could be modified by the lips and tongue, that the tone could be raised or lowered, and that it could take on a different quality by different uses of the vocal cavities. Hearing became involved as you found yourself enjoying certain sounds; hence, they were repeated. So, what began as random activity became perceived by you and then became somewhat consciously directed.

Along with the above activity, people entered the picture; your parents were making noises, too. Your ears and eyes became the avenues of social influence upon your speech. Your parents expressed pleasure at the sounds you made and perhaps imitated them. This stimulated you to repeat them. Then they made some sounds you had *not* made; hearing them, you were stimulated to reproduce what you had heard. Thus began your instruction in speech. You became an imitator of the person(s) who listened to you and talked to you; you knew nothing else about speech. To this day your speech bears the imprint of those first models, and the same thing will happen to your own children.

As you became older, your speech—like the rest of your behavior—became shaped by the approval or disapproval of other people. Some words or manners of speaking were accepted; others were rejected. It is not surprising, therefore, that now you are using certain speech reactions, words, and phrases that were a part of your early social environment. In realizing this, you should not blame your parents or others with whom you were closely associated—in case you think you have some of their "faults" of speech; rather, simply recognize how you acquired them and proceed from there.

SPEECH AND PERSONALITY

Other influences entered into your speech development. As you felt needs and desires, you used speech as a means of satisfying them. If your kind of speech succeeded, it was repeated on a later occasion, gradually becoming habituated. If it did not succeed, you probably reacted emotionally or you tried a different kind of speech. As your personality developed, certain traits began to appear. You became more emotional or less emotional; you became more dominant or more submissive; you became more confident or more self-conscious or fearful; you adopted a variety of attitudes and beliefs.

With development in personality came corresponding developments in your speech. The thoughts you uttered, the language you used, the pattern of your voice, and your physical manner all reflected in some way the kind of person you were becoming. Many of your experiences made a strong impact upon you, thus influencing your speech behavior. As you became aware of your own individuality—your uniqueness as a person different from other persons—you developed a sense of *self*. Your ego became significant in your relations with others. So, in your experiences, particularly your social experiences, your ego became affirmed or it became hurt. Your self-regard became heightened, making you more self-confident, or it became lowered, making you fearful or self-conscious—depending upon the circumstances. So, now, you may be able to recall situations in which you were shamed, frightened, angered; or you were made to feel strong, able, understanding.

The degree to which you have poise and confidence in speech situations now is a result of the conditioning you have experienced. The adjustment you are able to make depends upon the attitudes you have toward yourself as a speaker and those you have toward those who listen to you. If your attitudes are hindering a free and effective expression of yourself, the first step in changing these attitudes lies in understanding the experiences that caused you to acquire them.

EXPERIENCES—THEIR IMPACT

Some of these experiences, as we have pointed out, occur in the home. The relationship of parents with each other and the kind of talk they have with each other exert a profound influence upon their children's feelings and their speech. If the parents are considerate of each other and use speech that is intended to understand the other person, this pattern is readily picked up by the child.   Sad to say, the converse is also true.   The attitudes of parents toward their children is the other important factor.   Many children suffer from the attitude that children "are to be seen but not heard."   In a paper dealing with his speech background, a student wrote: "Between my father and my mother, they can and do take up 90 percent of any conversation participated in. . . ."   Another student wrote: "I can remember the fear I had talking to my father.   At this time the family situation was not a pleasant one. . . . It seemed that I was always trying to talk to Father at this time, but it seemed there would be a negative response given by him to what I said.   Most of the time he would not even take the time to hear me out.   At times he would even become violent."   Contrast those statements with another: "I have never had any speech difficulties.   In my home we were always free to speak."   These examples illustrate how home experiences condition us and shape the attitudes with which we meet speech situations.

Some of these experiences occur in school.   That is the place where parents hope their children's mental and social growth will progress faster and further than it would otherwise.   Many of the activities inside and outside the classroom and in the student's relationship with his teachers and administrators result in positive speech development; many times they seem to have little effect; often they have a harmful effect.   If you look back upon your own speech experiences in school, you can undoubtedly connect some of your present speech proficiencies or deficiencies with incidents there.   It might have been the kind of motivation you had for speaking in class or in special speaking events; it could have been the kind of reward given for success or the penalty inflicted for failure; the kinds of standards set by teachers or coaches could have been the influential factor in the experience. Studies show that many of the speech fears of college students had their origin in the elementary school, in junior high school, or in high school. In that case other undesirable aspects of personality and speech could also have had their beginnings in school; but desirable ones could have been developed there, also.

SELF-STUDY

You have now seen how your speech has developed and are aware of some of the factors which have played a part in making it what it is now.   You will find it helpful for your own view of your speech, as well as for your instructor, if you write what might be called a "biography" of your speech. No doubt you could do this better at the end of the course, but do the best you can with your present understanding of speech and its backgrounds.

Approach it with the question: From the beginning of my life until now, what people, what circumstances, what experiences have had an influence on my speech, and in what way?

It would be desirable, also, at this point to take an inventory of your speech. This can be done in two ways: (1) an evaluation of your speech equipment; (2) an evaluation of your speech skills. Evaluation of your speech equipment involves taking stock of the means or potential that you have to work with. In evaluating yourself on the items listed below, much will depend upon your own estimate; however, in some cases you might want to confer with some other person, including your instructor. Keep in mind certain facts about your medical history, as well as scores on tests you may have taken in the past.

YOUR SPEECH EQUIPMENT

(Check the column which represents your best self-evaluation.)

	GOOD	FAIR	POOR
1 *Thought* (mentality)			
a Sensory perception (ears, eyes, etc.)			
b Intelligence			
c High school grades			
d Background of knowledge			
e Memory (accuracy, length)			
f Listening (comprehension)			
g Listening (critical, creative)			
Specific comment:			
2 *Language*			
a Vocabulary (recognition)			
b Vocabulary (oral)			
c Grammar and usage			
d Fluency			
Specific comment:			
3 *Voice*			
a Larynx, throat			
b Mouth, nose			
c Strength of tone			
d Pitch: level, range, variety			
e Quality			
f Rate, rhythm			
g Articulation			

	GOOD	FAIR	POOR
h Pronunciation Specific comment:			

4. *Physical action*
  a   Physical build (height, weight, etc.)
  b   Limbs, organs, etc.
  c   Posture
  d   Facial expression
  e   Strength and grace of movement
  f   General health and vitality
Specific comment:			

YOUR SPEECH SKILLS

Consider now your ability to *use* your speech equipment.   The question here is: How effectively can you apply what you possess to five different kinds of speech situations?   These are sometimes called *forms* of speech. The ones chosen are those which are most frequently engaged in by teachers.   In each case, you should place a check mark under the heading which you believe is characteristic of your skill, using the last one for any explanation you wish to make.   It might be useful to check what you think is your skill in a particular form *before* studying it and participating in some practice; then check it again *following* the study and practice.

	GOOD	FAIR	POOR	EXPLANATION

1   *Conversation*
  a   Situations:
      Family
      Friends
      Strangers
      Different age level
  b   Special factors:
      Motives
      Interest in people
      Listening
      Techniques				

2   *Discussion*
  a   Types:
      Round table (committee)
      Panel (before audience)				

	GOOD	FAIR	POOR	EXPLANATION

      Forum (in large groups)
      Parliamentary
b   Special factors:
      Leadership
      Thinking with others
      Listening
      Objectivity

3 *Group leadership*
  a Situations:
      Own age level
      Older age group
      Younger age group
      Group of own sex
      Group of both sexes
  b Special factors:
      Poise
      Flexibility
      Listening
      Use of questions
      Response of members

4 *Exposition*
  a Situations:
      Informal
      Formal
      Own age level
      Older age level
      Younger age group
  b Special factors:
      Selecting materials
      Patterning ideas
      Being interesting
      Adaptability

5 *Oral reading*
  a Situations:
      Single person
      Small, informal group
      Large group, own age
      Large group, younger
  b. Special factors:
      Knowing materials
      Recreating ideas
      Responsiveness
      Sense of audience

YOUR SPEECH GOALS

It may seem that the above list presents a formidable task in speech improvement. It might be helpful, therefore, to focus on a few central goals. In a study of the speech characteristics of superior and inferior high school teachers, it was found that the following ten speech qualities correlated with effectiveness in teaching (listed in order of degree of correlation).[1]

1   *The ability to explain things well:* making points clear; keeping ideas in a helpful order; avoiding irrelevant material
2   *Being direct and communicative:* adapting material to the listener; keeping individuals in mind; being informal and enthusiastic
3   *Having poise:* being emotionally stable; being patient and understanding; being confident and positive
4   *Having an expressive voice:* ability to emphasize or highlight certain ideas; having variety of voice quality, pitch, intensity, and tempo; using a suitable rate
5   *Being intelligent and wise:* having a sense of what is important; knowing the subject matter; being broadminded and fair
6   *Using appropriate physical behavior:* having an expressive face; having a pleasing appearance; using meaningful gestures; having an appropriate posture
7   *Being easily heard and understood:* having a habit of speaking clearly and distinctly; using appropriate loudness; altering the loudness when occasion demands it
8   *Being a likeable person:* possessing a sense of humor; being friendly and warm; being sincere and natural
9   *Having a pleasant voice:* using a tone that is vibrant and colorful; using a pitch level that does not annoy; having a soft and friendly quality
10 *Having the ability to use language well:* using language that is clear and interesting; having fluency and ease in language use; employing acceptable grammar and usage

These cannot be achieved for you by your speech teacher; nor can they be achieved in your speech class alone. They can be achieved to a considerable extent *by you*—through the utilization of all your classes, all your reading and study, all your associations with people, and all your experiences. For "Any man who is educated," said Mark Hopkins, "is self-educated."

---

[1] Albert B. Becker, "The Speech Characteristics of Superior and Inferior High School Teachers," unpublished doctoral dissertation, Northwestern University, Evanston, Ill., 1949.

FOR FURTHER READING

Association For Supervision and Curriculum Development, N.E.A.: *Perceiving, Behaving, Becoming*, National Education Association, Washington, 1962, chaps. 2 and 3.

Black, John W. and Wilbur E. Moore: *Speech: Code, Meaning, and Communication*, McGraw-Hill Book Company, New York, 1955, chap. 1.

Brown, Charles T. and Charles Van Riper: *Speech and Man*, Prentice-Hall, Inc., Englewood Cliffs, N.J., 1966, chap. 3.

Bryngelson, Bryng: *Personality Development Through Speech*, T. S. Denison & Co., Inc., Minneapolis, 1964.

Eisenson, Jon, J. J. Auer, and J. V. Irwin: *The Psychology of Communication*, Appleton-Century-Crofts, Inc., New York, 1963, chaps. 1–3.

Frankl, Viktor: *Man's Search For Meaning*, Washington Square Press, New York, 1963.

Gray, Miles W. and Claude M. Wise: *The Bases of Speech*, 3d ed., Harper & Row, Publishers, Inc., New York, 1959, p. 24–37.

Hopkins, L. Thomas: *The Emerging Self in School and Home*, Harper & Row, Publishers, Inc., New York, 1954.

Rahskopf, Horace E.: *Basic Speech Improvement*, Harper & Row, Publishers, Inc., New York, 1965, chaps. 1 and 2.

Sarett, Alma Johnson, Lew Sarett, and William T. Foster: *Basic Principles of Speech*, 4th ed., Houghton Mifflin Company, Boston, 1969, chap. 3.

PART TWO

IMPROVING
SPEECH ESSENTIALS

CHAPTER THREE

IDEAS AND THINKING

An idea is a concept that results from conscious thought. It may be an impression, an image, an opinion, or a belief. Thinking is purposeful mental activity engaged in to find the answer to a question or to satisfy a curiosity. Thinking, therefore, is the process; ideas are the product.

As a teacher, you will deal with ideas during every hour of the day. The more significant they are and the more pertinent they are to the growth of your students, the more effective will be your teaching. If you conceive of your task as being the development of disciplined, creative minds in your students, then the quality of *your* thinking—and, therefore, your ideas— becomes of paramount importance to you.

The quality of your mind will be apparent to your students chiefly through what you say to them. Your speech can be no better than your ideas. That is the reason for the advice: Think twice before you speak, especially if you are going to say what you think. Improved thinking, then, will result in better speech; but good speech improvement should also result in better thought. Then your speech will become "better than silence."

THINKING AND THE TEACHER

FOR INSTRUCTIONAL EFFICIENCY

A teacher working with from twenty to forty minds and dealing with a variety of subject matter each day is quite aware of the continued need for information, as well as the ability to use this information to good effect in his thinking. The best possible use of thinking is needed for the purposeful planning that must be adapted to each group and situation. It is required if lectures or explanations have meaning for the varied types of mentalities receiving them. It is called upon in the leading of discussions and in giving an opinion. It is demanded when evaluation is needed— whether it be of the pupil's or the teacher's efforts. It should be present when discipline problems arise or when an individual pupil needs counseling.

FOR STUDENTS' OBSERVATION

A teacher would rarely say, "Now this is the way I think." He doesn't have to. Students become aware, consciously or unconsciously, of how a teacher's mind works whether he wills it or not.   They note what he considers important; they see how he solves problems as they arise; they feel satisfaction with orderly sequences or frustration with haphazard ones.   They sense that they are being led by a fertile, creative mind or by one that is rutted or unimaginative.

FOR PERSONAL GROWTH

As a person, you have desires for self-fulfillment at the highest possible level.   That means you wish to expand your capacity to understand, to increase your efficiency in solving the problems of living, to grow in your ability to adapt to whatever your environment may be.   Therefore, a great part of your satisfaction with life will come from establishing better attitudes and habits of mind.

FOR STATUS AMONG PEERS

Too often a teacher is thought of in his community as a person who may know the contents of certain books but is not sought after as a person who can deal with problems outside the classroom.   If a teacher has a good mind, he is needed in connection with school affairs and professional issues. Likewise, community organizations and civic groups should profit by having members who can think.   If your education has made you a better thinker, you should have some prestige with your peers, both in your profession and among other adults in the community.

HOW WE THINK

KINDS OF THINKING

It will aid your understanding of thinking if you are aware of the different kinds of thinking.   The kinds differ according to purpose, but their processes vary also.   Even though there is this differentiation, one kind might merge into another.   Also, it is likely that more than one kind would be used in any session of thought.

DAYDREAMING. This is sometimes called "reverie" or "content of consciousness."   It is usually an uninhibited free play of ideas, therefore without conscious purpose.   Taking their own course, our ideas will be determined by personal intangibles.   These would include our likes and dislikes, our loves and hates, our desires, our hopes, and our fears.   So when a person says to you while you are daydreaming, "A penny for your thoughts," he would buy at a ridiculous price some of the most intimate aspects of your personality.

Even though there is no pattern in daydreaming, it can be useful.   If you were to retrace all the ideas that went through your mind during one period—e.g., while driving a car alone between two cities—you could discover some of your real ambitions, problems you fail to face up to, your points of insecurity, your feelings about certain people.   Thus, an analysis of your daydreaming could make it an asset to you.

Daydreaming can be of value in another way.   Because it is uninhibited, it gives free flight to the imagination, which is a necessary factor in achievement.   A trip to the moon was considered to be idle fancy not so long ago, but not so today.   To make present trips possible, someone had to dream about it.   Daydreaming, then, can be the prelude to positive action; but daydreaming that always leads to simply more daydreaming can be a detriment to mental health.

CRITICAL THINKING.   The central purpose of this kind of thinking is to *evaluate.*   It subjects ideas to careful scrutiny, to determine whether they are true or false.   Thus, it involves making judgments, and as such it is often considered to be synonymous with intelligence.   It is interesting to note that the word *intelligent* is derived from the Latin verb, *intelligere,* which is derived from *inter* (between) and *legere* (to choose).   Thus, literally, the meaning of intelligent is the ability to choose well.   The critical thinker perceives the difference between the good and the bad, between values that are transient and those that are permanent, between genuineness and superficiality, between the relevant and the irrelevant, between unsupported beliefs and those founded in fact.

Watson and Glaser, in their *Critical Thinking Appraisal Manual,* list three things that are involved in critical thinking:

1   *attitudes of inquiry that involve an ability to recognize the existence of problems and an acceptance of the general need for evidence in support of what is asserted to be true;*
2   *knowledge of the nature of valid inferences, abstractions, and generalizations in which the weight or accuracy of different kinds of evidence are logically determined; and*

3   *skills in employing and applying the above attitudes and knowledge.*[1]

What are some of the typical situations requiring critical thinking?   A juryman is always confronted with the question: Do the facts and testimony as presented indicate the innocence or the guilt of the defendant? A member of an audience evaluates a speaker's ideas, his support for those ideas, his sincerity, and his purpose.   We need critical thinking whenever we make a judgment or a decision.   A prospective car buyer evaluates the type of car, its particular features, and its performance against the price that is asked for it.   In selecting a textbook a teacher must decide to what extent this book will make a desirable contribution to the education of his pupils.

CREATIVE THINKING.   The purpose behind this kind of thinking is to produce an idea that did not exist before—at least not in relation to the present need.   Its basic element is imagination.   The word indicates that we use images of what we have previously observed to arrive at a new image (idea).   The inventor of the windshield washer on an automobile did not use any new materials; but he put a jar or a bag, some tubes, and vent all together and arrived at something new.

A curious mind always has the possibility of creating new knowledge through having the yeast of curiosity.   James Harvey Robinson pointed this out when he wrote: "... this kind of meditation begets knowledge, and knowledge is really creative inasmuch as it makes things look different from what they seemed before and may indeed work for their reconstruction."[2]   He noted the fact that a person does not indulge in creative thinking unless he has curiosity—that "idle curiosity" (seemingly idle to other people) which asks questions about things and which may lead to discovery through a systematic examination of them.   Robinson gave the example of the seventeen-year-old Galileo watching the swinging lamps as he sat in the cathedral of his native town.   He wondered whether or not a long oscillation would take the same time as a short one, and he timed them with his pulse.   Robinson then pointed out:

This observation, however remarkable in itself, was not enough to produce

---

[1] Goodwin Watson and Edward M. Glaser, *Watson-Glaser Critical Thinking Appraisal Manual,* Harcourt, Brace & World, Inc., New York, 1964, p. 10.

[2] James Harvey Robinson, *The Mind in the Making,* Harper & Row, Publishers, Incorporated, New York, 1921, p. 49.

a really creative thought.   Others may have noticed the same thing and yet nothing came of it.   Most of our observations have no assignable results.   To be really creative, ideas have to be worked up and then put over so that they become a part of man's social heritage.   The highly accurate pendulum clock was one of the later results of Galileo's discovery. He himself was led to reconsider and successfully to refute the old notions of falling bodies.[3]

There seems to be considerable agreement that there are four steps in the process of creative thought.   They are:

1 *The preparation stage.*   This involves surveying the problem, or looking the situation over, followed by making a specific statement of the problem, probably in the form of a question.   It utilizes the motives of the person who is thinking, as well as his knowledge of images and ideas relevant to what he is seeking.

2 *The incubation stage.*   In this stage the person may seemingly drop the subject from conscious attention, but apparently some kind of unconscious thought takes place.

3 *The illumination stage.*   This is the moment of sudden insight, the arrival of the bright idea.   There is no predicting it, but it usually comes when the individual is not forcing himself to think.

4 *The evaluation stage.*   Here the thinker will examine what he has, critically, and may decide to stop, with the feeling that this is it, or he may revise or refine what he has done.

Here is a problem which confronted a United Nations committee.   In its new building one room was to be designated as a "meditation room."   This room was to be open to representatives of all of the member nations; it was to be suitable, therefore, for members of practically any race or religious faith, as well as for any person not identified with a religious faith.   It was felt that there should be some symbol or symbols at the front of the room. What would be appropriate?   Whether you think about this alone or with a group of persons, you are likely to go through all of the four steps in the creative thinking process.

Before leaving the subject of creative thinking, a word should be said about what is called "re-creative thinking."   This is a necessary part of any interpretation of music, drama, poetry, prose—anything which was the result of

[3] *Ibid.*, p. 53.

another person's creative thinking. It may not involve the above steps in just the same way that the creator used them, but it requires that the reader, listener, or observer walk the way of the creator in order to appreciate adequately what he is trying to interpret for others. It is this lack of effort to enter into the mind of the original writer or artist that produces so much hollow mouthing of the words when people repeat such passages as the Lord's Prayer, "The Gettysburg Address," and the Beatitudes. We note it, too, when we hear quoted such familiar sentences as "To thine own self be true," "As a man thinketh in his heart, so is he," and "Give me liberty or give me death."

PROBLEM SOLVING. Even though problem solving may be considered as the application of critical thinking and creative thinking to a specific question or situation, we shall deal with it separately. The purpose behind problem solving is usually to find a procedure for doing something. For example, solving the following problem is essentially finding a procedure.

> Suppose you were given an empty 5-gallon can and an empty 3-gallon can, neither of which has any graduated markings on it. You are asked to go down to the lake and bring back exactly 4 gallons of water. How would you do it?

The statement of a problem generally begins with the word How or the word What. We ask, How can I get better grades? How can I get all of my work done? How should I teach this unit of study? Or we ask, What is the best curriculum for me to pursue? What should be done to improve labor organizations? or What training should be required for certain teaching certificates?

The central factor in problem solving is the choice of alternatives. A person who thinks a great deal finds many alternatives. You will know a good thinker by the quality of those alternatives that come to his mind. You can detect the pattern of a person's thinking by the similarity of the alternatives that he presents in various problem-solving situations. For example, the religious fanatic may have one answer to all social and moral problems; the man on the street thinks "there ought to be a law"; some teachers believe that the home is the solution to most of their problems with pupils; and some parents think the schools should have all the answers. These seem to be extremes, but just consider how often we think that the answer to any problem is another committee—or how often we say, "If I just had more money, everything would be all right."

In connection with problem solving one hears much about the "scientific method." While much *critical* thinking is involved here, the word *method* implies that again there is concern with procedure. In *Your Most Enchanted Listener*, Wendell Johnson says that there are four basic steps in the scientific method: question, observation, report, conclusion. A more elaborate exposition of the scientific method is presented by Stuart Chase in *The Proper Study of Mankind*. "The Scientific Method in Action," he says, is as follows:

1 *Eliminate human emotions or feelings.*
2 *State clearly the problem to be solved.*
3 *Formulate a hypothesis based on exploration and classification of available evidence.*
4 *Test the hypothesis by experiments and observation.*
5 *Relate the verified hypothesis to other knowledge.*
6 *Compare only facts of the same order.*
7 *Continue to suspect the findings, making changes if necessary.*
8 *Consider no propositions as self-evident.*
9 *Make final decisions based on observation and experiment on the non-verbal level rather than on logic.*
10 *State conclusions honestly, without slanting or bias.*[4]

It can be seen that Chase's steps are similar to Johnson's, with the addition of the concept of objectivity and that of suspending judgment. Thus, the scientific method, in essence, is the honest use of careful procedure.

THE PROCESS OF THINKING

Now that we have seen the forms in which man thinks, according to his purpose, let us look at the psychological processes that take place as we try to think. We shall consider these processes from the aspects of the tools employed and the use of patterns.

THE TOOLS EMPLOYED

MUSCLES. In considering the process of thinking, we must regard it not as something which takes place in the brain alone, but rather throughout

---

[4] By permission from Stuart Chase, *The Proper Study of Mankind*, Harper & Row, Publishers, Incorporated, New York, 1948, pp. 20–22.

the whole body.   We have a concept for this which we call "the mind."
Ashley Montagu defines mind as follows: "Mind represents the expression of
the social organization of the nervous elements of the whole body."[5]
Laboratory tests have shown that when a person "thinks" raising his arm,
the muscles in that arm contract even though he doesn't actually raise it.
Likewise, the speech muscles contract when a person thinks the word *ball*.
Muscle action, then, is often a concomitant of thinking, but it would not
be safe to say that it is a necessary factor in all thinking.   When Rodin
made the statue of "Le Penseur," he made him appear to be motionless;
however, an examination of it reveals that there is muscle tension throughout
the man's body.

One may conclude, therefore, that with much of our thinking, muscle action
occurs.   In many instances it seems to help thinking—just how, we are
not prepared to say.   But since thinking is done with our mind, which
includes our total nervous mechanism, it would appear reasonable that we
should think with all of ourselves.

IMAGES.   In the classical Greek language *idea* and *image* were the same
word, *icon*, which is translated as *idol*.   This is somewhat consistent with
the definition of *image*—representations of things which are not present to
the senses.   To say that they are "mental pictures" is a bit misleading, since
we may have images of hearing, touch, temperature, taste, smell, pressure,
etc.   One has no image about a thing unless he has had experience with it;
therefore, the image is the memory of the original sensation.   Even though
images do not closely correspond with the original sensation, we use them
for many kinds of thinking.   In *The Art of Thinking*, Dimnet says, "Inevitably people will reveal in their thoughts and speeches, in their outlook on
life and in their lives themselves, the quality of the images filling their
minds."[6]   Consider the images in the mind of a chef as he considers a menu;
note the possible images in the mind of the mechanic as he listens to the
unwanted noises in your car.   However, since there are no images for abstractions, it is necessary to consider a third tool used for thinking.

LANGUAGE.   This is your most useful tool for thinking; in fact, thinking
may be regarded as "talking to oneself."   And many times it is easier to
think if you have someone to whom you can verbalize a problem; then you

[5] Ashley Montagu, *On Being Intelligent*, Abelard-Schuman, Limited, New York, 1951, p. 6.
[6] Ernst Dimnet, *The Art of Thinking*, Simon and Schuster, Inc., New York, 1949, p. 58.

find yourself "thinking out loud."   As an example, notice what you do when trying to answer this question:

> Brothers and sisters have I none,
> But this man's father is my father's son.
> What is his relationship to me?

The average person will repeat all or some of the words several times in trying to figure it out.

Language provides a means of labeling.   If a composite of sensations has meaning attached to it, you have perceived something—i.e., there is a *percept*. For example, if someone hands you an object, and you see that it is round horizontally, somewhat tapered vertically, it is red and yellow in color, it feels smooth to the touch, it weighs about a quarter of a pound, it is about as large as your fist, it has a stem at the top, it smells like fruit—what do you perceive?   An apple.   Note that you combined all those sensations with the memory of similar sensations and found that the totality was a definite meaning.   On a higher level you arrive at *concepts*.   When you see apples, oranges, plums, peaches, and pears together in a basket, you call this collection *fruits*.   This is because there is one factor, or possibly more than one, which is common to all the objects.   So a concept has been defined as: "a word or other symbol which stands for the common property of a number of absent objects, acts, situations, or events."[7]   This is explained further by saying, "Concepts are always derived from primitive experience with existing things, but they represent no one thing capable of independent existence."[8]   Concepts enable us to think by means of *abstractions*—i.e., without reference to particular things.   Thus, we speak of community, beauty, justice, meaning, and faith with a general significance attached to each, but with reference to no concrete thing.   We can then think about such an assertion as, "Your speech reveals the quality of your thinking."

Language can be involved in thinking in various ways.   In the first place, it enables you to perceive better.   Having more words at your command increases your powers of discrimination.   You can make finer distinctions between colors; you can hear more of a symphony; you can better know a personality.

In the second place, it aids you in the conservation of your experiences. With a rich vocabulary you can listen to a speaker and better label and

---

[7] Floyd L. Ruch, *Psychology and Life*, 2d ed., Scott, Foresman and Company, Chicago, 1941, p. 396.
[8] *Ibid.*

categorize your perceptions of the speaker. You have terms which fit the speaker's ideas, his use of language, his voice, and his manner; thus, upon recall, the observations become more orderly and inclusive.

Thirdly, language makes possible your acquiring ideas and information from others through listening or through reading. You can experience vicariously many things through the words of a narrator, whether it be written or spoken. You do this when you watch a football game on television or when you read about what it is like to fly through a hurricane. You can also receive more abstract ideas in the same way. That is what you are doing now as you read this chapter. Thus you are entering into the thoughts of others by means of language.

This suggests one more involvement of language in your thinking: It enables you to use short cuts in your mental processes. You no longer have to refer to a multiplicity of concrete objects or experiences in order to relate them to another collection of such objects and experiences. For example, how much simpler and quicker it is to say, "our university" rather than to list all the people and things that are included under that term. Then you can more quickly think about such a question as, How can our university develop better thinkers?

THE USE OF PATTERNS

TRIAL-AND-ERROR. All thinking does not proceed in an A, B, C fashion. For example, what is the answer to this problem:

> Arrange four 9s in such a way that they equal 100.

Work it out on another piece of paper and then come back to this. Now, if you could put down all your thoughts on the above problem in the order in which they occurred, you would probably see that your thinking took long leaps, was circular at times, used back tracking, etc. It is likely, however, that the general pattern was one of trial and error. This is frequently the process; you propose one idea to yourself, test it mentally, reject it, propose another. That is the way many people play checkers. Sometimes, of course, they do not have to use the *mental* trial and error method; they have objects with which to work, and can try various solutions with their hands and eyes, rejecting those that do not work. This can be done with the following problem:

> Lay ten matches in a row, thus: 1 1 1 1 1 1 1 1 1 1
> Now get them into two's by picking up one at a time and jumping two others. You may jump only two, whether they be in pairs or as arranged.

INSIGHT. This is a more advanced process of thinking. The steps cannot be well defined because they are taken rapidly or because insight seems to arrive by unconscious thought. It could be the recognition of a *pattern* of things, information, or ideas. Perhaps in solving the problem of the matches, you got this insight after a few moves of the matches—in other words, you said, "Aha, I see!" because everything seemed to fall into place. The advanced checker or chess player does this. No doubt that is why the expert chess player can play several other players at the same time, moving from board to board. In an extensive series of experiments with monkeys and children, Harlow found that we get insight from one experience which can be applied to a similar experience; in other words, there is a transfer effect from one problem to another, which he calls "learning set." So we may say that insight develops as we "learn how to learn." And that is our central task in education.

LOGICAL THINKING. A discussion of the use of patterns in thinking would not be complete without considering the subject of reasoning or *logical* thinking. A useful definition of reasoning is: a tested method of thinking. This implies that it is a systematized procedure in which there are formalized patterns and to which definite rules apply. If you wish to study this in detail, you would need to consult books on logic or argument. Here we shall sketch briefly the two main types of argument and two related types that are commonly used.

Basically, logic uses the pattern of: *if . . . then*; in other words, if a certain thing is true or certain conditions exist, then something else is true or some other condition could exist. *Deduction* is one of the main types of reasoning using this pattern. It is a method of reasoning from the general to the particular. It begins with a general statement (major premise), proceeds to a particular statement (minor premise), and then draws a conclusion from the relationship of the particular statement to the general statement. Thus, you could reason deductively as follows:

All teachers are educated. (major premise)
Jane Smith is a teacher. (minor premise)
Therefore, Jane Smith is educated. (conclusion)

In this kind of reasoning, it is expected that you can prove both the major premise and the minor premise. If both are established, then the conclusion must follow. Our reasoning is often faulty because we neglect to make certain that one of the premises is true. For example, two boys of school age were sitting in a filling station on the last morning of school before the Christmas vacation. When asked why they weren't in school, one of them replied, "They're just having parties." It appeared that his major premise was something like: Parties are of no value.

A related type of reasoning which uses this general pattern is the *cause-effect* reasoning. Here it is assumed that a certain cause produces a certain effect. If this is accepted or established, then it may be applied to a particular instance. Thus, we say: If you study hard you will get better grades. Note that it is assumed that studying hard always results in better grades.

Sometimes the reasoning goes from *effect-to-cause.* Then, we say: You didn't get good grades because you didn't study hard. It is clear that the effect is produced by a definite cause. You can see from this example that one of the errors we fall into is that we assume that there is but *one* cause for a certain effect. In the case above, poor grades might have been caused not by the lack of effort, but by poor methods of study, defective eyes, emotional problems, or poor health. Another error is the failure to establish a clear relationship between the effect and the cause. For example, when a writer states that because college graduates earn more money in a lifetime than do non-college graduates, therefore the college education is the cause—he neglects to ascertain whether or not the people who go to college are the ones who would earn more money even if they didn't happen to go to college. In other words, he fails to establish that the college education produced the earning ability.

The second main type of logical reasoning is *inductive* reasoning. If a given number of particulars (instances) are true, then we can draw a general conclusion. Using this form, a person might say: Four out of five students who were interviewed said that teacher X was unfair; therefore, teacher X is unfair. In this instance a generalization was drawn on the basis of particular items. Think about the bases for the following generalizations: Athletes are poor students; girls are not good in mathematics; plumbers forget their tools; redheaded people have quick tempers. We err in the use of the inductive method when we generalize from too few instances or from instances which are not typical.

In your conversations and in more serious discussions you have observed a related form of induction used—reasoning by *analogy.* In this form a person concludes that if one thing resembles another in a number of points (characteristics), then it must resemble it on another point. So people draw conclusions from comparing minds with machines, schools with industry, people with monkeys, and the United Nations with our federal government. It is possible to draw false conclusions by this method if you fail to compare things on essential points or if you neglect the points of difference. It might be unwise, therefore, to conclude that because teacher A taught with a certain method, teacher B could teach with the same method.

In summing up how we think, then, we can say that in the process we implement the tools of muscles, images, and language in patterns of trial and error, insight, and logical thinking. These are involved when we are trying to do critical thinking, creative thinking, problem solving, or perhaps even in our daydreaming.

HOW TO IMPROVE YOUR THINKING

There are many pitfalls in thinking, many faculty tendencies that all of us seem to have. However, instead of dwelling upon these, we shall point out some positive practical ways by which you can improve the quality of your own thinking.

TAKING INVENTORY

Taking inventory, we admit, is not easy to do. But there are some means at your disposal for determining your assets as well as your needs. These questions will suggest some of the means available to you.

1 Have you taken a test—such as the Watson-Glaser Critical Thinking Appraisal?
2 How well did you solve the problems that were presented earlier in this chapter?
3 What kinds of thinking are revealed by papers you have written for other courses?
4 What kind of mind is revealed by your activities for a day or for a week?
5 How does your thinking compare with that of others:
   a Your peers—in conversation groups, committees, class discussion?
   b Your instructors, clergymen, lecturers, politicians?
6 How well have you been able to solve your personal problems:
   a In your everyday life, such as health, money, clothes?
   b In your job, such as planning work or study, budgeting time, methods of work, relations with others?

USING BASIC REQUIREMENTS

UNDERSTAND THE PROBLEM.   Most of your thinking is aimed at answering a question or deciding what to do. Before looking for a solution, it is important that you see why the problem exists and the kind of answer that is needed.   It helps if you can recognize the parts of the problem, their relationship to each other and to the total problem.   Note, too, how much of your own ego or your emotions is involved in the problem. If you cannot keep these in perspective, you have little chance for a rational solution.

BECOME INFORMED.   This implies that you should withhold an answer until you know the facts pertaining to a problem.   We see too many instances of protest marches, editorials, and letters to editors which are triggered by only a little information or by one person's experience.   When you are asked to give an immediate opinion about something, keep your self-respect by labeling your answer as a tentative one or as only a guess.

IMPROVE YOUR USE OF LANGUAGE.   This requires accumulating a wide vocabulary, especially in the realm of abstract language.   Beyond that, it requires the use of apt words—words that most accurately express an idea or a relationship between ideas and that are pertinent and precise.   It is important, too, that your language in sentence form expresses clearly your perceptions, your information, and your logical processes.

AVOID STEREOTYPED THINKING.   To do this, you first have to be able to recognize when your thinking is stereotyped.   For example, if you are asked to plan a program for a father-son banquet, it is so easy to think: We need a toastmaster, a main speaker, a toast by a father, and a toast by a son.   Suppose, instead, you asked, Isn't there some other way of developing a program?   A psychologist wisely reminds us that if we are to keep our minds unrigidly alive, we should not take the usual for granted and we should always be seeing an alternative.

HAVE AN OPEN, QUESTIONING MIND.   This means, first of all, that you need to have a mind that is hospitable to new ideas, a mind that will at least give a new idea a hearing. It requires, also, that you examine ideas before accepting them; this should be true regardless of the source of the idea.   Often you may believe something simply because it is in print or because a person with considerable status utters it.   Remember that the wise men who sit in our Supreme Court often arrive at different conclusions based on the same evidence.   Finally, if you are to keep an open, questioning mind, be willing to question your own beliefs.   You can practice this easily by starting to question your belief about some person whom you dislike.

TAKE TIME TO REFLECT.   Recently we heard a faculty member exclaim, "Teachers don't have time to sit back and think!"   Perhaps we don't *take* the time to think.   There are many times when we might.   For example, after a conversation, after a lecture, after reading, after any experience, you can ask yourself, What does this mean?   What else might it mean?   Why did so-and-so come to the conclusion that he did?   Why is my own conclusion different?   Carlyle once wrote, "Sit still and label your thoughts."

PRACTICE, PRACTICE, PRACTICE

Ernest Dimnet says, "The more a man thinks the better adapted he becomes at thinking."[9]   Many people learn to think on their own; but it is probably true that one of the chief reasons we have schools is that we want to confront young people with tasks in which they have to think.   If you wish to practice thinking in a variety of ways, we can make several suggestions for your practice.

PRACTICE BETTER PERCEPTION.   We perceive with any or all of our eleven or more senses.   If you were to practice the better use of just one of them—sight—there are several means for doing it.   First of all, practice seeing all that is there.   Louis Agassiz taught this thoroughly.   To one of his pupils he gave a preserved fish and asked him to see what was there.   In an hour of looking at it the pupil thought he had seen everything.   Agassiz demanded more than this.   So the pupil spent over a hundred hours looking at it some more and taking notes.   After his report to Agassiz, he was told, "That is not right."   So he spent another week of ten hours a day examining it some more before Agassiz was satisfied.

Another aspect of your practice in perception is to see more than meets the eye.   Try to see what others do not see.   This might be in a flower, a shrub covered with snow, the reaction of a person in a conversation, or a moment in a play.   Take a lesson from a mechanic who listens to sounds coming from your automobile or from a doctor who looks at a patient or listens to the sounds that come from his thumping different parts of the patient's body.   Notice what the artist sees in an old wind-beaten pine or in a human face.

Further, try taking notes on your observations.   Many writers and artists do this.   See if you can put into language the sights, sounds, smells, tactile

[9] *Op. cit.,* p. 58

sensations, joys, pains, and moods that enter your life. When you have an idea about something, jot it down, even if it means getting out of bed. You may never use it, but the practice will be valuable.

PRACTICE OBJECTIVE THINKING.   You are thinking objectively when you consider an idea without being influenced by your own needs or emotions.   For example, a person who was convicted of first-degree murder would be objective in the extreme if he could decide that capital punishment would be desirable in his state.   In practicing objectivity, you should try to recognize when you are just being emotional rather than thinking.   You could do this in such situations as losing your purse or receiving a low grade on an examination.   Another way of practicing would be to identify the steps you have taken in trying to make a decision and be aware of the stage you are in at the moment.   A third means is that of testing your conclusions about a problem; this may be simply by exposing them to the thinking of other people; it may be by trying them out in practice.

LEARN TO ASK QUESTIONS.   "The art of asking questions—" says Wendell Johnson, "the art without which clear thinking and good will may never quite be joined—is to be come by only through discipline beyond that to which we are accustomed."   The value of asking questions increases when you ask the *right* questions, and to ask the right questions you will need both curiosity and imagination.   One thing more is needed—courage.

If you want better answers than you now have, you may have to discard the answers you have always believed in, even though they came from those you respect and admire.

PRACTICE TAKING A FRESH LOOK.   Don't be like the chicken that is trying to get back into the chicken yard; it runs up and down the same path time after time, always trying the same way to get in.   Step back and try to see the idea or the problem from a *new* angle.   This is what a member of a school board did when they were planning a new elementary building; he simply asked, "Why do we have to have corridors in the building?" Try this method when studying for a test or in financing an education.

THINK WHILE YOU LEARN.   It has been found that learning that is most similar to thinking is the best kind of preparation for good thinking. You have opportunities for practicing this in many classes.   As you listen to an instructor, you can mentally test what is said or relate it to other ideas you know about.   As you read assignments for various courses, you can do this; here you have more time to trace the reasoning of the writer, as well as to examine the facts.   As you review for an examination, you can discard the memoriter method of learning and substitute inductive or deductive thinking.   Do you practice thinking while preparing and writing a term paper?

ASSOCIATE WITH PEOPLE WHO THINK.   This association may be real or it may be vicarious.   It may be real as you walk from class with another student, as you discuss matters in the dormitory, as you become an active member of a club or a debate squad.   It may be vicarious as you listen to a visiting lecturer or read a book or magazine.   It requires that you think with the speaker or writer; but you will be free either to appreciate his qualities of thought or to disagree with him.   In any case, you are comparing your thinking with that of others, learning from their conclusions and profiting by their errors.

IMPLICATIONS FOR TEACHING

Just because you are a person, a social being, a citizen in a democratic society, you would be interested in what we have been saying about ideas and thinking.   But there are implications that pertain especially to the teacher. We would like to point out some of them.

A RICHER "SOIL FOR THINKING"

We cannot subscribe to the belief held by some that a good teacher can teach anything well, regardless of what he knows about the subject being taught.   A good teacher, little informed about a subject, might well stimulate more learning in a pupil than would a poor teacher who is informed; but that is not enough.   As a teacher of truths and as a teacher of pupils, you will need all you can acquire of a rich surface soil as well as a good subsoil.   This means an active, acquiring, and inquiring mind—one that knows the sources of information that your pupils utilize and one that has gone into areas that their minds have not yet explored.

To develop such a mind there are more means at your disposal than you can possibly use to the full.   If you wish "a full mind," the libraries, the periodicals, and the newspapers are teeming with opportunities.   If you are still in college, this may be your best chance to read many things just because you *want* to read them.   Indeed, it would be unfortunate if you were to read only the things that you are required to read.   The same applies to your listening; you may be expected to listen to classroom lectures or discussions, but you also have the *choice* of listening to speakers who come from the outside to your college community.   So, too, can you listen to debates, panels, plays, interpreters of literature, and musical programs.   You may not always learn facts, but you will acquire concepts, ideas, and tastes—along with mental stimulation.

GROUP THINKING

A great deal of your thinking as a teacher will be done in group situations; the group may be a class you are teaching or it may be a teaching staff, a council, a committee, or a conversational group.   How can you best utilize these situations?   One way is to use them as a "sounding board" for your previous thinking.   Often when a person is trying to express his ideas to others, they become clarified or modified in his own mind.   Another way is to listen to the thoughts of others as they pertain to a subject on which you have been thinking.   Of course, this latter implies that you have a receptive mind so that your thinking can be both critical and creative.

The interchange of ideas in a group can provide stimulation for your own thinking which you cannot always get when alone. The mental alertness of people varies with the situation in which they find themselves. Other things being equal, you will find yourself to be most alert when taking an examination. Rated along with this would be your alertness in an important interview situation.   Your alertness is also sharp when you are participating in group discussion.   It has been said that a person thinks because he speaks. If this is true, it would seem most likely to occur when the person is in a group where he not only listens but is also expected to speak.

SOLVING INDIVIDUAL PROBLEMS

Edwin T. Sandberg asserts:

All prospective teachers should be taught to think for themselves.   The necessity for such emphasis is immediately obvious: if an individual has never done any real thinking for himself, he can hardly be expected to know how to simulate it in his students.[10]

[10] Edwin T. Sandberg, "Teaching the Teacher to Think," *Education*, vol. 71, p. 610, June, 1951.

This seems to be logical.   And yet, as we pointed out at the beginning of this chapter, the teacher evidences his thinking by the way he solves his own problems.   The state of his classroom or his office reveals something of how his mind works; his purposes, his planning, and his methods of teaching are further revelations.   But in addition to his teaching problems, he must be able to solve his personal financial problems, his family problems, his emotional problems, and his communication problems.   We hope that what we have said in the foregoing pages will be of some help to you in thinking more effectively regarding all of these.

In conclusion, we would like to pass on the word of encouragement given by the psychologist, William James:

> *Let no youth have any anxiety about the upshot of his education, whatever the line of it may be.   If he keep faithfully busy each hour of the working day, he may safely leave the final result to itself.   He can with perfect certainty count on waking up some fine morning to find himself one of the competent ones of his generation, in whatever pursuit he may have singled out.   Silently between all the details of his business the power of judging in all that class of matter will have built itself up within him as a possession that will never pass away.   Young people should know this truth in advance.   The ignorance of it has probably engendered more discouragement and faint-heartedness in youths embarking on arduous careers than all other causes put together.*[11]

---

[11] William James, *Talks to Teachers on Psychology.*   All rights reserved.   Holt, Rinehart and Winston, Inc., New York, 1939, p. 78.

FOR FURTHER READING

Alexander, Hubert G.: *Language and Thinking*, D. Van Nostrand Company, Inc., Princeton, N.J., 1967.

Brown, Charles T. and Charles Van Riper: *Speech and Man*, Prentice-Hall, Inc., Englewood Cliffs, N.J., 1966, chap. 6.

Carroll, John B.: *Language and Thought*, Prentice-Hall, Inc., Englewood Cliffs, N.J., 1964, chap. 6.

Chase, Stuart: *Guides to Straight Thinking*, Harper & Row, Publishers, Inc., New York, 1956.

Dimnet, Ernest: *The Art of Thinking*, Simon and Schuster, Inc., New York, 1949.

Flesch, Rudolf: *The Art of Clear Thinking*, The Macmillan Company, New York, 1962.

Johnson, Wendell: *Your Most Enchanted Listener*, Harper & Row, Publishers, Inc., New York, 1956.

Montagu, Ashley: *On Being Intelligent*, Abelard-Schuman, Ltd., New York, 1951.

Sargent, William: *Battle for the Mind*, Penguin Books, Inc., Baltimore, 1961.

Thouless, Robert H.: *How to Think Straight*, Simon and Schuster, New York, 1939.

CHAPTER FOUR

LISTENING

From radio, television, films, the telephone, conversation, discussion, and speakers appearing before us in audience situations, we receive a stream of stimuli to which we must *listen* during all our waking hours. In our society, listening is essential to the development and survival of the individual. It has a significant role in interpersonal communication; also, mass media of communication have rapidly made all of us dependent upon listening in order to live successfully in an electronic age. The great competition for the minds of men will be won or lost through listening, primarily.

THE EXTENT OF LISTENING

We gain most of our general knowledge through listening. The Columbia Broadcasting Company states that over 90 percent of our knowledge of current events comes through our listening to radio and television. Surveys by Rankin[1] and others indicate that we spend almost 70 percent of our day in verbal communication. He also found that our use of the four language arts during waking hours revealed that we spent 45 percent of our time in listening, 30 percent in speaking, 16 percent in reading, and 9 percent in writing.

In *business*, the American Management Association states that executives devote 80 percent of their day to verbal communication, and more than half of it to listening.

LISTENING IS VITAL IN LEARNING AND TEACHING

In education, listening and reading are at the heart of all learning. As a *student*, a role you have had for years, you are already aware of this fact. Listening to lectures, discussions, and demonstrations is an inherent part of student activity. You spend as much as 80 percent of your time in class listening. The wide use of the lecture method in college instruction accounts for much of this.

---

[1] See Ralph G. Nichols and Leonard A. Stevens, *Are You Listening?*, McGraw-Hill Book Company, New York, 1957, p. 10.

As a *teacher*, you will be responsible for initiating and developing learning experiences. This cannot be done by your doing all the talking. Conservative estimates by elementary and high school teachers indicate that they often spend 60 percent of their day in listening. After you have taught a while, you will learn that many of the frustrations of teaching develop because the teacher feels that *pupils* have not listened well. Similarly, some of the failures in teaching result because *teachers* are not careful, courteous, and understanding listeners.

THE MEANING OF LISTENING

Most of the messages that come to us from others are received by either our eyes or our ears. With our eyes we receive much information from the printed page; but what we see there are the representations of sound combinations that we could also hear a speaker utter. Hearing, however, is not necessarily listening. Hearing is only the sensation of sounds as they are registered in the brain. Listening is a mental process which is initiated by the sounds heard. Since it depends so much upon our present ideas and habits of thinking, the chapter dealing with those was presented prior to this one.

DEFINITION

A dictionary definition of listening might include such phrases as "the conscious use of the sense of hearing" or "paying attention." This is more amply expressed by Nichols in his explanation of what listening means:

> *Remembering that apprehend means "to become aware of through the senses" and that "comprehend" means "to embrace or understand a thing in all its compass and extent," perhaps one could say that hearing is the apprehension of sound and that listening is the comprehension of aural symbols.... Let us assume, then, that in communications work we are primarily interested in listening rather than hearing, and that until a better definition is devised listening may be defined as "the attachment of meaning to aural symbols."* [2]

---

[2] Ralph G. Nichols, "Listening: Questions and Problems," *Quarterly Journal of Speech*, 33, p. 84, February, 1947.

To complete a concept of what listening involves, we would add the following idea expressed by Baird and Knower:

> *As we use the term here "listening" includes visual as well as auditory perception. It includes watching the speaker and observing his actions and his use of visual aids as well as hearing what he says.*[3]

PURPOSE FOR LISTENING

What is meant by listening depends to some extent upon the purpose for listening. Your mental processes will vary according to whether you are listening to a radio news report, a play, a debate, or a sermon. There are at least four purposes for listening—four reasons for a person's giving attention to sounds.

LISTENING FOR COMPREHENSION. Just as comprehension is one of the goals in reading, so it is in listening. This is the kind of listening that is usually referred to when people discuss listening; it is the kind most easily tested, also. Since the listener here has no other purpose than to know what was said, it has been referred to as "submissive" listening. It includes knowing the central idea or point of the speaker, as well as the pattern of supporting ideas and facts. It is not enough, however, merely to understand these things while one is listening; there must be some retention of them if one claims he has listened well. Therefore, the listener must attach significance to things he hears, he must grasp relationships among the things said, and he must have an adequate memory. Failure in these often causes a listener to say, "The speaker jumbled everything up," when it was the listener, himself, who "jumbled" things.

LISTENING FOR APPRECIATION. This could also be called listening for enjoyment, for pleasure, for gratification, or for relaxation. Of course, a person doesn't appreciate what he hears unless he first comprehends it. Note how this is true in listening to a funny story, a poem, a play, or a concert. It has been said that we listen with what we are; in that case, what we bring to the things we hear determine the extent of our appreciation. This suggests the incident in which the woman said to an artist, "I don't

---

[3] A. Craig Baird and Franklin H. Knower, *General Speech*, 3d ed., McGraw-Hill Book Company, New York, 1963, p. 223.

know much about art, but I know what I like and what I don't like." The artist merely replied, "Yes, madam, and so does a cow!"

CRITICAL LISTENING. The key idea in this kind of listening is evaluation. What was said in the previous chapter regarding critical thinking applies here. Therefore, the critical listener is not necessarily a faultfinder. He listens to judge what is said. He compares assertions with the support given for them. He evaluates the quality of the thinking done by the speaker. He assesses the validity of facts given in the light of his previous knowledge and experience. He may also analyze the speaker's motives, his selection of material, and his manner of speaking. This kind of listening is required of the debate judge, the reviewer of musical or dramatic presentations, and the teacher of speech. However, any teacher listens in this way almost every hour of the day. Whenever it is used, it may result in approval of what is heard, it may result in disapproval, or it may result in partial approval. In any case, it can be the basis for either helpful or hurtful response by the listener.

CREATIVE LISTENING. A person cannot do creative listening unless he can think creatively. As we pointed out in the previous chapter, in creative thinking something new to the thinker results from putting things together in a different way. This can happen when one is listening. Thoughts such as the following come to his mind: That explains why I feel as I do about . . . I wonder if that could be applied to . . . What would be another use of this in my field? During creative listening, one does not want to take many notes on what is said; rather, he should feel free to let his mind rove and explore. Sometimes a teacher gets fresh ideas for teaching just by listening creatively to a student. Often a new idea comes from a conversation with another teacher; this is a good by-product from the teacher's lounge.

LISTENING IN LEARNING

To aid students in their learning, colleges and universities provide libraries; but they also provide classrooms, dormitories, and student centers. In the last three places students learn by talking and listening. If it were ever proved that students could learn without listening, there would be thousands of unhappy teachers. However, it is doubtful that it will be proved. We learn our culture largely through listening; we learn to think by listening;

we learn to love by listening; we learn about others and about ourselves by listening. And yet, we do not listen well.

EFFICIENCY OF STUDENTS' LISTENING

Students are among those who do not listen well.   Studies done at Michigan State University by Dow and Irvin with 2,800 students showed that 37 percent comprehended 25 to 60 percent of the material presented. The majority of students had 50 percent efficiency in recalling factual material from a lecture.   Brown, at the University of Minnesota, found only 49 percent of freshman students able to get the central idea of a selection heard in a standard listening test.   Nichols reported the average student listener at the St. Paul Branch (Engineering) at Minnesota understood about 68 percent of materials presented, but some got as little as 20 percent.   Nichols, Brown, and Bird reveal that immediately after the average person listened to someone talk, *no matter how carefully he had listened*, he recalls only about half of what he has heard.

REASONS FOR POOR LISTENING

Like many other people, you may be laboring under some wrong assumptions about listening.   One of these is that a good reader will be a good listener.   This has not been proved to be true.   One probable reason is that reading is a private activity, while listening is a social one; another is that the reader sees visual symbols, while the listener hears sound symbols; a third is that the reader sets his own pace, while the speaker sets the listener's pace; a fourth is that the listener can add the speaker's vocal meanings and his physical actions to the words he hears, whereas the reader has only the black print and the punctuation marks.   Another wrong assumption is that intelligent people are always better listeners than are unintelligent ones.   This, too, is not borne out in fact.   A third assumption is the great amount of listening that we do should make us good listeners.   The data given earlier regarding students' listening disprove this assumption.   A fourth assumption is that if we can hear well, we will listen well.   The truth is that the percent of our population that listens poorly far exceeds the 5 or 6 percent who have serious hearing problems.   What, then, are the real reasons for poor listening?

YOUR ATTITUDES. Often you have a lack of desire to listen.   You may be in a class, for example, when you would rather be catching up on your sleep. Or you may have been "dragged" to church. Or you may be caught in a conversation from which you cannot gracefully escape. So you "fake" listening—giving all the signs of listening, but having your mind far away. Another attitude is having a mental set against the speaker or his subject. You may not like the speaker as a person or you may dismiss the subject as uninteresting to you. A third attitude is similar to the second—having a self-centered approach. You tend to listen only to those things which feed your ego, or you are so wrapped up in petty concerns about your personal life that you are not interested in another person's ideas about the world outside yourself. Finally, there is the attitude which results in making only emotional responses to the speaker. Perhaps you resent one word or one idea of the speaker, and this triggers emotions that becloud your perception of all the rest that is said.

YOUR METHODS. Poor listening often results from going at it in the wrong way. A commonly observed mistake is that of the lack of effort. The passive listener wants to be withdrawn, comfortable, and inactive. He is like the tennis player who wants to play without perspiring.

A second ineffective way of listening is to listen for facts only. The attention to detail will obscure your perception of the purpose and the central thought of the speaker, as well as the *ideas* he is developing in support of his central thought. Also, being obsessed with remembering one fact interferes with your grasping the next fact.

A third mistake in listening is that of giving attention to the irrelevant. When you have more concern for the speaker's appearance or his delivery, for the person who walks in late (note this in the next class you attend), or for other distractions, then you have forfeited your chance to know what the speaker has intended for you.

A fourth tendency is that of wasting time. It has been found that usually you can listen about four times as fast as the speaker can utter his thoughts. During that time, you could relate what he is saying to his previous ideas, you could evaluate his thinking or his evidence, you could relate his ideas to other things you know, or you could anticipate what he may say next. Instead, are you just sitting there?

A fifth method of listening poorly might lie in the way you take notes. Trying to write down verbatim what is said is almost impossible unless you are good at shorthand. Making notes on an idea before you have heard all of it is also ineffectual. Making unstructured notes hinders not only your current listening, but it also makes a later review of them more difficult.

Finally, you might ask yourself if you practice difficult listening. Is your listening to radio and television programs limited to popular music or variety shows, or do you frequently listen to thoughtful news analyses, discussions of current issues, sermons, or speeches by people who have done some thinking? Do you take advantage of visiting speakers on the campus? Do you attend the production of campus or community drama? Listening always to that which is light or entertaining will keep your listening ability on that level.

LISTENING CAN BE IMPROVED

Definite training in listening is the best way to improve efficiency. It should not be left to chance, or given only incidental attention. Rewarding results can be obtained, even with short periods of planned instruction.

Krueger at Whittier College reports college freshmen improved from 18 to 56 percent in listening comprehension after a very brief instructional period. Dow and Irvin at Michigan State University, working with 2,800 students previously reported as deficient in listening, reported that one year of instruction produced gains of 12 to 25 percent in better comprehension. They also noted that students who were extremely poor listeners made the greatest gains, often as high as 50 percent.[4] Nichols, reporting results of his work for fifteen years in teaching a twelve-week listening course to freshmen scoring in the lowest 20 percent on a listening test, also indicates consistent improvement. These low scorers improved their listening ability to a point where they equalled or surpassed those who were not required to take the course. Every group improved at least 25 percent in its ability to understand spoken language. Some gained as much as 40 percent.[5]

HOW TO IMPROVE LISTENING

What we have said thus far can give you a basis for improvement. At this point we shall present you with some direct approaches and methods for working at the problem.

FIRST STEPS. Although it may seem quite obvious, any improvement in listening assumes that you have adequate hearing. If you consistently

---

[4] Clyde Dow and C. E. Irvin, *Syllabus: Communication Skills*, The Michigan State University Press, East Lansing, Mich., 1954, p. 116.

[5] Ralph G. Nichols and Leonard A. Stevens, *Are You Listening?*, McGraw-Hill Book Company, New York, 1957, p. 15.

have trouble hearing speakers in conversation or in an audience situation, you should have a hearing test. Your speech teacher will be glad to arrange it for you. If you find that you have a serious hearing deficiency, your therapist will advise you regarding a hearing aid or special training, or both.

A second step is to know what mental equipment you need for better listening. It has been found that the chief things which make a difference in listening ability are the following: ability to think clearly (developed in the previous chapter), size of vocabulary, knowledge of English usage, reading comprehension, ability to see the structure or oral discourse, and a sense of the significant. All of these can be developed, not only in your listening, but also in your reading, writing, and speaking.

A third step is to know what your needs are. This can give you some motivation for trying to improve. There are several ways of getting this information. One is to recall your personal experiences as a listener to class lectures or as a participant in discussions. Did you grasp all that was said? Did you fail on certain kinds of items—such as main ideas, facts, inferences drawn by the speaker? Another way is to recall the comments of your friends, family, or instructors about your ability as a listener. Do they ask you to be attentive? Do they have to repeat things for you? Do they complain because you don't follow instructions? A third way is to take a standardized test of listening comprehension. There are two quite well known, and a third that has had extensive use in California: the Brown-Carlsen Listening Comprehension Test,[6] the STEP (Sequential Tests of Educational Progress) tests of listening ability,[7] and the California Auding Test.[8]

If tests such as those above are not available, try answering the following questions with one of three answers: Yes—No—Doubtful.

1   Can you follow directions after hearing them only once?
2   Do you listen primarily for ideas rather than for facts?
3   Do you try to differentiate facts from opinions when you hear people talking?
4   Can you anticipate another person's next ideas when you listen?
5   Can you summarize the remarks of another person to whom you listen?

[6] World Book Company, Tarrytown-on-Hudson, N.Y., 1952.
[7] STEP, Princeton, New Jersey, 1954, publishers (four forms).
[8] Available through Don P. Brown and John Caffrey, Council on Auding Research, 146 Columbia Avenue, Redwood City, California, 1952.

6 Do you easily remember ideas you try to carry in mind as you listen to others?

7 Do you have a desire to ask questions of a speaker?

8 Can you listen to an argument without becoming emotionally upset?

9 Do you suspend judgment for a time on new arguments which you hear?

10 Are you aware of things the speaker might have said but avoided saying?

11 Do you remember the idea that was illustrated by a story?

12 Do you recognize a speaker's transitions from one idea to another?

13 Do you notice any digression of a speaker from his main line of thought?

14 After listening to someone, are you more inclined to discuss his ideas rather than his manner of speaking?

15 Can you listen without being distracted by other sights and sounds?

16 Can you listen to a speaker without thinking about other listeners?

17 Can you notice violations of good speech without disliking the person speaking?

18 In a conversation, do you hear the last comment of another before you speak?

19 Can you receive value from a speaker to whom you are required to listen?

20 Do you tend to change your attitude toward the speaker as you hear more from him?

21 Can you listen well to a person whose racial or religious background is different from yours?

22 Are you aware of why you do or do not listen to someone?

23 Do you get new insights regarding yourself when you listen to others?

24 Do you listen objectively to criticism of your efforts?

25 Do your friends ask you to listen to their problems?

Checking over your answers to the above twenty-five questions will give you at least a partial insight into listening tendencies as a whole; noting the unsatisfactory answers you gave will help you to decide the areas for your listening improvement.

DEVELOPING CONSTRUCTIVE LISTENING METHODS.[9] By now you may be aware of your need for better listening. We hope that you have

---

[9] Adapted from E. C. Buehler and Wil Linkugel, *Speech: A First Course*, Harper & Row, Publishers, Incorporated, New York, 1962, pp. 94–99.

taken the first steps discussed above. We now offer you some positive methods which you can use. Of course, they will not work unless you do.

1 Prepare in advance for listening. By anticipating your listening activity, you can develop an attitude or "set" that will carry you through the experience that is to come. Such a favorable predisposition helps you to recall more completely. You listen with a purpose. You can strengthen your whole listening activity by checking your own obstacles, by learning something about the speaker, by relating his subject to your previous knowledge, and by anticipating any distractions that may be present. Thus you will be ready to listen more efficiently.

2 Give your whole attention to listening. Realizing that concentration is the key to good listening, you need to dedicate your energies to a full-scale effort that will not tolerate faking attention, and allows you to take full advantage of thought speed. Spurn any thought of not wanting to listen.

3 Keep an open mind. Again, this echoes an admonition in the previous chapter on thinking. Wait for the content of the speech to develop; suspend judgment on new ideas or arguments; be alert to any tendency to resist ideas emotionally; break out of your occupational shell or your previous point of view; look for interesting points. In other words, give the speaker a full opportunity to reach you with his ideas and information.

4 Resist distractions. Why give any priority of attention to what another listener is doing, to a door opening, or any other distraction? When these occur, work harder at concentration. *Do not tune out the speaker; tune out the offensive distractions.*

5 Look for the speaker's purpose and central idea. Does he intend to entertain you, inform you, convince you, impress you, or persuade you? Then find the *specific* purpose of his talk as he relates his general purpose to his subject, the listeners, and the occasion. Note what he says by way of introduction. Follow his development carefully, and then you will usually have little trouble in knowing where he is headed.

6 Concentrate on key points. By accurate listening, you can usually relate the main points of the speaker to his specific purpose and central idea. Develop in your notes your outline of his talk. With this framework, you can fit in subpoints and supporting materials.

7 Look for between-the-lines meanings or implications. Not all meanings in a talk are literal. As you listen, try to make judgments on the *exact* meanings the speaker intends. The language, the delivery—with par-

ticular inflections in the voice, changes of voice quality, certain kinds of pauses—can change the literal meaning subtly to figurative or emotionally toned slantings that reveal his real meaning, his attitude, or his true purposes. Note whether or not he reveals by his delivery any particularly sensitive areas in his subject. Check your accuracy of interpreting these by questions, if possible, or by comparing ideas with other listeners.

VARIED FORMS OF SPEECH—A CHALLENGE TO LISTENING SKILL. As you read the constructive suggestions above, they may have appeared to stress listening to a single speaker who gives a planned, continuous talk (lecture, address, sermon). It is true that this situation is most typical of your listening role in a college classroom or as a member of an audience for a speaker outside school. However, you should realize the great range of your listening experiences, even during a single week—all determined by situations employing many forms of speech.

Consider your participation in an important telephone call, an interview for a job, your conference with an instructor about a paper or your work in his class, your participation in class discussion, your membership in a student organization which is hearing a committee report, your leadership of a panel discussion in a student convocation, your appearance in an intercollegiate debate, your role as a representative of your college in a national conference— all of these require concentrated, accurate listening if you are to fulfill your role. You will have to refine and adapt your listening methods to fit new and changing conditions.

In all of these situations, you start by overcoming listening obstacles and developing the constructive habits indicated earlier; but you must continually refine, polish, and perfect listening abilities to meet the varied, specific, and often difficult situations. You have an opportunity for continued growth in your listening skills.

LISTENING IN TEACHING

We have gone to some length to discuss your listening needs as a student, and to show you how you can develop better listening while in school. We hope you have been asking, But what about my listening as a teacher? We fear, however, that too many teachers think of their role as being a talker, and that of the student as being a listener. We doubt that real education is taking place where that is true. In education we have too much faith in the power of telling and not enough awareness of the need to listen.

THE TEACHER'S ROLES AS LISTENER

It may surprise you to have us say that your first role will be that of a learner. On second thought, you realize that there is so much that you still do not know, especially in these days of the "information input overload." Also, you may some day come to realize that if the teacher is not still learning, his classes have less meaning for his students. One fine teacher whom we know has testified, "I do my best teaching when I am learning with the kids." And there is much for you as a teacher to be learned by listening—from information about school policy to the problems of the custodian, from the news of the world to the junior play.

A second role is that of being a leader of learners. You will need listening skills in the leading of class discussions, in handling questions following your presentation of material, in being a sponsor for a club or a student council, in directing a play or other speech activities. What you say in those situations will be helpful in proportion to the way in which you have listened.

A third role will be that of being a member of an adult group. It may be a faculty meeting where critical issues are being discussed; it may be a planning committee; it may be a professional conference; it may be a parent-teacher association meeting. In these situations, as well as in others, it will be more important than you now realize that you implement many of the ideas we presented earlier in connection with listening and learning.

LISTENING TO STUDENTS

Here is where instruction either rises or falls. "Tellin' ain't teachin!" said Grandpa Slagle. Then what is teaching? It is talking *with* students. Earl C. Kelley, well-known author of *Education for What Is Real* and *In Defense of Youth*, once pointed out that one of the fundamentals for human growth was good communication between at least one adult and the young. We submit that good communication includes the adult's doing his share of listening. Yet one study showed that the teacher in a typical classroom listened only 31 percent of the time. To what ends or purposes does the teacher listen? We shall discuss what we consider to be the four most important purposes (reasons) for his listening.

FOR INFORMATION. If it is true that before you can teach a student, you have to "learn him," then you can never know too much about him. Listening to the student—outside the classroom as well as within the classroom—can tell you much about his home, his parents and their wishes, his knowledge of the subject you are teaching, his hobbies, and his participation in sports and other activities. We have learned much from taking students to other schools for debates and similar activities just by driving the car and letting them do the talking.

In the classroom, students present their ideas in the form of questions, answers to questions, suggestions, replies to others in discussion, class debates, and special reports. In these your first concern is to know what they mean. In the case of reports, students will often testify later that they, themselves, did not know what they had said. When that occurs, it would be well if you would reconsider why and how you made the assignment. In other cases, even though the student does not express his ideas in your language, try to grasp what he means and how he sees significance in it. Note, too, if he sees relationships between pieces of information, between ideas, and between ideas and life. Your first concern, then, should not be his mistakes in grammar, his pronunciation, his use of "uh," or his posture, but rather what is going on in his mind.

FOR HELPING WITH LEARNING. Just today, in answer to a question, a student began talking to the point but then threw in some other ideas that were not pertinent, indicating some confusion about the subject area being discussed. We were in a position, then, to help her to put things back into proper relationship. Sometimes your listening will enable you to help students to develop a sense of ideas and the ability to couch these in sentence form—thus requiring them to think clearly and to express the meaning to others.

Often the help you can give is in connection with the meanings of words; knowing how the student sees a word may be the starting point. For example, when one of our students referred to *abominable* muscles instead of *abdominal* muscles, we were quite sure that his learning had gone awry.

Listening to students will also tell you something about *their* listening. You might begin to suspect that one of them has a hearing loss. The cue might be the peculiar nature of his voice or articulation; it might be in the kind of answer he gives. But, since many people with good hearing have listening problems, you might be able to determine the particular nature of the problem—difficulty with language, susceptibility to distractions, indifference, inability to retain ideas, etc.

FOR UNDERSTANDING. The normal human being wants to feel that he is understood; he wants to feel that he has some qualities that are appreciated by others. The student often craves this from a teacher because he does not get it at home. But he wants it from both. You, as a teacher, will find many opportunities to find out what a student really is—if you listen. In elementary grades there are the "sharing periods," the art and music lessons, the sessions in creative dramatics, the plays prepared and produced, the room parties, and the activities on the playgrounds. In the secondary school there are similar situations and activities. We have always valued those times when we worked with students on scenery, or when we were coaching the tennis team, or when we were invited to a student's home for dinner.

What is the kind of listening we need to do in order to understand a student as a person and to perceive how he relates to others? Carl R. Rogers has expressed it for all of us. He says, "Real communication occurs . . . when we listen with understanding. What does that mean? It means to see the expressed idea and attitude from the other person's point of view, to sense how it feels to him, to achieve his frame of reference in regard to the thing he is talking about."[10] This means that you do not listen with your defenses up; it means that you do not listen with your intellectual claws ready; it means that you do not listen primarily with your emotions. Instead, you listen with empathy; you learn something of what it is like to be the student who is talking.

The effect of this kind of listening, says Rogers, is the following: "It is the most effective agent we know for altering the basic personality structure of an individual and for improving his relationships and his communications with others. If I can listen to what he can tell me, if I can understand how it seems to him, if I can see its personal flavor which it has for him, then I will be releasing potent forces of change in him."[11]

Listening in this way will enable you to understand better the feelings that your students have about you and your class. It will help you to perceive their assets and their limitations, their deeper purposes, their personal needs, their social relationships. Most important, it may help you to realize more closely the feelings they have about themselves. Knowing these things will put you on the ground floor for helping them to learn.

---

[10] From Carl R. Rogers, "Barriers and Gateways to Communication," appearing in *Human Relations: Rare, Medium, or Well-done?*, Harvard College, 1954.
[11] *Ibid.*, p. 28.

But listening of this kind is not easy. You will have to hold back your biases, your prejudices, your preconceived ideas, and your previous judgments. You will have to listen with some humility and readiness to accept ideas that may be upsetting. It will take courage, too, since you might find yourself in the position of taking the student's attitude—one that is opposed to the one you held. But, if you can do it, the student will eventually find that you are on his side, and when that happens, he will feel that the doors are open for him to be what he can be. You will find it most difficult to listen in this way when your own emotions are involved. Perhaps that is when it is most needed. You may be helped in such a case by calling upon a third party who can listen without your emotional involvement.

Perhaps all of us could listen better and have more fruitful communication if we could lay aside our predisposed notions and our attitudes toward the person talking and if we could just see ourselves in other people.

FOR MAKING BETTER RESPONSES. It might be assumed that, if you used your listening for the above three purposes, then you would make better responses. However, let us point this up more specifically. If we may play with words a little, we would ask, What is your response-ability? We have heard so many students tell of the damage done to them by a teacher's response that we feel compelled to stress this aspect of teaching. Along with the ability to explain and the ability to ask questions, we know of nothing more important in the teacher's role than the ability to make the right response after he has listened to a student.

In the matter of asking questions, you will usually have a question you had planned, but the follow-up questions depend upon your listening. If your listening has been the kind described above, your follow-up questions will indicate your responsiveness as a communicator, thus promoting freedom and responsiveness in the student. In addition, it is telling other members of the class or group that they may feel safe in their answers or in raising questions of their own. It doesn't take students long to know whether or not it is safe to ask questions or to express forthrightly what they are thinking.

Now, just what do you say when a student answers your question? We know of a teacher who used just one response if the answer was correct; she said "Good." But one day when she put the problem of $2 + 3 = ?$ on the board and asked a first grader (who often rode a milk truck with his dad) what the answer was, he curtly replied, "Five." Her response, again, was "Good"; but she was not prepared for his rejoinder, "Hell, that's perfect!" What other responses might be given to students' answers?

Often these do not have to be long. It may be only a "mmm-hmm," a "Yes," or a "I see what you're getting at"; or it may be more negatively a "Oh, no," a "I wonder if...," or a "But, wouldn't...." These responses with an attitude of interest, expressed in the voice and the visual expression of the teacher, will encourage the student who is speaking. Faking listening while you are thinking of your next question or consulting your notes will dry up the stream of information or thinking.

Of course, responses may be longer. One of these could be your attempt to paraphrase what the student has said. This lets him know that you were listening, and it may also help the listening of the others in the class. Sometimes you may want to ask another student if he understood what the first student said; then ask him to express it as he sees it. Another longer response would be your interpretation of what the speaker said. For example, it might be a generalization based on a student's information; it could also be a statement of the meaning of an experience or a story, such as "What a wonderful gift for a parent" or "That's the reason we have some required subjects in college."

If you are really listening, then, your responses will produce stimulating questions; they will be a source of encouragement to your speaking-listening students; they will promote learning and a better communication atmosphere. In your responses the student will see a reflection of himself as a speaker.

LISTENING TO ADULTS

Needless to say, as a teacher you will be listening to adults as well as to students. Since this is important listening, and since they may be more critical of listening weaknesses, we feel that it would be an oversight to omit a consideration of this area of listening. You will be listening to teaching colleagues, to custodians, to administrators, to parents, and to other adults in the community. Unless your listening changes, you will probably listen to them as well as you now listen to your school associates.

Where will this listening occur? Sometimes it will be in the teachers' lounge, sometimes in the corridors, sometimes in an office, and sometimes in called meetings. Each situation will require its own kind of listening. Good listening will be rewarding. We hear principals complaining that their teachers do not listen; likewise, we hear teachers saying that the principal wants their opinions, but he doesn't listen! Teachers meet in a committee and find that the chairman didn't come to listen to their ideas; or a member of the committee makes comments totally unrelated to what someone else has said.

What can we say about your listening to adults? Obviously, the first thing is that you *try* to listen. The second thing is to apply what we have said up to this point: (1) Use the methods of listening that we have set forth for the student; (2) use the kind of listening that we have urged you to use when students talk. Some of the best conversationalists have been regarded as such simply because they were good listeners. So often there is the cry, "If only somebody would listen!"

SELF-LISTENING

By now you are probably exclaiming, Do I have to listen to myself, too? And why not? Wendell Johnson has written a book entitled, *Your Most Enchanted Listener*; it deals primarily with what you hear yourself say. We have heard of the woman who could start her tongue talking and go away and leave it running! Such a person has a self-listening score of close to zero. She is listening neither to her ideas (if there be any), her language, nor to her voice. And yet, these are listening circuits, all of which a person can employ.

Self-listening should be of help in self-understanding. You sometimes talk to yourself in order to hear the language associated with your thoughts; this seems to aid you in understanding what you mean or in making next steps. But there is also the use of implicit speech when you are communicating desires, values. and problems to yourself. This is necessary in order to maintain our mental health; in fact, Carl R. Rogers points out that the neurotic person is the one within whom the communication process has broken down.

Besides listening to your self-talk, you need to listen to what you say to others. Sometimes this listening should be on the idea-circuit—listening to the accuracy of your statements. Have you noticed how often people will say "left" when they are thinking "right," or they will say "east" when they mean "west"? These are simple instances; more complex ones are the judgments one makes or the opinions one gives in a committee meeting or a business meeting—to say nothing about conversations. A way of guarding against ill-advised remarks was once given by Lionel Barrymore, the great character actor. He suggested that before you uttered something, you should ask yourself, How would I like to *hear* what I am about to say?

It pays, also, to listen occasionally to the voice you are using. Is it tending to rise in pitch, to increase in intensity, to become harsh or nasal or strident? This is important in your talking to students, as well as in your talking with adults. Their ears are sensitive to the cues they get from your voice, and often this will tell them more than your language will. No doubt that is why Emerson's remark is so often quoted: "What you are speaks so loudly that I cannot hear what you say."

We conclude what may have seemed a long chapter to you. Yet we do not apologize for its length because of the fact that communication requires two persons, a speaker *and* a listener. Therefore, if you are to communicate well in the many roles you will have as a teacher, the effort you put into better listening will improve your speaking and will make you more effective in the interaction between you and others. You can begin by understanding and practicing the art of listening as a student. Then, as a teacher, you can be more adaptive in listening to students, to adults, and to yourself. You will be a person that others like to be with.

FOR FURTHER READING

Baird, A. Craig and Franklin H. Knower: *General Speech*, 3d ed., McGraw-Hill Book Company, New York, 1963, chap. 15.

Barbara, Dominic: *The Art of Listening,* Charles C Thomas, Publisher, Springfield, Ill., 1958.

Buehler, E. C. and Wil A. Linkugel: *Speech: A First Course*, Harper & Row, Publishers, Inc., New York, 1962, chap. 4.

Erway, Ella: *Listening: A Programmed Approach*, McGraw-Hill Book Company, New York, 1969.

Johnson, Wendell: *Your Most Enchanted Listener,* Harper & Row, Publishers, Inc., New York, 1956.

Lee, Irving J.: *How to Talk With People*, Harper & Row, Publishers, Inc., New York, 1952, chap. 1.

Nichols, Ralph G. and Leonard A. Stevens: *Are You Listening?*, McGraw-Hill Book Company, New York, 1957.

Rahskopf, Horace G.: *Basic Speech Improvement*, Harper & Row, Publishers, Inc., New York, 1965, chap. 3.

CHAPTER FIVE

PREPARATION FOR SPEAKING

Teachers who speak effectively are not just "born" with this ability, nor is it the result of coincidence or accident. Their wealth of interesting ideas, use of appropriate language, and skill in delivering their message impressively is *learned*. It rests upon careful study, experience, and extensive preparation. What you hear may have taken weeks or months to prepare. The poised, confident presentation you enjoy results from such continued effort.

The best teacher-speaker is a master of the extemporaneous method. He does not memorize, orate, or recite his materials in an elocutionary manner. He does not read mechanically from manuscript. He speaks conversationally and directly *to* and *with* his listeners. He is fully prepared and well organized, but he has developed facility in wording his ideas and thinking on his feet. He can express himself simply, clearly, and effectively. His manner of speaking is flexible and adaptable. He can meet changing conditions on the spot. He feels self-sufficient and assured. He can use this basic ability in a class lecture, a question period, a discussion, or can adjust to meet any other speaking situations that arise.

These basic steps in preparation are most practical in developing the extemporaneous method:

1 Select the subject.
2 Analyze the audience and the occasion.
3 Determine the purpose, adjusting it specifically to the analysis you have made.
4 Investigate and gather necessary material.
5 Organize the material into a usable outline with introduction, body, and conclusion.
6 Practice the speech aloud, wording it properly, with the outline as a guide.

SELECT THE SUBJECT

Many of the speeches you give as a teacher will cover subjects within your field of specialization. Your principal job will be to select the particular portion of the material that is appropriate. You will be concerned with the length of your talks because of the time limits imposed by the class situation. You will be influenced by your interests and those of your audience.

In this speech course you may also select some subjects from your field of concentration. To this extent you will be holding a series of dress rehearsals for occasions that will come later in your actual teaching. Here you will select, restrict, and adapt to the conditions of this particular situation. In addition, you will deal with other subjects outside your teaching field—public issues or community problems that command your attention and expression of your ideas.

There are certain suggestions helpful to you in this task.

SUITABLE TO THE SPEAKER

Choose a subject that interests you, about which you know something, and on which you are qualified to speak. It should also fit your background, personality, character, and reputation with your audience. In a situation outside school, you should be sure it fits your role as an educator in a community situation.

SUITABLE FOR THE AUDIENCE

The interests of your audience should greatly influence your choice of subject. Even your handling of classroom subject matter can appeal to such interests. Your subjects for out-of-school audiences should always be relative to their basic interests. Your knowledge of the composition of your audience will reveal age group, cultural level, grade level, and occupational interests that you can use effectively.

APPROPRIATE TO THE OCCASION

You will present your speech under certain conditions in the situation where it is given. Your subject should fit these conditions. Be sure it suits the theme or purpose of the meeting, and is in keeping with the prevailing mood. An after-dinner occasion usually requires a light touch with a subject of similar type. A meeting of parents on school integration necessitates a serious subject and treatment. A commemorative occasion demands a specific subject closely related to the particular significance of the ceremony.

The size of the room, its location, the hour of the meeting, the nature of the program, the subjects of the other speakers appearing, and the time limits also may influence your choice of subject. Reliable information about all factors in the occasion aids you in making an intelligent selection, and contributes much to your success in speaking.

ANALYZE THE AUDIENCE AND THE OCCASION

Having chosen a suitable subject, you must next consider *in detail* the audience and the occasion. Analysis of these factors is basic to determining your purpose, selecting and organizing your materials, and wording the speech.

THE AUDIENCE

Careful analysis of your audience is one of your best investments in preparation. In a class you are able to do this with much accuracy because you see and work with your listeners every day. You can add to your *basic* analysis by continued observation. Although classes differ, they are quite homogeneous. You can, therefore, be reasonably sure of your general findings, can adjust your talks to them, and adapt specifically later to new information you obtain about your listeners.

In an audience outside school, you have a greater variety of listeners with wider differences in interests. Usually you speak once to such a group. Your analysis for such a talk must be done very thoroughly and in advance of your talk.

Certain questions are very relevant as guides for your analysis. What do you know about the *age* of your listeners? Is there a wide range or are they nearly all the same age? Wide differences in age cause you to adapt in both subject and information. What is the size of your audience? Is it *a mixed audience* or all of *one sex*? What are the *occupations* represented by your listeners? What is the *intelligence* and *education* of your audience? Wide variations are possible here. Are they *members* of *professional, social,* or *business groups*? Does your audience belong to the *same religion*? What is the *economic status* of your audience? Does your audience contain many *nationalities* or *races*? If so, what are they? What are their characteristics? What are the *political beliefs* of the group you are addressing? Are they inclined to be liberal or conservative?

What do you know about the audience that relates *directly* to the subject of your speech? How much do they know about it? If they are very well informed, you will have to prepare more carefully, gather more material, be especially accurate, and develop means of making your talk more vivid. What is their position on your subject? Are they opposed, in doubt, or favorable to your stand on the question?

All these details influence your preparation. They should help you to plan your approach, restrict your subject, and make specific adaptation to your listeners.

THE OCCASION

Equally important is your knowledge of the occasion and your use of this information in preparation. Certain questions can help you in this analysis. Where and under what conditions will you speak? Assuming that most speaking occasions are indoors, in what kind of room will you speak? Are the acoustics good? Can the speaker be seen easily in this room? Will you be on a platform, stage, or at floor level? Where will the audience be situated? Directly in front of the speaker, on either side, or widely spread out? Will they be standing or seated? Will you be using a public address system? Will you be located behind a speaker's stand? Will there be noise or distractions within the audience or from conditions outside it?

What is the purpose of the occasion? Does it have any special purpose— a homecoming, an awards dinner, a commemorative ceremony? Are you the single, principal speaker, or are there several speakers? Is this a regular meeting of an organization? Is the meeting formal with a definite agenda, or is it casual or unstructured? Is your talk restricted by a special event, or do you have free choice of your subject and purpose?

Are there rules and a procedure that must be followed? Is your speech part of a regular order of business or a feature of a special program? Who will introduce you? Are you to acknowledge any officers, visiting guests, or prominent members of the group? Will a question period follow your talk?

Specifically, what are the details of the program—the date, the hour? After dinner? After luncheon? What are the events immediately before and after your talk?

All these questions help you to develop a practical basis for your preparation. Your ability to get the answers and adjust to the conditions will ensure the success of your talk.

DETERMINE THE PURPOSE

Nothing is more frustrating to an audience than listening to a speaker who talks aimlessly, never making his purpose clear. Effective oral communication, whether in conversation, in a classroom, or before a public audience, requires that a speaker have something to say and is controlled by a *general* purpose, which he adjusts *specifically* and *definitely* to his audience and the occasion. Such a clear goal controls his content, organization, and delivery.

There are five possible *general* purposes: *to inform* in order to achieve understanding; *to convince* in order to gain acceptance of one's beliefs or argument; *to persuade* in order to cause people to take action, to do something; *to stimulate* in order to inspire or stir the emotions; *to entertain* in order to give pleasure or enjoyment. Not every speech has a single purpose. Your talk may have more than one purpose. However, one of these is a *primary one.* For example, you could talk of your experiences in a teaching position in Africa. This talk would be primarily to inform, but could also entertain, or perhaps persuade your audience. Plan your talk around the primary purpose.

You also adjust this general purpose specifically to your audience and the occasion. This means that you have a possibility of many more *specific purposes* because of the numerous details you have to consider and the body of facts you assembled in your analysis. In each case you adjust the general purpose very definitely and concisely. State the specific purpose in terms of the exact response you wish from this particular audience and occasion. Thus, your general purpose to inform members of your class about your teaching experiences in Africa could become specific purposes: (1) *to inform your freshman speech class of the educational needs of the people of Kenya* and (2) *to interest your classmates in teaching abroad.*

Subject:	Teaching in Africa
General purpose:	To inform.
Specific purposes:	To inform the speech class of the educational needs in Kenya, and to interest them in teaching abroad.
Specific audience:	Students in Section 20, "Speech for Teachers" at Northwestern University, Evanston, Illinois.
Specific occasion:	Final talks, five minutes in length, to be given March 8, 9, and 10, in room 22. Centennial Hall at 8:00 A.M. Introduction by student chairman. Other talks by class members to follow.

This list applies this specific adjustment of general purposes further:

GENERAL PURPOSE	SUBJECT	SPECIFIC PURPOSE ADJUSTED
To convince	Audiovisual aids	To convince Section 22 of "Psychology for Teachers" that overhead projectors produce more rapid, more permanent learning

GENERAL PURPOSE	SUBJECT	SPECIFIC PURPOSE ADJUSTED
To persuade	Discussion leadership	To persuade all sophomores in Education to take the elective "Discussion Leadership"
To stimulate	Albert Schweitzer	To stimulate (inspire) university students at opening convocation with the life and example of Albert Schweitzer
To entertain	Samuel Clemens (Mark Twain)	To provide enjoyment and pleasure to a senior literature class with a talk on the humor of Mark Twain

INVESTIGATE AND GATHER NECESSARY MATERIAL

You have now limited your subject and adapted it with a specific purpose to your speaking situation. You proceed next to gather materials for your talk. Your methods are: take inventory of your knowledge and read extensively.

TAKE INVENTORY OF YOUR KNOWLEDGE

The best place to start is with what you know already. Take inventory by making a simple list of the points you know about your subject. Suppose that you are going to develop the subject of Group Leadership as a speech to persuade. Your list might include such items as Needs for Leadership Training in Teaching, Qualities of a Leader, Excellent Leaders I Have Known, Poor Leaders I Have Seen, and Leaders Can be Trained.

On a similar list you might include items you do not know: Techniques of Leadership in Discussion, Courses Offered on Campus, References and Readings on Group Discussion, Faculty Instructors in Leadership, Films and Other AV Aids, Opportunities for Training through Campus Activities. With these lists you can quite systematically use other methods to get materials you need.

READ EXTENSIVELY

Much information on the question of Group Leadership is available in printed sources available in the library. A logical next step then is to make a systematic investigation of these sources. Your own training and work methods will determine how you proceed. A series of steps often recommended goes from *general* sources to *specific* items covering your particular subject:

1 Start with a general reference such as the unabridged dictionary. Webster's *New International Dictionary* would help you in a definition of terms and a start on your subject.

2 Check the encyclopedias for an authoritative article on your subject and note well the bibliography at its conclusion for additional sources. *The Encyclopedia Americana, Encyclopaedia Britannica,* and *World Book* are among the best compilations.

3 Examine thoroughly the card catalog in the library by author and title. Add other entries from the subject entries relating to your speech. For example, under Leadership, Group Leadership, and Group Discussion you would find many items.

4 Procure the most recent works on your subject from the circulation desk. Be sure to read the descriptions on catalog cards before writing your call slips. This will help you to find relevant materials. Examine the bibliographies at the ends of chapters or footnoted items that appear prominently.

5 Get specialized bibliographies from the reference library; they may be available in various fields such as education, sociology, political science, history and others. Also check the file of master's or doctoral dissertations and government publications.

6 Review the listings in *The Reader's Guide to Periodical Literature* and in the *Education Index.* They may provide extensive magazine and journal articles on your subject. With this list you can procure bound volumes containing items you need.

7 Read the *New York Times Index* to find useful items published in that newspaper.

8 Consult the clipping file, the vertical file, and the pamphlet file for additional possibilities.

9 Visit the audiovisual section to find listings of available tapes, disks, kinescopes, films, filmstrips, and video tapes.

10 Look through the bookshelves and magazine racks for possible special displays containing materials you need.

11 Ask the librarians for further help. They are generally most cooperative.

Of course, you need not follow all of these steps. However, they represent an organized procedure to guide you.

Take adequate, systematic notes, using a card or notebook method to guarantee you accurate information—easily available and flexible for purposes of organization.

ORGANIZE THE MATERIAL INTO A USABLE OUTLINE

Organization of your material requires you to formulate the basic sequence of your talk: develop the introduction, body, and conclusion; select the best materials for supporting ideas; and determine the form of your outline—all in relation to the specifically worded purpose of your speech.

TYPES OF OUTLINES

Outlining rests upon good thinking. You need to see relationships, be able to coordinate or subordinate points and supporting materials, and develop the form of outline that best suits your needs in preparation and delivery. Individual differences exist in the process of note making and note use. Some persons can speak very successfully from a *simple list* of words on a card. Others do well with a *key-phrase* outline. Some prefer the *complete sentence* outline. Here are two outlines to illustrate ways of developing a subject:

INSTRUCTIONAL SPEECH

Fractions

Introduction

I   Today's lesson—something new
  A   Fraction—new word
  B   Familiar—end of lesson

Body

II   Halves—paper
  A   Square—fold
    1   Two sections
    2   All sections same size

3 Terms—half and whole
B Circle—same as square
III Fourths—paper
  A Square—fold again
    1 Four sections
    2 All sections same size
    3 Terms—fourth and whole
  B Circle—same as square
IV Halves—real object—yarn
  A Two sections
  B All sections same size
V Fourths—real object—apple
  A Four sections
  B All sections same size
VI Fraction—part of a whole

Conclusion

VII Summary
  A Halves
    1 Two sections
    2 All sections same size
  B Fourths
    1 Four sections
    2 All sections same size
  C Paper and other objects as well
VIII Concluding remarks
  A Learned—fraction
    1 Part of a whole
    2 Half or quarter—tests for each
  B Throughout year—learn many other numbers—call fractions

Growth of the United States

Introduction

The United States was formed by three wars and six acquisitions over 115 years.

Body

I Louisiana Purchase (1803)

   A $15,000,000.
   B   Put an end to Napoleon's dream of controlling the Mississippi
        Valley.
   C   This was the first step towards United States expansion to the
        Pacific.
II   Florida Acquired (1819)
   A   Acquired from Spain.
   B   A few years previously the United States had annexed the narrow
        strip of land that constituted West Florida.
III   Texas Annexation (1845)
   A   Republic of Texas had been established nine years previously after
        the American settlers' victory over the Mexicans.
   B   The state of Texas, part of the states of Oklahoma, Colorado,
        New Mexico, and even Wyoming.
IV   Oregon Country (1846)
   A   Was subject of frequent negotiations between the United States
        and Great Britain for almost thirty years before they adjusted
        their rival claims.
   B   This treaty extended the boundary along the 49th parallel from
        the Rocky Mountains to the Pacific Ocean, deflecting southward
        around the end of Vancouver Island.
V   The Mexican Cession (1848)
   A   Boundary claims of Texas upheld by military action.
   B   California and New Mexico ceded to the United States.
VI   Gadsden Purchase (1853)
   A $10,000,000.
   B   Secured enough territory for the proposed southern railroad route.
VII   The Alaska Purchase (1867)
   A $7,200,000.
   B   Acquired from Russia.
VIII   Hawaiian Annexation (1898)
   A   Taken from Spain in the Spanish American War.

Conclusion

So, today because of these acquisitions, the United States reaches from the
Atlantic Ocean to the Pacific Ocean.

These outline types are directly related to the method of delivery. As we
observed earlier, a teacher is most effective if he masters the *extemporaneous*
method. This requires his development of outline notes into a fully worded

presentation "on the spot." The amount of support he needs from notes will depend upon his vocabulary, his ability to verbalize ideas orally, his fluency, and his knowledge of his material. The sentence outline affords the most complete wording of his points. Beginning speakers usually start with such notes but later reduce the length of their notes after they achieve greater security through experience.

Some persons try to gain mastery over content and language by writing out the entire talk as a manuscript. They then read it rather than speak it. This practice is not encouraged as a desired method for one's fundamental delivery. Although it ensures exact wording, it has numerous disadvantages: (1) It tends to become a crutch, never allowing the speaker necessary freedom; (2) it cannot be adapted easily to conditions that arise in the speaking situation; (3) in delivery it usually pins the speaker down so that he cannot keep eye contact with his listeners; (4) in most cases, it invites mechanical, meaningless, monotonous communication of ideas. Any person who relies greatly upon manuscript notes should become an expert oral reader as well as a good extemporaneous speaker.

Under certain conditions, manuscript speeches are forced upon a speaker: (1) when his material must be cleared by his superiors; for example, an army officer might have to get his talk approved by the commanding officer; (2) when his material must be edited or checked before publication in a magazine or book; (3) when the speech must be timed exactly, as on radio or television; (4) when the speaker insists upon accuracy in a verbatim quotation for a newspaper or news film. The President of the United States almost always uses a manuscript speech. In general, a teacher does not have to meet such conditions. However, he may find reading from manuscript very convenient for quotations for closely worded principles he is teaching.

THE INTRODUCTION

This section of the speech is of great importance because it determines whether the audience decides to listen or not. Introductions have these purposes: to establish contact, to arouse interest, and to state the subject.

ESTABLISHING CONTACT. The speaker's first responsibility is to gain the attention of the audience by establishing contact in some definite way. His actions as well as his speech content contribute to this purpose—his movement to the speaker's stand or to a position in front of the room, his quiet pause before speaking, his salutation—all have to gain attention. The content of the introduction is the means of establishing a common bond between him and the audience so that they will be interested in his message instead of their own affairs. Successful methods use content related to something in the speaking situation:

1   Refer to a preceding speaker.
2   Compliment the audience.
3   Acknowledge warmly the speaker's introduction.
4   Express genuine pleasure simply and sincerely.
5   Refer to local conditions—the weather, the place, the occasion, the reason for the talk.
6   Mention a specific event that has just taken place or is now in process— a baby crying, a late arrival, an airplane passing, the excellent food.
7   Refer to a recent public event or an idea prominent in the minds of the listeners.

GAINING ATTENTION AND AROUSING INTEREST. Next, get the attention of the audience and arouse interest in what you are saying. This step is critical and marks the beginning of a series of efforts to maintain such interest throughout the talk. A teacher-speaker is particularly aware of this need and should utilize a variety of ways to meet it:

1   Develop a series of questions about the subject.
2   Use an appropriate story or narrative.
3   Present a startling statement or striking fact.
4   Utilize a humorous story or joke that is relevant, novel, and in good taste.
5   Relate the subject to the particular interest of the audience.
6   Cite a familiar, compelling quotation that relates to the subject.
7   Use a chalkboard or other visual aids.

Any of these methods will gain attention and arouse interest. Be sure to avoid trite, overworked material; concentrate on developing vital, creative ways of arousing interest. Relate them closely to the basic content of the body of your talk. Your introduction then will have maximum effectiveness.

STATING THE SUBJECT. Finally, your introduction must reveal to the audience clearly, concisely, and directly the purpose of your talk. Your statement will be very close in wording to the specific purposes developed earlier in this chapter. If you were to speak on Albert Schweitzer, your statement could very well be: "Tonight I want to share with you information and experiences of one of the truly great men of our times—a man who renounced a brilliant career as a writer, musician, and philosopher in Europe to serve the spiritual and medical needs of his fellow men in Africa. That person is Albert Schweitzer." Such a statement could very appropriately be placed in your outline as a lead-in to the main body of your content. Thus, it would inform the audience definitely of the scope of your speech. In a classroom situation, teachers become skilled in revealing a specific subject as they introduce the work for a particular day or lesson.

THE BODY

This section of the talk contains the main part of your content. Your basic message is found here, developed to fit the specific statement given in the introduction.

If you have followed well the steps in preparation, you should have no difficulties with this section. Your subject has been carefully selected, your audience and occasion analyzed, your purpose clearly formulated and specifically adjusted to the needs of your speaking situation, and your supply of ideas and information gathered. Your principal task is the arrangement of your main and subpoints with their supporting materials in an order most suitable for you as a speaker, the audience, and the occasion. In short, you have all of the raw materials; you must decide now upon the arrangement or particular kind of "package" in which your product will be most successfully contained. A knowledge of the various ways of arranging (ordering) ideas will help you at this point. You can select the best one or combinations to fit your speaker needs in your situation:

1   *Time order.* In a process, narrative, or chronological relationship, you will find time arrangement most useful. A description of an experiment in making oxygen could follow this order. An account of your trip through a steel rod mill or a report of your attendance at a performance of the Metropolitan Opera would also be well organized with a time order arrangement.

2   *Space order.* Any exposition or description of objects in physical or geographical location involves the use of space order. Details of a trip through the Prudential Building, the Statue of Liberty, the state of Hawaii, or the United Nations Building, could be done most clearly and effectively in space order as you relate your observations from top to bottom, east to west, north to south, or outside to inside. In some cases, time and space orders may be combined, as in your account of the operation of the steel mill.

3   *Topical order.* Some subjects are most effectively arranged according to their natural parts or divisions. One of these categories leads readily to the next as you would find if you discussed a new secondary school. Such topics as architecture, classrooms, athletic plant, landscaping, faculty, students, budget, and curriculum are natural divisions for such a talk.

4   *Problem-solution order.* This arrangement develops an analysis of the need for a change (problem), followed by the details of a plan to take care of the need (solution). It is especially effective in an argumentative speech although some informative talks can be arranged, using this order. An explanation of a new fire drill plan in a school could employ this arrangement very successfully.

5   *Climactic order.* This sequence begins with the least important point and builds gradually to the most significant idea. A series of arguments can be arranged effectively in climactic order. Descriptive material, starting with minor details, can also be developed in climactic order with increasing vividness until major points are reached. In each case the listener receives the impact of ascending strength or importance in such a speech.

6   *Simple to complex order.* Similar to climactic arrangement, this order begins with the simplest detail or principle and builds to the more difficult or complicated content. Thus, an explanation of the game of tennis to a physical education class might start with a simple principle: "Hit the ball over the net into the opponent's court so that he cannot return it." From this simple statement you could develop all the facts about service, receiving, team play, and rules of the game.

7   *Cause to effect order.* In this pattern, you describe certain circumstances or forces and then indicate the results that follow them; or you may reverse the order and describe conditions or results and then point out the factors that *caused them.* For example, a talk might explain a new chemical spray and could then reveal results of its success in fighting the Dutch elm disease in trees.

8   *Logical order.* Most commonly used in proving a proposition or main argument deductively, each supporting point becomes supporting proof or a reason for the acceptance of the major argument it supports. The best example of such an arrangement would be a brief in which all arguments and evidence are arranged so that they *logically* support and prove the major contention of the lawyer or debater.

As a teacher-speaker you will find among this list of possible arrangements of ideas those that fit *almost* every need for organizing the body of your talk.

You may wish to combine, or even create, new ways of arranging ideas to suit your particular situation.   The essential thing in your preparation is that you must have *some* systematic way of organizing materials so that you can handle them effectively and your listeners can respond readily to them.

THE CONCLUSION

The conclusion performs two functions in your speech: It summarizes and it brings your speech to a close.   In both instances its content and delivery are related directly to you the speaker, to your subject, to your purpose, and to the occasion.   In preparing your conclusion, you make a summary of the major points in the body of your talk and formulate an appropriate closing statement.

THE SUMMARY.   Brevity and simplicity describe the best summaries; however, these qualities may have to be modified if the talk has been long or its content complex.   A simple listing of main points, relating them to the specific purpose of the speaker, is usually sufficient.   However, your summary may be reinforced by repetition or restatement in order to clinch basic ideas with the audience.

THE CONCLUDING STATEMENT.   This sentence should be a planned "sign-off" and is of as great importance as the opening words of the speaker. It is good insurance for you to write this critical sentence in your outline, relating it to your purpose and basic content and to the response desired of your audience in the situation.   The statement should be definite and should sound final.

OTHER POSSIBILITIES FOR TEACHER USE.   Certain other means of concluding a talk are sometimes employed to make the closing statement more vivid or concrete.   They include: a conclusion that *applies* your ideas to particular audience interests; one that proposes specific procedures for applications of your materials; a conclusion that *appeals to local interest, to higher motives,* or to the *emotions* of the audience; one that *predicts* better things to come; a conclusion that strikes a *humorous note* (in a speech to entertain); and one that *epitomizes* the main ideas through a quick *overview* of the speech, expressed in an appropriate description, narrative, or quotation.   As a perceptive speaker, you will know when such modifications are appropriate.

PRACTICE THE SPEECH ALOUD,
WORDING IT PROPERLY

Your preparation thus far should have produced a body of ideas and information, organized so that you have a *deliverable* speech. Now it is your task to express that content in the best oral language you can master. To accomplish this aim, you will need some oral practice, using your notes or outline. Like nearly all effective speakers, you will find that such activity helps you to get the verbal "bugs" out of your presentation *before* you face your classroom or outside audience. Breaks in fluency, inaccuracies, hesitations, and repetitions can be almost entirely eliminated. You can then proceed smoothly, use suitable transitions, check and recheck word choice. Develop language that will have four desired qualities: clarity, persuasiveness, correctness, and accuracy. Thus your oral composition will be strengthened, and you will gain the benefits of the extemporaneous method of delivery, spontaneity and adaptability. As you practice your speech, your language may not be identical each time. However, your ideas will be verbalized, your sentences formulated, with correct, coherent relationships established throughout the content of your presentation.

Skill in wording your ideas comes with study and experience, both in practice sessions and before audiences. Work at it carefully and patiently, and you will note interesting improvements in your ability. For further study of language and style, be sure to read Chapter 6.

You have now completed the steps in preparing a speech. Each time you face a speaking situation, restudy your methods, improve them, and adjust them so that you will gain better results. Some speakers utilize a tape recorder to help them study organization, wording, and vocal delivery. Try using any such aids you find practical for you.

FOR FURTHER READING

Baird, A. Craig and Franklin H. Knower: *General Speech*, 3d ed., McGraw-Hill Book Company, New York, 1963, chaps. 3–7.

Bryant, Donald C. and Karl R. Wallace: *Fundamentals of Public Speaking*, 3d ed., Appleton-Century-Crofts, Inc., New York, 1960, chaps. 5 and 6.

Buehler, E. C. and Wil A. Linkugel: *Speech: A First Course*, Harper & Row, Publishers, Inc., New York, 1962, chaps. 5–9.

Gray, Giles W. and Waldo W. Braden: *Public Speaking: Principles and Practice*, 2d ed., Harper & Row, Publishers, Inc., New York, 1963, chaps. 12–18.

Hance, Kenneth G., David C. Ralph, and Milton J. Wiksell: *Principles of Speaking*, 2d ed., Wadsworth Publishing Co., Belmont, Calif., 1969, chaps. 8–11.

CHAPTER SIX

ORAL LANGUAGE

In comparing inferior and superior high school teachers by means of students' reactions, we found that among ten main items there was less difference between the good and poor teacher with respect to language than any other item. In analyzing this, however, we found that it occurred because students did not notice that inferior teachers were particularly poor in grammar or in fluency; but it is significant that among the thirty-one subitems on which the teachers were rated, the ability to use language that was clear and interesting ranked third as a factor which distinguished the good from the poor teacher.

Here are some typical comments made regarding the language use of both kinds of teachers:

SUPERIOR TEACHER	INFERIOR TEACHER
"She makes it clear."	"Makes any topic uninteresting."
"Her picture words and phrases are never tiring."	"Can't express herself."
"Talks the language of the students."	"Makes it clear, but uninteresting."
"You never wonder what she said."	"Talks too much."
"I never heard her make a mistake in grammar."	"She is kind, but hard to understand."

It would seem to be just good sense, then, to approach the use of language from the viewpoint of the student. We teachers are often unaware that the meaning which words have for us is not the same as their meaning to children. For example, while the family was out for a ride one Sunday afternoon, five-year-old John asked, "Dad, does this road belong to us?" Dad was taken aback for a moment, but replied, "No, John. This road is for everyone to use." He understood what John meant, however, when John next asked, "Well, are we going to take this road home?" Then Dad explained to John what *he* had meant! If you don't appreciate the difficulty a child has in learning the many words he needs to know, read Helen Keller's account of her own experience as related in *The Story of My Life*. For instance, learning that two objects could be different in many respects and still both called *doll*, or learning the difference between *mug* and *water*— these were difficult enough; but learning the meaning of *love* was something else again. As teachers, unless our language conveys an idea to the student similar to the one we have in mind, our talking is in vain.

Several questions thus arise. What is language anyway? How does the listener "make anything" out of what he hears? What kinds of meaning do we convey by language? What factors alter the kind of language we use? How can we improve the wording of our questions? How can we improve the wording of our explanations? How can we develop a better vocabulary?

WHAT IS LANGUAGE?

Yes, anybody knows what language is! Then, how would you define it or describe it? To do so would surely involve the term *symbol*. A symbol is a sign; it is not the thing, but it represents the thing. Thus, the sign at the outskirts of town may say "Battle Creek"; this only means that Battle Creek is in this vicinity—not that the sign is Battle Creek. In a similar way, a robin may be a "sign" of spring, or a track may be a sign of a deer. The word has meaning, then, as it refers to something else. Of course, it will still have no meaning if the "something else" (the referent) is unknown to the listener. Meaning depends upon something being *significant* to the listener; it is somehow a part of his past experience. How futile, then, to ask children to memorize the Preamble to the Constitution before they have concepts of justice, domestic tranquility, ordain, and constitution!

Our concern, then, is how to use language which will reveal to the listener the meaning we have in our own minds. And what is the process of transmitting that meaning? It is not like the system of wires and boxes formerly used in department stores. There, the clerk put the customer's money and the sales slip into a container, attached it to a "cart," pulled on a rope, and dispatched it via the wire to the cashier's cage. In the case of oral language, the meaning is not so unmistakably delivered. As the speaker, you utter a series of words which you must regard as only stimuli. You have not "sent" anything; you have merely tried to stir up some images or concepts in the mind of the listener.

Even though you assume that he understands the "code" you are using, you cannot be sure that he will respond as you wish. You may have said to a class, "Your assignment for tomorrow is to write a letter to a friend telling him about our assembly program." However, you were not prepared for the letter which merely gave a review of all of the assemblies for the year; nor did you expect Willie would *mail* his letter to his friend. Likewise, when you utter such words as *home, dinner, learn,* and *ball,* are you sure of what has occurred in the mind of the student?

Stirring up meaning by the use of language is even more difficult when the listener is not using the same "code" that you use. In this morning's mail was a reminder to attend a meeting of the Netherland-America University League. The program includes "Folk Songs," with the added line, "Kun je nog singen—Zing dan mee!" Would this have the same meaning for you that it did for the writer? Anne Morrow Lindbergh observed this problem in Alaska during a church service. The Eskimos had no word for *sheep,* or for *oxen,* or for *power;* so the minister had to explain passages from the Bible by substituting words such as: *reindeer, dogs,* and *dynamite.* A little child one day was playing near the stove in the kitchen. He grasped the handle of a pot which was extremely hot, and seemed unable to let go. His aunt, who is a native of Georgia, seeing his plight, almost yelled, "Turn it loose!— turn it loose!" He still clung to the handle; but when his dad said, "Let go of it!" he promptly released his grasp. We have trouble talking with the Russians because in their "code" the word *democracy* does not mean what it does to us—and yet what does it mean to us?

Another factor in the problem of stirring up meaning by oral language is the fact that it is *oral.* Often you have found that another person cannot appreciate a letter you have received from someone you know very well; this is due largely to the fact that when you read it, you "can just hear her saying that." In another case, when you say to someone, "That's the right answer," he would be more sure of understanding what you meant than he would had you written it instead of saying it. For, in saying it, you might mean, "You got the correct answer, but I question *how* you got it." Or, "Your classmate gave the correct answer; yours was not correct." This simply brings into focus the close relationship between the language you use and the manner in which you speak it.

Language was oral to begin with. Many languages or dialects still exist which were never written down by their users. However, as man became more civilized and society more complex, it became profitable to invent a means of converting sound-symbols into sight-symbols so certain observations could be relayed to others without the observer being present. Thus, on this page, we say to you what we would have said to you a year, or four, or five years before you now read it. Of course, printing has enabled the writer to say it to the thousands, separated by thousands of miles.

Even though we resort to the printed word on a tremendous scale, we usually prefer the oral. That is why we will leave our homes to go to an auditorium and listen to a man speak, even though he is a better writer than he is a speaker. He may only repeat some of the ideas we have read in his books or published articles; but having heard him speak them enables us to better understand what he meant.

CHARACTERISTICS OF ORAL LANGUAGE

What, then, are the differences between the written word and the spoken word? There are two kinds: One lies in the language usage itself; the other lies in the media by which the language is conveyed. People do not usually say things in the same form in which they write them. You will be shocked into believing this if you ever see a typed transcript of some remarks you have made as you spoke impromptu.

ORAL LANGUAGE IS ADAPTED TO THE RECEIVER. This means that the speaker talks to the kinds of listeners he has. He is aware of their motives for being present to listen to him. He knows something of their background on the subject he is discussing. He is (or should be) conscious of their general attitudes toward him. He speaks according to the size and makeup of the listening group. But the speaker also considers the place in which he speaks. Is he sitting at his desk with one or two persons standing by? Is he talking to a class in a typical classroom? Is he talking at a dinner table? Is he addressing a student body in an auditorium? These conditions should influence the oral language of the speaker. You can, of course, name other reasons for variation in the oral language caused by the need to adapt to the receiver of your idea.

THE SENTENCES OF ORAL LANGUAGE ARE INCLINED TO BE SHORT. This may be due to the speaker's inability to construct effective long sentences on the spur of the moment. But, from the standpoint of the listener, that is probably a good thing; for, with the necessity for him to grasp immediately what the speaker is trying to convey, he can easily get lost or confused by the long sentence. Note this quality in the following:

I recall the case of a man I once knew who certainly was not a great talker. He would say good-morning to you if you insisted upon it. He would go so far as to reply "yes" or "no" when he could not well avoid it. This man and his wife worked all the time. They had no children to sup-

port. They never went anywhere. They never bought anything. They both worked as hard as they could from morning till night. But the harder they worked the poorer they got.[1]

ORAL LANGUAGE IS VARIED IN SENTENCE FORM. Even though the sentences are characteristically short, they have variety in their length. There are also frequent questions, exclamations, and imperative sentences. Carl S. Patton illustrates this further on in the material referred to above.

Have you ever had, at times, an ambition to become the silent man who does great things? Did you ever draw a picture of yourself in your mind's eye, just as you thought you would some time look, after you had built a great building, or conducted a great campaign,—with a lot of people standing around you to compliment you or to ask you how you did it,—and you not saying a word,—as if it was too small a matter for you to talk about? as mum as General Grant when he looked over the city of Vicksburg? Well, that is a pretty good ideal; only you want to remember that merely keeping quiet doesn't make anyone great. There are lots of people who are very quiet and very useless. The things that we say are merely the paint and trimmings; the deeds that we do are the houses in which we live.[2]

ORAL LANGUAGE IS LESS ORTHODOX IN SYNTAX. We are accustomed to think of a sentence as having a subject, a predicate, and modifiers— with the possibility, also, of having direct objects, predicate nouns, phrases, clauses, etc. But in oral language a sentence fragment or a compression of a sentence will often serve our purpose well enough. To a comment we may say only, "Fine!" To a question we may reply only, "Yes" or "No" or "Certainly" or "Of course." We may greet someone by saying, "Good morning" or "Lovely weather, isn't it?" We may say to a class, "Any questions?" or "Good work" or "Not so good." We do not consider these expressions faulty because in the oral situation they communicate effectively and quickly what we have to say.

ORAL LANGUAGE USES FREQUENT REPETITION AND RESTATE-MENT. We do not mean to condone the repetition of phrases such as

[1] Carl S. Patton, *Speech Improvement*, F. S. Crofts & Co., New York, 1936, p. 151.
[2] *Ibid.*

I mean, you see, I says, in that regard, more or less, as far as that goes, it seems to me, well frankly. Nor do we approve the overuse of *grand, lovely, nice, swell, O.K., great, cute,* etc. We do mean that, since the listener must get the idea now or not at all, oral language needs to repeat the idea, if not the words. It is often said that a teacher feels he must say a thing three times to be sure the class understands it. He may, of course, say it in different words: he may use a comparison; he may use an example; he may even ask a student to restate the idea. It is done also in everyday life. While a person is explaining something, he may say, "Well let me put it this way..." or "What I'm trying to get at is..."—indicating that he is not quite satisfied with the reception he thinks his idea is getting.

ORAL LANGUAGE IS MORE PERSONAL AND DIRECT. In the first place, it abounds in pronouns such as *I, my, you, your, we, us,* and *our.* Our cue is what we hear in conversational speech. It is replete with these pronouns. These indicate the sense of personal relationship with the listener. This sense also causes the language to be more direct. There are fewer long generalizations and high-level abstractions and more use of specifics and concreteness. Teachers, as well as other professional and business people, too often talk "like a man walking on stilts." In its extreme form it is labeled *gobbledygook*—a term invented by Congressman Maury Maverick of Texas. Among the examples cited by Stuart Chase is the following "pedageese":

> *Realization has grown that the curriculum or the experiences of learners change and improve only as those who are most directly involved examine their goals, improve their understandings and increase their skills in performing the tasks necessary to reach newly defined goals.*[3]

Does this mean, "Pupils will learn more if they are sure of what they want and know how to get it?" An example of a less direct statement being understood because it is preceded by statements that are more direct is found in a speech by Dr. Ralph W. Sockman:

> *If my neighbor allows his garden to grow up with weeds how can I keep*

---

[3] Stuart Chase, *The Power of Words,* Harcourt, Brace & World, Inc., New York, 1954, p. 253.

those weeds out of my property? I cannot fence against weeds when the seeds are in the air. The only way to keep a garden a garden is to cultivate it. And the only way to keep America a free democratic society is to cultivate our civic, social and spiritual institutions.[4]

ORAL LANGUAGE APPEALS TO THE EAR AS WELL AS TO THE MIND. Of course, all sensations stimulate the brain, but here we mean that the spoken words have more sound-appeal than do written words. They are more euphonious and are more often combined into rhythmical patterns. Note the sound-values in such passages as: "Then heaven tries earth if it be in tune." "The next gale that sweeps from the north will bring to our ears the clash of resounding arms!" "I hear the feet of Sleep-eye go Tip-toe ... tip-toe." Note, also, the lingering effects of the rhythm in these passages: "The world will little note nor long remember what we say here, but it can never forget what they did here," "A date which will live in infamy," "Ask not what your country can do for you." If you listen to the talk that goes on about you, you will hear language that grates on the ear and sentences that sound awkward and jerky; but you will also hear words whose sounds leave an echo, and you will hear sentences you remember because they moved in rhythm.

YOUR VOCABULARY

For a word to be yours, you should know its spelling, its pronunciation, and its meaning(s) in various contexts. Here we shall deal only with the aspect of meaning. Students so regularly complain that their vocabulary is not large enough. However, while none of us has the richness of vocabulary that we would wish, the college student is quite likely to have a vocabulary of 20,000 to 50,000 words. So the first goal in working with vocabulary is to use well what you have.

If you examine memorable examples of verbal expression, you can see that there is very little difficulty in understanding the individual words. For instance, below are four columns of words, which are really scrambled quotations. Using those simple words, construct a sentence which has significant meaning. You may (and probably will) end up with an idea that people cherish.

---

[4] Ralph W. Sockman (Minister, Christ Church, New York), "The Worth of One," *Vital Speeches,* Aug. 15, 1949, p. 655.

I	II	III	IV
is	thought	Caesar	that
thing	our	you	loud
fear	those	I	what
the	of	so	are
we	songs	were	you
itself	saddest	born	speaks
only	sweetest	was	I
to	tell	free	say
have	are	as	so
fear	that		hear
			you
			cannot
			what

The above are four memorable passages, couched in a total of thirty-five different words, and twenty-nine of them are one-syllable words! In Lincoln's Gettysburg Address the most difficult words are probably "conceived," "dedicated," "proposition," and "consecrated."   It is the combination of simple, common words that makes Lincoln's "remarks" a cherished bit of American literature.   So, at the outset, keep improving your ability to use the vocabulary you now have.

But, with the great wealth of English words at your disposal, you ought to feel challenged to come into possession of more of them—much as a child explores a box of toys.   Henry Chester Tracy once wrote:

In childhood we were eager for words. They were significant to us. We gathered them as choice and important prizes. We offered them naively to our friends. That was a love that should have been caught and perpetuated, bred into an intelligent and growing capacity; for it was the first organization of the mind in its effort to appreciate and express a world.

Let us, then, look into the means of making more words our own.

VOCABULARY ENRICHMENT

When one embarks upon a new program or course of action, he may need some stimulation that serves as a kind of "kick-off."   In thinking of vocabulary development, we know of nothing more arousing than Helen Keller's account of how she learned her first word, actually the dawn of a whole new life for her. We quote one paragraph, hoping you will read it all in *The Story of My Life*.

> *The morning after my teacher came she led me into her room and gave me a doll. The little blind children at the Perkins Institution sent it and Laura Bridgman had dressed it; but I did not know this until afterward. When I had played with it a little while, Miss Sullivan slowly spelled into my hand the word "d-o-l-l." I was at once interested in this finger play and tried to imitate it. When I finally succeeded in making the letters correctly I was flushed with childish pleasure and pride. Running downstairs to my mother I held up my hands and made the letters for doll. I did not know that I was spelling a word or even that words existed; I was simply making my fingers go in monkey-like imitation. In the days that followed I learned to spell in this uncomprehending way a great many words, among them pin, hat, cup, and a few verbs like sit, stand, and walk. But my teacher had been with me several weeks before I understood that everything has a name.[5]*

TAKE AN ATTITUDE. The above paragraph and the one by Henry Chester Tracy suggest that you need to begin vocabulary growth with an attitude that is positive and motivating. It is essentially an attitude of "I wonder," a feeling that just ahead is something new and interesting, something to be explored. Then it involves the sense that, having explored and found, we have a new tool, a new device, with which we can better express our understanding of the world about us and better relate ourselves to those with whom we live. For example, did you recently hear the word *nasturtium* and wonder why they would give that name to a flower? What did the announcer mean when he used the word *fugue?* Is *moot* really a word?

USE YOUR EARS AND YOUR EYES. The above suggestions indicate that in every hour of the day there can be opportunities for the acquisition of new words. Just yesterday, while our twelve-year-old was watching a television show, he turned from the set and asked, "Dad, is an ambush the same as a bushwhacker?" Are the words you hear on radio and television a part of your vocabulary? How about the words you see on billboards, in magazine advertising, on the front page of your newspaper—to say nothing of

---

[5] Helen Keller, *The Story of My Life*, Doubleday & Company, Inc., Garden City, N.Y., 1954, p. 35.

words you hear in lectures and sermons or those you think you understand in the textbook you are studying or the novel you pick up to read before going to sleep? Have you increased your vocabulary any by reading this chapter thus far?

GET THE DICTIONARY HABIT. We know you have heard this before; but maybe heretofore you have thought the dictionary was frowning at you from its place on your desk. Could you imagine it is looking hopefully, invitingly at you? We like the story of the old lady who said she found the dictionary very interesting, although she had trouble following the story! If you are going to acquire any habit, you know that it involves repeated activity until you do not need conscious mental effort to perform the act. So let it be with your dictionary. Keep it always in the same place so your hand can reach it automatically. It need not be an unabridged dictionary, but it ought to be a recent edition of one of the three most frequently recommended dictionaries. After you have had it a year, you will know by its appearance and the way it handles whether or not you have the habit.

USE SPECIAL DEVICES. An obvious device is a pencil and notebook— to be carried with you at all times. Use it when you hear unfamiliar words so you can find out about them later. Some people make lists of words, adding from one to five each day and reviewing them daily. They use words from their reading as well as from their listening. An important suggestion is in order here. When you do look up a word in the dictionary, find out as much about it as you can; don't be satisfied with finding one synonym. Note that it has different meanings in different subject areas; note its etymology and its antonym; note its spelling and its pronunciation; note the family of words to which it belongs.

This suggests what might be called another device—learning the etymology and the history of words. For example, once you have learned that the Greek word *chronos* means time, think of the possibilities of extending your vocabulary to include such words as *chronic, chronicle, chronological, chronometer, synchronize, synchronous,* and *synchrotron.* This study, of course, involves not only learning the meaning of stems, but also the meanings of prefixes and suffixes which occur so frequently, particularly in words of Latin or Greek origin.

Related to using the etymology of words is the device of trying to define words yourself. Start with an easy word, like *pencil.* What can you say about it that would contain all the pertinent facts about it and make it distinct from such things as crayon, pen, or typewriter? Then proceed to abstract words such as *hunger*, or *honesty*, or *love*. It can be a game to see how your definitions compare with those in a dictionary. (Of course, you can define dictionary!)

No doubt you have received one or more Christmas cards containing some verse composed by a friend or relative. Upon reading it you may have thought that it was not a literary gem; but have you ever tried to write poetry? We believe it is an excellent way not only to tax the vocabulary you have but also to send you looking for better words to express what you are trying to think. You find you need new words to say things you could not say without them—or at least to say them more accurately. You don't have to look far for a subject. Just shut your eyes and listen to the noises in the building; or open them and look at the traffic outside on the street. Write about an episode in class or a particular moment in your relationship with a pupil or a friend or a member of your family. Don't feel bad if it isn't worth publishing; it will be worth doing for itself.

There is a parallel device in your use of speech. How often do you try to express exactly what you observe, or feel, or think? We are all inclined to use trite expressions rather than to speak more precisely. What do we *really* mean when we say, "It's been so nice...," or "Take it easy...," or "The food was wonderful," or "They have a nice home"? In our conversations we could use more of those words from our recognition vocabulary than we do, thus increasing our active oral vocabulary. When talking to groups, we can do the same. Too often a person feels that he must have a talk written out so he won't be at a loss for words. That is no solution for improving our oral vocabulary. We must put ourselves "on a spot" and trust ourselves to be able to use words at the moment which will convey our ideas. In the process you may hesitate or fumble a bit, but it is no great harm. A high jumper does not learn to clear 6 feet by keeping the bar down at 4 feet, where he is sure he won't miss!

Some people avoid taking vocabulary tests because they can't face the score they may receive. We recommend taking as many as you can, following up on all of the mistakes, as a kind of game for improving your vocabulary. You can find one each month in the *Reader's Digest*. Some news magazines provide them in their supplemental publications. Occasionally you will find one in a newspaper. You will find one at the end of this chapter. As a check on your fluency or word-readiness, we suggest a specially constructed synonym test which must be done within rigid time limits. The Educational Testing Service once constructed a sample verbal comprehension test for

Colliers. It is in four parts, each part presenting a different kind of problem.

Then there are word games. We do not know whether or not the inveterate crossword puzzle addict has increased his vocabulary to a marked extent, but it is probable that he has. The game of Scrabble is another provocative word game. Here, again, we know of no study of the effects of this game upon a person's vocabulary, but we are sure it can do no harm, and it ought to be more beneficial for your vocabulary than playing cards for three hours or even watching typical entertainment on a television show. Perhaps you know of other stimulating word games.

Besides the devices we have described above, there are books which deal with vocabulary building. Two such books are *Word Resources* by Frieda Radke and *How to Enlarge and Improve Your Vocabulary* by Richard D. Mallery. Each has material for making an inventory of your vocabulary, as well as some specific procedures for vocabulary enlargement. In *Word Resources* there is a test included in each of the first eleven chapters. The book itself is designed "as a text in vocabulary self-teaching." In *How to Enlarge and Improve Your Vocabulary* there is much useful material on the use of words and the means of learning new words, but it is also a handy source of information on synonyms and antonyms as well as on prefixes, suffixes, and roots of words. A third book, called *Vocab*, is really a little pocket-sized booklet described as "a fascinating solitaire or group diversion for alert minds." It is based on the idea of patterns of words according to whether the letters are formed on a vertical line or a curved base. Its use would at least tax the vocabulary you now possess.

PRACTICE. We have already pointed out how you might use writing and everyday speaking to cultivate your vocabulary. In working on your *oral* vocabulary there are some specific activities you could use. One of these is to paraphrase (restate in your own words) what you have just read or heard. This can be done profitably while studying a textbook. First, read a given paragraph swiftly to get the main idea that is developed. Then reread the paragraph to see how the author explained, amplified, reasoned, or illustrated the idea. Then lay the book aside and *say* what you would say if you were expressing that idea to another person. Don't try to remember sentences or phrases. Naturally, you will use some of the vocabulary the author used, but you will also use synonyms and phrases not used by the author. After you have done this, read the paragraph again and repeat your oral expression of it.

Another type of practice is to do something similar when you are listening to a person speak. You can do this most easily while listening to a radio talk or sermon. Here, of course, you have only one chance to understand what the idea is that is being developed. Listen carefully to the speaker's development of the idea, turn the volume down, and then say it yourself with the attitude that you have an audience listening. Then turn up the volume and wait for the speaker to begin the development of another idea, after which you paraphrase again. You will find that this process will do something for your listening, too.

A third method of practice is similar to the above. While engaging in a conversation or a discussion, listen carefully to another person's discussion of a person, idea, experience, etc.; then try to restate what that person has said, using his vocabulary as much as possible. Then ask the person if he would accept your statement of what he said. Again, this is an excellent device for improving your listening as well as your speaking.

Finally, as we have advised earlier, practice saying *exactly* what you mean. Discriminate in your use of verbs, adverbs, and adjectives. For example, did the person *walk* to school, or did he shuffle, amble, stride, or trip? Was the singer's voice *beautiful*, or was it resonant, rich, colorful, lilting, or clear? Did the wind blow *hard*, or did it blow like a gale, in gusts, or incessantly? Use words that discriminate, thus giving the listener an image similar to your own.

PRONUNCIATION

In the use of oral language the pronunciation of a word is of next importance to the meaning of it. We have said that when you investigate a word, you should find out as much about the word as you can, including its pronunciation. (How do you pronounce *pronunciation?*) It is one of the refinements of good speech, and is analogous to how a woman wears a flower or a bow she has chosen or how a man ties a tie he has selected. Your listeners may get your meaning whether you say *ak sept* or *as sept*, but they may be annoyed by your carelessness or ignorance, thus lowering their attention to your next sentence or discounting whatever else you say. For you as a teacher it is important, too, because you assume that if your pupils learn what you know (and more, we hope) and use the language as you use it, they will have made progress. For further discussion of pronunciation, consult Chapter 8.

GRAMMAR AND USAGE

The amount of space we shall devote to this problem is not proportional to its importance. If you are quite deficient in this aspect of language, we recommend that you study a text such as *Guide to American English* by L. M. Myers or Chapters 2, 3, and 4 in Porter G. Perrin's *Writer's Guide and Index to English*. If you are interested, but not particularly deficient, we would suggest the chapter entitled, "Schoolroom Talk," in *The Power of Words* by Stuart Chase or *The Structure of English* by Charles C. Fries.

Let us, at least, make the following assertions for you to ponder:

1   Language should convey meaning as clearly as possible.
2   Language expresses the person—his personality, his intellectual status, his social status.
3   Whenever a person violates accepted grammar and usage, he should know what he is doing.
4   Language is a function of time, place, circumstance, age, sex, and status.
5   Our use of language affects the way we think.
6   Language was made for man, not man for the language.

The Department of Communication at Michigan State University once made this statement: "Good communication . . . is clear when it is unambiguous in vocabulary and structure; effective when it is forthright, simple, specific, and adaptable to the audience; socially acceptable when it is appropriate to the community in which the user lives and works."

FLUENCY

Here is a problem which is inadequately treated in most speech books. Yet it is one of the great concerns of so many students who feel the need for speech improvement. It means the ability to speak readily, and has its origin in the Latin participle *fluens*, which means flowing. It means, then, a flow—but of what? Ordinarily, we think of a flow of words; but we believe that, rightly considered, it should mean a flow of *ideas*. The listener is not satisfied with flow of mere words; he is more likely to be satisfied with a flow of sense. That does not require a continuous outpouring of words. It is assumed that there are frequent pauses, and of varying length, in normal speech. If those pauses do not detract from the flow of meaning, the speaker is fluent enough. In fact, pauses are used to keep the meaning clear or to enhance certain aspects of it.

What are the factors involved in fluency? All of them are not language factors. This is true because we use language to represent meaning. Words are signs of percepts and concepts, and these are mental phenomena. There-fore, we cannot disassociate language from thinking. And, if fluency is a flow of meaning, the problems involved in it are bound to consist of lan-guage and thought—interrelated.

CLEAR CONCEPTS. Students in speech classes will say, time and again, "I can talk well about things I know about." They mean that they have sharp mental images about such things as how to tackle in football, how to do a dance step, or what kind of parents they have. They mean also that they understand clearly certain relationships in such areas as camp counsel-ing, drag racing, or student government in their high school. They have these clear concepts usually because of firsthand experience with them. They become less fluent on subjects in which they must get the concepts from word symbols, particularly if these are abstractions.

Since you are expected to talk about things other than your experience, you are faced with the question, How can I acquire clearer concepts about things I read and hear about? One answer is to immerse yourself in the subject. A veteran professor of history once said, "If you want to know history, you'll have to read a lot of it." It should be obvious, then, that you cannot be expected to talk fluently about a topic when you have read only one article on it. If you read from various sources or listen to more than one speaker, you will find that with each source you are increasing your ability to under-stand the next one; your vocabulary is being sharpened and enriched and your grasp of ideas is becoming more secure.

Another help in developing clear concepts is to ask questions. Ask questions of yourself while thinking about a subject; ask an author or a speaker ques-tions (to yourself) before you read or hear what is said under a certain title; ask yourself questions *as* you read or listen; ask questions of other people—after a speech or in conversation. Worse than not understanding something is to do nothing about it. A boyhood friend of ours had a ques-tion he would often ask, chiefly in a facetious vein, "Do you understand what you know about it?" Let that be your guide in asking questions.

FOCUS OF THOUGHT. With reference to the speech of children, Van Riper and Butler state: "Some of the most common fluency disrupters are these: interruptions, hurry, competition for the listener's ear, the loss of a listener, an unfavorable reaction on the part of the listener, and noise."[6]

---

[6] Charles Van Riper and Katharine Butler, *Speech in the Elementary Classroom,* Harper & Row, Publishers, Incorporated, New York, 1955, p. 108.

These distractions are not peculiar to children. College students and teachers are beset by them, too. How can you become immune to them? One way is to strengthen your thought pattern in your own mind. Keep aware of your key ideas, but also keep a strong sense of the relationship of points to the main idea and a strong sense of the relationship of points to each other. This means, to begin with, you should have a mental picture of your subject—whether it be a time-order arrangement, a space-order arrangement, a cause-effect arrangement, a general-to-specific arrangement, or a specific-to-general arrangement.

You will maintain your fluency better, also, if you keep your purpose for speaking in the foreground of your thinking. Do you want your listeners to see that there are three aspects to an assignment? Do you want them to understand the four steps in a process? Do you want them to believe that a certain statement is true? Do you want to stimulate them to think for themselves or to respond in some other way? If you are aware at all times of what your target is and where it is, you will be less sensitive to the distractions that may crop up.

You can utilize the above suggestions by setting up situations for practice. For example, use a radio as a distraction. Tune in a program where one or more persons are speaking; adjust the volume to a level where it will be a challenge, but not too great; then recite something you know from memory, such as a poem or a paragraph of a speech—but try to say it as though you were expressing its meaning to some listeners. (You may have listeners present.) A more difficult variation of this method is to talk extemporaneously while a program of music (at a distracting level of volume) comes from the radio.

You can also devise situations in the speech classroom. One suggestion is to try to talk with uninterrupted continuity in a small group discussion while two others in the group fidget with papers, books, pencils, etc.—or while all the others in the group look anywhere but at you. You might talk to the whole class while two members of the class visit with each other, another person is opening a window, another is reading a paper. Also, it is a real challenge to talk to the class when all of them are looking at the floor. Perhaps as difficult a situation as any is to talk to the class while another student is also talking to the class, each trying to get the interest of the majority of the listeners.

In any of the practice situations suggested above, after you have tried it, make an appraisal of it yourself or with the help of others. Note the places in your talk where you felt successful, trying to determine what enabled you to be; note also the places where the distractions shunted off your thinking, trying to analyze the cause—whether it was in the type of distraction, your concepts, your purpose, or some other factor. Then repeat the attempt, correcting the error in your attitude or mental processes.

EMOTIONAL CONTROL. It is difficult for anyone to be fluent when he is fearful, insecure, or self-conscious. Negative emotions will inhibit thought processes—an indication that thought and emotion are interrelated. The effects of even a mild emotional disturbance were revealed in an experiment reported by Morton M. Hunt. In the experiment fifty university students were asked to translate various sentences into a simple code. It was found that when students had to deal with sentences whose content caused a personal uneasiness (e.g., "My family does not respect my judgment.") they took longer to code such sentences and there were 50 percent more errors. It is to be expected, then, that when a person is talking to a group and has feelings of inadequacy, fear of social disapproval (being laughed at), or apprehension regarding his appearance or speech habits, he is liable to the same kind of mental block.

The whole problem of emotions cannot be dealt with here, but we shall point out a few practical means for alleviating inhibiting emotions. In the first place, you should realize just what your significance is in the speaking situation. If you are speaking to classmates, they do not expect you to be anything but a classmate. Posing as something else, just for the occasion, is just asking for trouble. If you are a teacher talking to your class, your pupils expect you to take the role of leader, adviser, and helper—not a walking encyclopedia or a paragon of virtue. If you are talking to parents, they expect you to be a human being, who has a college education (perhaps as they have), and who likes children and wants to see them grow in all respects. Therefore, in approaching a speaking situation, assess it accurately and do not try to be something you are not expected to be.

Too many people think of a speech as a crisis. We do not wish to encourage indifference or careless efforts, but let us face the fact that very probably "the world will little note nor long remember" what you say on a given occasion. You should hope that you have ideas that are good enough and well enough expressed so they will be remembered in part for at least a week. If they can make a lasting impression on your listeners, you can take great satisfaction from it. But, in any case, the world will go on in some fashion whether you speak or not.

Some students, of course, take a speech course only for the grade they can get in it. For them, each speaking opportunity is for a grade. They confuse the symbol for the thing it represents, like thinking the map is the territory it portrays. If you are inclined to do this, it means that you are talking only to the instructor. We believe, however, that most speech instructors want to know how well you can communicate with your fellow students. After all, it is of first importance that you be able to talk to your peers. After that, learn to talk to those older or younger than you or to those of different rank or status. When you show that you are effective in leading the thinking of the whole group, the grade will probably be taken care of.

Fear of not having anything to say is a common occurrence among people who are confronted with the necessity for speaking. We have dealt with this somewhat under the heading of "Focus of Thought." However, here we shall give some techniques which will reduce that apprehension. We assume that you are as well prepared as the situation permits, that you have a pattern of ideas, and that you have a desire to communicate them. Now, if during your speaking, you have a "blank" moment, you will not be disgraced if you admit it candidly. That helps to relieve the tension among your listeners and the pressure on yourself. You may also ask yourself, "What was that *last* idea I was speaking about?" If you are familiar with the pattern of your ideas, often the next one will come to mind simply by association, particularly if you have rehearsed or thought through your material as a *whole*, not by parts.

Sometimes students say, when they seem stymied, "I know what I mean, but I can't say it." When asked what they do mean, they proceed to tell it and the mental block is dissipated. The cue for you, then, is to realize that if you pause a moment to ask yourself what it is you are trying to say, you stand a good chance of being able to go on—provided you are not obsessed with having to say it with the exact wording you had planned.

WORD-READINESS. The last suggestion above indicated that you should rely upon yourself to be able to select words and construct sentences with facility. Van Riper and Butler state: "According to several researches, verbal fluency is in part a function of the richness of word associations and the speed of word association."[7] We have discussed how you might increase your richness of word associations under "Vocabulary Enrichment." How can you increase your speed of association? We suggest again the use of para-

---

[7] *Ibid.*, p. 98.

phrasing, as described earlier.   Another technique, in connection with the use of the radio, is to listen to a speaker with your hand on the volume control.   At a given point in the speaker's sentence, turn the volume down quickly and finish the sentence yourself with as little hesitation as possible. You can do this many times during one speaker's talk.   Even better might be the use of a tape recorder.   Have a speech recorded on tape and play it back, stopping the recorder partway in a sentence and then completing the sentence yourself.   Then play the rest of the sentence as it was given by the speaker on the tape.   This will give you a chance for comparing yours with his.

Another technique is to work with another person.   Choose a topic about which both of you know something.   Let one person start talking about it, the other listening closely.   Suddenly the speaker stops and points at the listener.   That is his cue to pick up the discourse and carry it along until you feel you have pretty well covered the topic.

You can use other methods while working in pairs.   One of these is to talk to your partner (while he times you) for two minutes on a familiar topic.   Whenever you hesitate on the choice of a word, he should insert one if possible before you use one.   You might want to take turns and keep score.   You can also use the paraphrasing of proverbs or epigrams.   One person gives the other a proverb, such as "A word to the wise is sufficient"; the receiver then must express the same idea in as many ways as possible within a certain time limit, one or two minutes.   For this, you will want to come prepared in advance with proverbs and epigrams.

One more suggestion.   Either with a tape recorder or without, do a radio broadcast of some event, describing things just as you see them.   It might be a homecoming parade, an athletic event, a street scene, the goings-on in the "Union" lobby, or what you see through the window of your room.   Try to keep the "faucet running" as you give an imaginary listener verbal pictures of what you see and hear.   It would be much like Rebecca's narration of the battle in Scott's *Ivanhoe* or what you commonly hear on your radio. If you use a tape recorder, of course, you will have an opportunity to play it back to note your successes and failures, perhaps making verbal improvements as you listen.

SELF-TALK.   In much that we have said about fluency and how to improve it, there has been the intimation that, after all, we need to be able to listen to ourselves.   As Wendell Johnson points out, "... any speaker is his own

CARL A. RUDISILL LIBRARY
LENOIR RHYNE COLLEGE

listener, often his own most responsive and vulnerable listener."[8]   Being an
alert listener to ourselves enables us to exercise control over the language we
use so that the language may not be the governor of our thinking.   For, as
Johnson says further on, "The more automatically or thoughtlessly we employ
the forms of our language, the more thoroughly and automatically they
determine the thoughts we have and the statements we make.   It follows
that the more fully aware we are of the language forms we are using, and
the kinds of relationships we are representing and stressing, the more of
a say we have in what we have to say."[9]   It resolves itself into the proposition stated by Humpty Dumpty in *Through the Looking Glass,* "The question
is which is to be master—that's all."

You have ample opportunity to listen to yourself through the use of self-
talk.   Now a person talking to himself may be a subject of ridicule if he
does it in the wrong places, but let us face the facts as stated by Van Riper
and Butler:

> *Actually, self-talking goes on throughout our whole lives.   It is vitally*
> *necessary to all thought.   Many psychologists feel that it is thought.   The*
> *stream of consciousness is a verbal stream.   We solve problems by first*
> *stating the problem, by asking questions of ourselves.   Then we try*
> *out one possible solution after another, thinking it out in words if we can,*
> *or silently commenting on our various attempts as we carry them out.*
> *The more fluent one's self-talking, the better he can think.*[10]

So you will have to lose some of the inhibitions imposed upon you by
our culture and once more, as you did when you were a child—and happy
because you could be naturally self-expressive without penalty—use self-talk
for both your thinking and your fluency.   It may be loud enough to be
heard by your ears, or it may be what is called "inner speech"—the kind
we have been using before we wrote these sentences.   You can do this
readily in many of the moments when you are alone, whether walking, riding,
or sitting by yourself in a corner.   The fact that people are often heard
"singing in the shower" suggests that it would be a place where they could
most readily indulge in self-talk also.   A skillful and highly fluent college
debater once said that he practiced refutation of opponent's arguments while

[8] Wendell Johnson, *Your Most Enchanted Listener,* Harper & Row, Publishers, Incorporated, New
York, 1956, p. 171.
[9] *Ibid.,* pp. 175–176.
[10] *Op. cit.,* p. 117.

shaving in the morning. So, do not be overly self-conscious about using self-talk and self-listening as you seek to improve your fluency.

THE TEACHER'S QUESTIONS

There have been many quips and comments about the questions teachers ask. And yet, a teacher without the ability to ask useful questions cannot go far in motivating pupils to learn, in teaching them to use what they already know, and in helping them to be expressive of their ideas.

The problem that arises here is, How do I ask the question? The answer depends upon why you *want* to ask the question. If you want to know the extent of a student's information, you will probably begin with such words as *who, what, when, where, why*—the newspaper reporter's questions. So, you would ask, for example, Who was the first American novelist? What is the formula for sodium chloride? When was our state admitted to the Union? Where did Albert Schweitzer establish his hospital? Why does your face get red in cold weather?

If, however, you were trying to stimulate your students to use what they know in some creative or reflective thinking, you would ask questions that were worded similar to these: If you had been in Washington's place, do you suppose you would have accepted the leadership of the colonial armies? What could have caused Samuel Clemens to be pessimistic about life? What would be the easiest way to figure the height of a flagpole? How can you decide whether or not a speech is effective?

Listed below are five questions actually asked during one period in an English class and five questions actually asked during one period of a mathematics class. Which ones, do you think, would be the most effective?

1 Would you be weary if you listened to this three hours every Sunday, or would you think twice?
2 Don't you wish you had a chance to talk to Johnathan Edwards personally to see why he felt this way?
3 Any questions on this? Do you understand it?
4 Did you like Sarah Kemble Knight? Why?
5 What were some of the examples of humor in Colonel William Byrd's *A History of the Dividing Line*?

1 Does that mean that 2 and A are to the negative power?
2 How did we do on that? How many got it right?

3   If you multiply the denominator by xy, do you have to multiply the numerator too?

4   How would $\frac{1}{6^3}$ be written with a negative exponent?

5   Do you know how to find the fifth root of 6?

THE TEACHER'S ANSWERS

One occasionally wonders whether the questions the pupils ask are more important than the ones the *teacher* asks. The very fact that the pupil asks a question probably indicates that he is not just a passive listener, and learning takes place much more readily when a person *wants* to know. The teacher's response to these questions is important, and we believe it should have at least three characteristics.

AN HONEST ANSWER

One honest answer is, "I don't know." Even a teacher does not know everything! But if you, the teacher, *should* know the answer and do not, you must take your choice between being regarded as not knowing enough or being regarded as a bluffer or a dishonest person. You may evade the question by saying, "That's a good question! Look up the answer for tomorrow." Or you may say, "That doesn't pertain to the lesson." Neither one really "gets by." Sometimes a teacher is asked for his opinion on a locally controversial matter. In this case his answer may arouse controversy with parents, for many of these are relayed home. However, an honest answer could be, "I'll be glad to tell you privately, but I don't think I should here." Another could be, "Of course, I may be wrong about this, but I think... However, I can see why some people think..." This opens the way for the pupils to do some thinking; then the wise teacher listens well and asks more questions.

A SATISFYING ANSWER

The pupil does not want an answer to another question, nor does he want a long preliminary discourse. If he asks, "How was the earth made?" he will get some satisfaction out of a brief explanation of one hypothesis. If he asks, "Why isn't Mrs. _____ our teacher any more?" the satisfying answer might well be, "She's going to have a baby." Information is most significant when it is most wanted.   Therefore, when a pupil has a question, there is your opportunity.

AN ANSWER IN LANGUAGE
SYMPATHETIC WITH THE QUESTION

Sometimes a teacher may want to restate the question to see if he has clearly understood what was asked.   Sometimes he may inquire into the reason for the question.   (A favorite game of some high school students is to sidetrack the teacher on a pet subject so he won't ask *them* questions.)   In either case, the language of the response ought to reveal the teacher's interest in the question.   It should include some of the words used by the pupil. For example, suppose a pupil asks, "Do people get money for being on the City Council?"   The teacher's reply could be something like the following: "Yes, Jimmy, they usually do get some money for it.   Sometimes they are paid a certain amount for each meeting."

Questions, answers, explanations—these are the chief channels through which the teacher's oral language flows.   Can you use this symbolic representation of ideas so your pupils get new concepts, new meanings, changed behavior? Can you induce them to seek for further information about themselves and their world? Can you provoke them to think critically and well? Rarely will you feel that you have spoken just the right word, but you will succeed oftener if you try oftener—avoiding the tendency to repeat trite phrases and trying to find the words that will stir up significance in the minds of your listeners.

FOR FURTHER READING

Alexander, Hubert G.: *Language and Thinking*, D. Van Nostrand Co., Inc., Princeton, N.J., 1967, chaps. 1–4.

Brown, Roger: *Words and Things*, The Free Press of Glencoe, New York, 1958.

Carroll, John B.: *Language and Thought*, Prentice-Hall, Inc., Englewood Cliffs, N.J., 1964.

Crowley, Ada Fuller: *Magic in Words*, Exposition Press, New York, 1955.

Dance, Frank E. X., ed.: *Human Communication Theory*, Holt, Rinehart and Winston, Inc., New York, 1967, pp. 116–129.

Eisenson, Jon, J. J. Auer, and John V. Irwin: *The Psychology of Communication*, Appleton-Century-Crofts, Inc., New York, 1963, chap. 7.

Fraenkel, Gerd: *What Is Language?*, Ginn and Company, Boston, 1965.

Hayakawa, S. I.: *Language in Thought and Action*, 2d ed., Harcourt, Brace & World, Inc., 1964.

Laguna, Grace A. de: *Speech: Its Function and Development*, Indiana University Press, Bloomington, 1963.

Oliver, K .A.: *Our Living Language*, distributed by Occidental College, Los Angeles, 1957.

Pei, Mario: *Language For Everybody*, The Devin-Adair Co., New York, 1956, chap. 1.

CHAPTER SEVEN

VOICE FOR SPEECH

Everything a teacher says is influenced by his voice and personal speech habits. In the first place, they make an impact upon the feelings of his pupils. In the case of elementary pupils, Kramer describes this effect as follows:

> *When the child enters school, he spends the greater part of the day with the teacher, whose voice and speech ... tend to influence not only the voice and speech but the personality and general well-being of the child. The teacher who has a high-pitched nasal, thin, flat voice very often affects children in such a way that they become high-strung and excited. On the other hand, the teacher with a quiet, well-pitched, well-supported voice, pleasing in quality, usually creates for the child a feeling of calmness and security, which is essential for his emotional and mental health.*[1]

Beginning teachers often have one great fear—that they may have discipline problems. Whether or not you have them will depend in great part upon your use of voice. Just recently we heard of a student teacher who was deeply interested in the fact that pupils at one end of the building were noisy and uncontrolled, while those at the other end seemed businesslike and content. He noted that the teachers at the noisy end of the building "yelled" at the pupils, while those at the other end spoke in a friendly, yet controlled manner.

We suspect, also, that the quality of learning done by those pupils differed according to the teachers' use of voice. Teaching efficiency may often lie not so much in the word as in the way in which the word is said. The teacher's real meaning, his emphasis, his ability to stimulate depend so much on his mode of utterance. As was said long ago, "It's not so much the word you say as the tone in which you convey it."

The teacher's vocal capabilities are important, too, because of increasing demands for teachers to teach by television, speak over radio, make tape recordings, and to appear publicly as representatives of the field of education before community audiences. Nor do we forget what the teacher does or does not convey by his voice among his colleagues and with administrators.

---

[1] Magdalene Kramer, "Speech in the Elementary School," *Teachers College Record*, vol. 62, p. 509, March, 1941.

They may not be aware of it, but the way in which one's associates accept him or his ideas are strongly colored by the kinds of sounds that come to their ears.

THE SOUND OF YOUR VOICE

Do you remember the first time you heard your voice from a recording? Your first—and very typical—remark quite probably was, "That doesn't sound like me!" And that is quite true, because before that time you had not heard yourself as others hear you. You were accustomed to hearing the sound of your voice through two channels: the sound waves coming into you outer ear by air conduction; the sound waves reaching the inner ear by bone conduction. The recording, if it is made with fidelity, enables you to listen to yourself as others hear you. You can do this also with a little instrument called a Tok-bak, a plastic device which channels the voice directly from the mouth to the ear—much like cupping one hand around the ear and the other hand at the opposite side of the mouth so that the voice is somewhat "tunneled" from mouth to ear.

THE NATURE OF SOUND

In order to understand the sound of your voice, you need to know some basic things about sound itself. We have said that you use voice to make sounds for others to hear. However, sounds are made in other ways. They are made by a vibrating string, by a vibrating bar, by a vibrating reed, by a vibrating membrane, and by a vibrating column of air. You can name an example of each of these.

REQUIREMENTS FOR SOUND. As was implied above, in order to have sound, there must be something in vibration. Of course, in order to have a body vibrate, some energy must be applied to it. Therefore, the first requirement is a source of energy. This may be a hammer, a finger, a bow (as with a violin), breath pressure, or even gravity. After the source of energy causes a vibration, there must be a transmitting medium—some means for carrying the sound. This is usually the air. However, sound will travel through any gas, liquid, or solid. It will not travel through a vacuum. The fourth requirement for sound is a receiver. For speech purposes that is either the ear or a microphone. We say there is sound when we can *hear* the vibrations. The physicist, however, says there is sound when there are vibrations which *could* be heard if an ear were present. He deals with the phenomenon of vibration; we are concerned with the perception of those vibrations.

HOW SOUND TRAVELS. In the paragraph above we said that sound travels through a transmitting medium. Do you know how it does this? In the first place, the medium must be elastic. If a body is elastic, it tends to return to normal position after it has been moved. It is much like a pendulum that swings back after it has been moved from its position of rest. This elasticity is possible because bodies are made up of billions of molecules, all in a state of motion. When energy is applied, they are propelled in the direction that the energy is moving, and then they bounce back.

In the air, this movement of molecules produces a condensation of molecules, followed by a rarefaction of them, similar to this: . . . .
. . . . These are called *sound waves*. However, keep in mind that they travel, not in one straight line, but in all directions from the vibrator. Thus, you are able to hear a sound if it is to your left, your right, above you, or below you. Perhaps you have felt the pressure of these waves on your fingers if you were carrying something like a carton when a truck went by. A moving picture film, such as *Sound Waves and Their Sources* (*Encyclopaedia Britannica*), would aid you in understanding this.

THE FOUR ELEMENTS OF SOUND. Sound has four properties or elements, all of which you have some knowledge. The first of these is *pitch*. It is the ear's perception of the frequency of vibration. The more frequent the vibration, the higher is the pitch. It is much like the sound of an automobile motor—the faster it runs, the higher is the pitch of its sound. You do not perceive any vibration as a sound, however, unless its frequency is more than 16 vibrations per second; nor will they be heard by the typical ear when they exceed 20,000 vibrations per second.

The second element of sound is *loudness*. One sound is heard as louder than another largely because of the amount of energy applied to the vibrator. The physicist thinks of this as intensity, resulting from greater or less amplitude of vibration. Amplitude, in terms of the pendulum, would be the length of the swing of the pendulum from its rest position. In sound waves it would be the amount of pressure exerted by the wave upon something like the eardrum. Loudness is also influenced by the reaction of a resonator— a concept that will be discussed in connection with voice production.

A third element of sound is *quality*. If two sounds are alike in pitch and loudness and still are different, we say that the difference is in quality. (The word *timbre* is often used as a synonym.) Thus, the same note may be played on two different musical instruments with the same loudness, but one may be recognized as different from the other because each has its own characteristic sound. To explain this we should point out that a given sound has its own basic pitch level—called a *fundamental tone*. But besides this, it may have several tones (frequencies) that are multiples of the fundamental. The number of these added tones (overtones), the relative strength of each, and their relationship to the fundamental will determine the kind of quality that the sound will have.

Time is the fourth element of sound. In a sense, the only aspect of time in a sound is its duration: how long does it last? However, since sounds so often appear in a series (as in speech or music), we are concerned with the interval between sounds. In speech we call this a *pause*. The term used in speech for the duration of the sound is *quantity*. Together, quantity and pause determine the *rate* (tempo), as well as the *rhythm* of related sounds. It is interesting to note individual differences in both rate and rhythm in listening to the footsteps of different people.

HOW VOICE IS PRODUCED

It should now be easier for you to understand how your voice is produced and why it sounds as it does. Your voice is essentially the result of a vibrating column of air. To produce it, four physiological agents are necessary: an energizer, a vibrator, some resonators, and some articulators.

THE ENERGIZER. This is the breath pressure that you produce by the use of your breathing apparatus. This immediately calls to mind your lungs—two spongy masses, one in each side of the chest, or thorax. The basic element in the lungs is the tiny air sacs, or alveoli, which are inflated and deflated as you breathe. There are about 800,000 of these, each connected by a tube, which is joined to a larger tube, which, in turn, is joined to a still larger tube, etc. Finally, there is one large tube leading from each lung. These tubes (the bronchi) join to form the windpipe (trachea) that you are familiar with. Think of a lung as being similar to a tree, with the leaves representing the alveoli, the twigs, branches, and limbs representing the tubes, and the trunk representing the bronchus.

Now, how is air inhaled and exhaled from the lungs? This involves a bony system and a muscular system. The most important bones are the twelve ribs on each side which form the rib cage. Seven of these are attached at the breastbone (sternum) at the front (three being fused to each other, and two being unattached at the front—the floating ribs), and all of them are attached to the vertebrae at the back. The collar bone (clavicle) and the shoulder blade (scapula) are involved as anchoring points for certain muscles. The ribs are capable of a movement outward and upward—an action like the raising of a bucket handle from the side of the bucket. The lungs, covered by a double-walled membrane called the pleura, tend to follow the movement of the ribs during inhalation and exhalation.

Of course, it is the muscle system which makes the whole process work. This system has three divisions: the thoracic muscles, the diaphragm, and the abdominal muscles. In the case of the thoracic muscles, there are, first of all, two sets of muscles between the ribs (hence, called *intercostals*); they are attached to the underside of one rib and the upperside of the rib below. Because of the angle in the shape of the ribs, when they contract, the ribs are pulled outward and upward, as described above. Other muscles along the vertebrae, in the neck, and at the shoulder bones assist in the movement of the ribs.

The second division of the muscle system is one muscle, the diaphragm. We know you have heard it mentioned often, but few people have a clear concept of what it is—or how to spell the word! Briefly, it is the floor of the chest. In its relaxed state it is a double-domed muscle, with one dome under each lung. Thus it has been described as being shaped like a lima bean or the top of a felt hat with a crease down the middle. It is attached to the sternum at the front, to the ribs at both sides, and to the vertebrae at the back. Contrary to what you may think, when it contracts, it moves down and forward toward a flattened shape. This contraction is for the purpose of inhalation.

The third division of the muscle system is the set of abdominal muscles. There are four of these, in layers. We shall not burden you with their names, but it is important to know that you contract these in order to sustain a long exhalation or to put the outgoing breath under greater pressure. Their contraction forces the viscera up against the diaphragm, thus helping to squeeze air out of the lungs.

Now, how do you inhale and how do you exhale? It will not do merely to say that you "draw it in" and then "force it out." Inhalation is achieved by the contraction of muscles. As mentioned above, the thoracic muscles pull the ribs outward and upward and tend to move the sternum forward.

The diaphragm contracts to lower the floor of the chest.   Both actions enlarge the chest cavity.   With the lungs following the chest walls, a partial vacuum is created, and so the outside air, with a pressure of fifteen pounds per square inch, rushes in to fill the vacuum.   It is much like a bellows, which is opened to acquire air and is squeezed to force the air out.

This brings us to the exhalation phase of breathing.   What forces are at work to force the air out, especially for speech?   The little air sacs in the lungs are made of elastic tissue; therefore, like a rubber balloon, their elasticity tends to force the air out.   With the relaxation of the chest muscles, gravity exerts some pull on the rib cage, helping to squeeze the lungs.   Since the diaphragm flattens when it contracts, for exhalation it relaxes and assumes its natural dome shape.   This also helps to reduce the size of the lungs, forcing the air out.   Another force results from the untorquing (untwisting) of the cartilages which join the ribs with the vertebrae and the sternum.   Since they are twisted somewhat when the ribs are raised, they are inclined to resume their untwisted state—just as your ear does when it is twisted.   Finally, as we have mentioned, the abdominal muscles contract for forced exhalation.   All of this is going on while you speak.

THE VIBRATOR.   The crucial organ for speech is the *larynx*—often called the "voice box."   It is really a valve made of cartilages, muscles, and membranes; it is situated at the top of the trachea.   It has a life-preserving function in that it helps to prevent food or other material from getting into the lungs.   It is also useful in lifting, pulling, pushing—in fact, in any kind of straining.

We shall not go into a detailed explanation of its structure.   When you feel your Adam's apple, you are touching a wedge-shaped cartilage which has within it your vocal cords.   These are not like two strings; they are more accurately called vocal folds.   They are two curtains of muscle and membrane which open and close like a "V."   Just as you can make a sound by forcing air between your lips, so you produce voice by forcing air between the vocal folds.   There are muscles which pull them apart for inhalation and other muscles which bring them together and tighten them for phonation (sound making).   Their length, thickness, and tension have much to do with the pitch of your voice.

Vibrations are produced by the alternate opening and closing of these vocal folds.   Being elastic and under muscle tension, after being blown apart by air pressure, they snap back together again.   This causes a puff of air to escape.   (Thus, a column of air is set into vibration.)   If these come at a rate of more than sixteen per second, we say that phonation, or vocalization, occurs.

The pitch of the voice is raised by bringing the vocal folds closer together, by increasing the tension on them, and by increasing the breath pressure beneath them. Loudness of the voice is increased chiefly by increased breath pressure, causing the vocal folds to emit stronger puffs of air. The voice quality is influenced by the condition of the membranes and the muscles. Inflammation, roughness, or nodes will tend to make the voice husky, raspy, or breathy. If muscles are not in good health, similar conditions may result. However, much of the quality of the voice depends upon the use of the resonators above the larynx, a subject to be considered next.

THE RESONATORS. Resonation is a kind of amplification or reinforcement of a sound or of certain aspects of it. An instance of one kind of resonance occurs when you pluck the tines of a tablefork and set the end of the handle upon a table. You notice that the sound of the vibrating tines is considerably louder. Tubes or cavities act in a similar way. You have noticed that if you have two goblets or water glasses, one having more water in it than the other, striking each lightly with a spoon will result in one having a different tone from that of the other. Similarly, if you blow across the top of two tubes, of the same size, except that one is longer than the other, different tones will be heard.

The explanation for the above phenomena is that every cavity has just one frequency of vibration to which it will respond. This natural frequency is dependent upon the size of the cavity, the shape of the cavity, and the size of its opening. The larger cavity has a lower frequency; the cavity with a longer neck has a lower frequency; the cavity with the smaller opening has a lower frequency. When one cavity opens into another, the frequency is changed. The kind of walls that a cavity has will also influence the tone.

Earlier we mentioned the resonators above the larynx. These are cavities, all connected with each other. The chief ones are the pharynx (throat), the mouth, and the nasal cavity. When you speak, the tone produced in the larynx is modified in various ways by these cavities before it comes out the mouth. The size of each cavity, its shape, its opening, the tightness of its walls—all of these play a part in making your voice what it is. They contribute, also, to the loudness of your voice. This is another way of saying that they enable you to project your voice or to give it volume.

THE ARTICULATORS. Sounds coming from the larynx and through the

resonators are not speech sounds until they have been changed by the articulators. These consist of the jaw, tongue, teeth, lips, hard palate, and soft
palate. In the formation of vowels, some of them act to change the
resonators—since vowels are primarily products of different resonating cavities
and openings. Consonants are the result of impeding or diverting the air-
sound stream that comes from the larynx. When you combine vowels and
consonants into continuous speech, the articulators are a busy team, working together with split-second timing.

WHAT YOUR VOICE REVEALS

Speech is a means of expressing both ourselves and our meanings. Sometimes the intent is to express mainly the self; more often the intent is to
express meaning. However, whenever you speak, you will be expressing
both. It is said that the listener always has two questions of the speaker:
What do you mean? How do you feel about it?

YOUR VOICE REVEALS YOU

Perhaps you have always assumed that the whole mechanism of speech that
we have described was designed or intended for speech. Upon second
thought, you can see that every part has as its first function the preservation
of life. Breathing is for the purpose of providing oxygen for the body;
the larynx is a protective valve for the lungs; the mouth and throat are for
the purpose of masticating and swallowing of food. Thus, you can see that
the speech organs and the speech process are close to life itself. It would
not seem strange, then, that the voice might reveal something of what
the person is.

Even though we have said that your voice reveals you, we will admit that
it is not safe to make judgments about a person without considering other
factors in the personality. It is almost impossible for you to separate the
physical behavior of the speaker, his thought processes, and his language
from his voice as you listen to him. Also, if he has a "trained voice," it is
more difficult to see beneath this veneer. Nevertheless, after we have listened
to a person, we may not remember many of the words he spoke, but we
can still hear his voice in memory. We shall state below what seem to be
the conclusions of people who have observed and studied the voice with
regard to what it reveals about the person.

BREATHING. The depth of breathing tells us something about the person. The energetic "go-getter" uses deep breathing, while the reflective, speculative person uses more shallow breathing. Breathing that is not deep, but balanced in amount, will be characteristic of the person with patience or endurance. A person who is in a state of inner conflict, trying to resolve an emotional problem, will be seen (and heard) taking deep, hard breaths. The rate of breathing changes with emotions. For example, a fearful person breathes frequently, while a person experiencing grief will breathe more slowly than normal. When a person feels joy or pleasure, he inhales with more energy; if he feels anger or pain, he exhales with more energy. The latter is also associated with the aggressive person. The shy person is inclined to use short exhalations, but a highly angry person may prolong his exhalation considerably.

PITCH OF THE VOICE. Most people have an optimum pitch level—or at least an optimum range. This is the pitch level at which the voice is most efficient. Persistent use of a higher or lower level often tells you something about the speaker. A low voice suggests the feeling of authority, of determination, or of stubbornness. However, a low voice that is warm in quality and flexible in pitch suggests confidence, intimacy, or sincere concern. We associate the high-pitched voice with a person under tension. The uncertain or fearful speaker often sounds as if he thinks the listener is far away or as if he were talking to space instead of to people or to a person. The use of pitch inflections tells you something else. When a male uses long, lingering inflections, he seems less masculine. When a person is unsure of himself, therefore indecisive, he uses more rising inflections, especially at the end of a phrase or a sentence. The assured or the dominant person uses more falling inflections.

VOICE QUALITY. This element of voice reveals the emotional state more fully than do any of the other elements. Sometimes the quality of a voice is poor because of severe laryngitis or some other illness. It may be poor because of abuse of the vocal folds or because of nodes which have developed on them. However, since quality is more often the result of how the resonators are used, it is interpreted as a sign of something in the personality. The voice with excessive nasality makes the listener suspect that the speaker is cynical or sarcastic. This may be a result of his need to attack others because of his fear of himself. Aggressive people are labeled so in part because their voices are harsh or strident. Since aggressive people are so because of a strong urge to excel or because they compensate by aggression for their feelings of insecurity, the result is tension and strain; the result of this tension is the harsh or strident voice. On the other hand, the healthy, poised individual is usually possessed of a vibrant, warm quality; it has richness and color.

VOCAL INTENSITY. The extremes of intensity in the voice are the unusually intense or loud voice and the abnormally weak or soft voice. A person's occupation has some influence upon this. The person who works out-of-doors or in a noisy environment is almost compelled to use a loud voice, whereas the librarian or the nurse learns to use a subdued voice. Likewise, the healthy, energetic person is inclined to use a vigorous voice, while the person who has chronic ill health or who expends less energy speaks softly. Beyond this, we see the person who has a need for power using voice of greater intensity than the person who feels self-sufficient. We associate unusual loudness, too, with the person who is angry; and yet, sometimes the anger of a man speaking softly may be greater than that of someone who shouts. The aggressive or the boastful person is inclined to use a loud voice; but so is the jovial, hail-fellow-well-met person. In general, the person who uses much intensity of voice suggests a more primitive, less sophisticated person. This is revealed by his tendency to use intensity as the primary means of emphasis on words, whether in speaking or reading aloud.

THE USE OF TIME. Here we are concerned chiefly with rate and rhythm. Excitement is associated with a rapid rate. Good news or high anticipation may arouse this. However, we often hear a person speaking or reading rapidly simply because he feels ill at east and wants to get it over with. The person with a slow rate is likely to be one who is deliberate or who feels that he has important things to say. On the other hand, a slow rate may result from the person's ineptness with language; it may result, also, from his efforts to repress strong emotions.

The rhythm of speech is the peculiar combination or pattern of quantity and pause. The normal rhythm of a person's speech is a result of biological rhythm patterns, his use of language, and his meanings. A person's emotions will change the normal rhythm. That is why the stutterer's problem is labeled as a rhythm problem. The cause lies deep in his emotions. It is interesting to note that the more regular or simple the rhythm of poetry is, the more it suggests the primitive. The very tense person will have a rhythm that seems strained and jerky. The person without tension will have a rhythm that is sluggish, suggesting the low swells on the ocean rather than the sharp, breaking waves. This comparison also seems to fit the extrovertive persons and the introvertive.

We have presented the above observations regarding the meaning of the voice with respect to personality for two reasons: The first is that it may help you to better understand the students you teach and the people with whom you work; the second is that it may help you to understand yourself. It will give you a basis for occasional self-listening, as well as a sensitivity to the feedback that you get from your listeners. It would be interesting to observe your present instructors and others to whom you listen for a week to see if you can confirm what we have said.

YOUR VOICE REVEALS MEANING

In the chapter dealing with language we pointed out the differences between oral and written language. One of these differences is that in oral language the voice can contribute much to the meaning. To appreciate this, you have only to ask yourself how many meanings there could be in such a simple sentence as Oh, is that so? For each way that you might say it, it would be impossible to indicate that meaning by written language. The voice can reveal two kinds of meaning: one of these is the intellectual meaning—the idea that is being expressed; the other is the emotional meaning—the subjective reactions of the speaker.

INTELLECTUAL MEANING. The voice expresses this kind of meaning essentially by making the idea as understandable as possible. One aspect of this is the use of emphasis. In the sentence, "I am going with John," any one of the five words could receive vocal emphasis, and the meaning would change in each instance. Many people, however, are unaware of how the emphasis is produced. In the first place, if the word has more than one syllable, the emphasis is on only one of the syllables. Secondly, that syllable will receive more time quantity; it will be spoken with greater intensity; it will have a marked pitch inflection. If you listen closely, you will note those three things happening if you emphasize *going* as you say, "I am going with John."

The voice can be used for making discriminations in meaning that may be more subtle than the emphasis of one word. Here time and pitch are the most useful elements of voice. The language of ideas comes in groups of words, or phrases; therefore the idea comes clearer where pauses come at appropriate places. Each sentence has its own rhythm; so here, too, the place-

ment and length of pause is important, along with the quantity given different syllables. Notice how this applies in the lines: He who knows not and
knows he knows not/He is a child; teach him. It would apply also in a
prose sentence, such as: There is a time in every man's education when he
arrives at the conviction that envy is ignorance.

The use of pitch is invaluable in making distinctions of meaning. The lack
of it is characteristic of the dull, unimaginative speaker or reader. Shades
of meaning can be revealed by key and inflection that cannot otherwise be
made evident. Let us illustrate it by the most remembered sentence in
Lincoln's Gettysburg Address. In part of the last sentence, he said, "that
government of the people, by the people, for the people, shall not perish
from the earth." Many people use a rising inflection (and more quantity)
on the prepositions "of," "by," and "for"; however, trained sensitive readers
use a rising inflection on the first syllable of "people" and use only a slightly
rising inflection on the prepositions, except for the last one. In reading
poetry, it is a common sin among untrained readers to use a falling inflection at the end of each line, clearly indicating that they are not thinking
the idea as they read. The idea would be nearly killed in the poem "The
Raven" if it were read in lines like these, with a falling inflection on the
underlined words:

Once upon a midnight dreary,
While I pondered weak and weary,
Over many a quaint and curious volume
Of forgotten lore.

This leads us to point out that pitch, as well as time, helps to show relationships of the parts of the sentence to each other. When a person begins a
sentence, he should know something of how that sentence will be constructed
and how it will end. Otherwise, he will use false inflections or poor phrasing
before he finishes. This is the reason that a radio newsreader often brings
off a sentence poorly. Note how the following sentence could be botched
up as to meaning if the pauses were placed where we put the dashes and
the underlined words were given a special rising inflection:

It is well—to note that pitch changes in speech—are almost infinite in
number,—while those of song are—very strictly—limited.

We have tried to show a few of the aspects of time and pitch as they help
to convey meaning. Even though the quality of the voice and its intensity
play their roles in the intellectual content of speech, it is through careful use

of time and pitch that fine discriminations can be made, delicate shades of meaning revealed, and the total idea of the sentence clearly presented.

EMOTIONAL MEANING. In discussing how the voice reveals your personality, we referred to some of a person's emotional expression. What was said there is closely related to the emotional meaning in the spoken word. When one speaks or reads, there is an overall mood in the content. It may be any of the following: reflective, humorous, anxious, vindictive, challenging, fearful, playful, loving. Of course, there are others. The language suggests the mood, but it is the voice that makes it unmistakable. One could say the following line with any of several moods:

I could not love thee dear so much, loved I not honor more.

Besides the general mood of the content of speech, there are the particular emotional meanings. When a person is speaking his own thoughts and feelings on a subject, the emotional content of what he says is inseparable from his own personal feelings; when he is reading aloud the expressions of another, the emotional content is largely in that which was written. In either case, the voice is the chief agent for conveying this meaning. There is emotion in the statement when a student says, "I've decided to drop out of college"; but there is almost a full charge of feeling when one soldier says to another, "You think I don't care—you think you're the only soul that cares!"

Every element of voice is called upon to express emotional meaning. While the quality of the voice seems to reveal the most, the pitch level of the voice and also the intensity and the time factors of quantity, rate, and rhythm make their contributions. You can observe these, isolated from the physical expression of the speaker, when you catch the emotions of someone you are talking with on the telephone. A person fails to communicate emotional meaning when he is inhibited by other conflicting emotions (such as fear of his audience), when he lacks the vocal flexibility to express the emotion, or when he lacks the sensitivity needed to perceive the emotion in the material itself.

IMPROVING YOUR VOICE

All of us can profit from the advice of King Lear given to Cordelia when he said, "How, how, Cordelia! mend your speech a little, lest you may mar your fortunes." With respect to voice, we consider it especially important for the teacher, since his pupils often have to listen to him for an hour at a time—or perhaps all day! If you are interested in improving your voice, we would remind you that there are many books which deal exclusively with voice. We urge you to use some of them. It is our purpose here to point out some ways by which you can discover your needs and begin to do something about them.

ANALYSIS

Since an analysis involves the separation of the whole into its parts, perhaps you can see now why we wanted you to read about the process of voice production and the elements involved in it. If you are to analyze your voice, you can do it better with that background. First of all, you will want to listen to your voice. In the chapter on listening, we urged that you do some self-listening. Now, you might do so again, paying particular attention to your use of voice. Try to hear yourself as you think others hear you. If you have a Tok-bak, mentioned earlier, try that, too. Make use of a tape recorder. Record various samples of your speech—such as informal conversation, oral reading, and talking before a group. Then listen critically to your use of breathing, your voice quality, your use of pitch, your loudness or intensity, and your use of the factors of time. It may help to listen closely to other voices, too, as a basis for comparison.

As a check on what you think you hear in your voice, ask others what they hear. Your family or friends could help—especially if you ask them particular questions about your voice. For example, do they think you talk too fast, too low in pitch, too soft in loudness, too harshly or with too much nasality, etc. If you haven't already talked with your speech teacher, don't overlook this opportunity. He will be your best source of help in determining which needs are greatest, as well as in helping you to decide what to do about them. Let us now look at six areas of your voice in which you may want to make some improvement.

AREAS FOR IMPROVEMENT

BREATHING. There are three main requirements for good breathing for speech: adequate lung capacity; quick and quiet inhalation of air (through the mouth); control of the outgoing air, with the ability to start and stop the exhalation whenever the demands of the idea or the emotions call for it. If you have to inhale too often—having the feeling that you are panting—

your air capacity might be low. However, the cause is more likely to be tension or excitement. In that case, consult with your instructor about ways of relieving some of the tension. On the other hand, if you do have a low air capacity, you can do nothing to enlarge your lungs; you can, however, make sure that you are inhaling deeply enough, making use of what capacity you have.

Few people have the problem of not inhaling quickly and quietly. You can inhale more quickly through your mouth; it would be ludicrous, anyway, to close your mouth while talking in order to inhale through your nose. If the inhalation is noisy, it is because you are causing air-friction with your teeth or you are not letting your tongue lie flat in your mouth. To help correct this, watch the opening of your mouth by means of a mirror; listen carefully, also, as you adjust the opening and as you find the tongue position which will result in noiseless inhalation.

The important aspect of breathing is achieving controlled exhalation. Your essential skills here are those of muscle control. As we pointed out, for inhalation, the diaphragm must relax. This relaxation must be smooth during the outpouring of sound; but it must hold whenever there is a pause, such as between words or between sentences. A similar kind of control is needed with the thoracic muscles. Since these muscles contract to lift the rib cage for inhalation, they relax for exhalation, with the pull of gravity, the elasticity of the air sacs in the lungs, and the untorquing of the rib cartilages acting as forces to expel the air. Their pausing in the exhalation process is noticed between the syllables of words. So, controlled relaxation of the muscles is again important for controlled speech.

One other factor in controlling exhalation is the set of four abdominal muscles. During inhalation these muscles relax, unlike the diaphragm and the thoracic muscles. Therefore, for exhalation they contract—especially when the reserve air is needed. You can feel these muscles tighten by placing your hand on your abdomen while you expel all of the air that you can. When an idea is sustained at some length or when strong emotion is involved, in order to provide the reserve air, the abdominal muscles contract to push the viscera up against the diaphragm in its relaxed position to aid in expelling the air. Obviously, then, the demands of speech may often require the controlled contraction of these muscles.

For the improvement of your breathing in speech, you can do two things: First, learn to control your emotions while speaking; second, learn to control the contraction and relaxation of the muscles involved. For the second part, you can find many exercises for practice; however, the practice of these will be of little value unless you can use them while you are speaking. This will take some conscious effort for a while; it is hoped that they will become habituated.

TONE PRODUCTION. Good tone production requires normal vocal equipment. This means that the larynx has no malformations and that it is in a good state of health. Abuse of the voice, sinusitis, laryngitis, and cancer naturally prevent the person from achieving proper closure of the vocal folds and also interfere with the fine adjustments of muscles and cartilages needed to ensure a good tone.

Related to the health of the larynx is the necessity for adequate relaxation of both the extrinsic muscles of the larynx (those which move the larynx as a whole) and the intrinsic muscles (those which function within the larynx). You have noticed that when your whole body is relaxed, your voice sounds more full, smooth, and in a better key. Sometimes you can relax the muscles of the neck and larynx by certain exercises, such as rolling the head, and massaging the neck muscles. This is a specific help when you cannot become totally relaxed.

A further help in tone production is making the right "attack" on vowels or voiced consonants. Your attack may be too soft or too sharp. If it is too soft, you are probably wasting breath instead of using all of it for vibration of the vocal folds. In this case, try the other extreme first; initiate a word such as *our* with definite vigor on the first sound—*ah.* Then listen as you use an unusually soft or breathy attack—saying something more like *hower.* Thirdly, make an attack that is about halfway between those two. If your attack is normally too sharp, do the above in reverse. You will need either a tape recorder or another person to listen in order to make the most of this practice.

As you see from the above, any discussion of tone production leads to the subject of voice quality. We pointed out earlier in this chapter that certain voice qualities often reflect personality characteristics. Obviously, if you have an undesirable voice quality that results from a present personality trait, you will want to do something about yourself. If the quality is simply a habit that originated from an earlier attitude or emotional problem, the approach should be toward establishing new habits. This can be done by the use of voice exercises and practice with the help of your instructor.

We have mentioned the voice that is either too soft and breathy or too sharp in its attack. Another undesirable quality is that of the harsh or strident voice. Usually the underlying cause here is tension. The tension may be due to fear of others or fears about your own inadequacy; it may be due to overaggressiveness on your part; it may be due to a strong urge for perfection. Relaxation is the key to overcoming this—whether by developing more healthy feelings or by using techniques for physical relaxation.

Another common defect in quality is hypernasality. While some of the cause for this may lie in the tone produced in the larynx, it appears that more of it is the result of faulty use of the resonators. There is undue use of the nasal cavity for resonating the tone. Physiologically, there are two causes for this: One is lowering of the soft palate so that the passage to the nose is too wide; the other is the failure to open the mouth enough. A person who is defensive, sarcastic, or resentful is inclined to have hypernasality. If you find that this is the cause in your case, you can see the kind of effort you will have to make. On the other hand, if the hypernasality is a result of habit, you will need to work with exercises and practice which will require more closure of the passage to the nose and more readiness to opening the mouth. Self-listening will be important here, as will the use of a tape recorder or a listener besides yourself.

LOUDNESS. Often referred to as intensity, loudness may be insufficient or excessive. Either defect could be due to a hearing loss, depending upon the type of loss. If you know or suspect that you have a hearing problem, the first step is a visit to a clinic or to an otologist. If, in conference with your instructor, you find that the seat of the problem lies in your personality adjustments to speech situations, you can begin there. The defect in loudness is usually one of insufficient loudness. If you work on that by exercises, keep in mind that your voice projects better with adequate breath support, by full use of the resonators, and by opening the mouth.

USE OF PITCH. As we pointed out earlier, each voice has a pitch area where it is most efficient (optimum pitch). If you find that your vocal pitch is too high or too low, try to find this optimum pitch. You can do this by humming from your lowest pitch to your highest and then back down. The point at which the tone sounds strongest is likely to be the optimum pitch. Some teachers of voice say that it will be about one-third of the distance between your lowest pitch and your highest. Any pitch changes should be both up and down from the optimum level. If your pitch level is a serious problem, you would do well to seek the services of a speech clinic, since it may be difficult to establish a new pitch, and forcing the voice may cause the tone to suffer.

The use of pitch inflections is often deficient. In flexible, cooperative speech more inflections are upward rather than downward. If downward inflections predominate, you should examine your concept of yourself and your attitude toward others, for it suggests that you are too assertive, aggressive, or inflexible. Of course, if you rarely use downward inflection, especially at the ends of declarative and imperative sentences, you may be too submissive, uncertain, or fearful. In oral reading, a person may use false inflections—changes in pitch which are not consistent with the relationship of words in the sentence or with the attitude or emotion being expressed. The solution here lies in closer study of the material for the intended meaning.

The most common fault in pitch inflection is that a narrow range of inflection is used—in both upward and downward inflection. This tendency is frequently labeled as the monotonous voice. If you have this fault, it may be because you are inhibited by fear, timidity, or self-consciousness. In many cases, the person does not hear himself do this—because of the feelings he has or because he becomes engrossed in using predetermined language for his ideas. You can improve in this respect by, first of all, sensitizing yourself to it through the use of a tape recording of some of your speech samples. Another help is to have a sharp appreciation of your idea as you utter it. A third help is to have a strong urge to communicate that idea to your listeners; show them that you want them to understand or to feel a certain way. One final suggestion—one that accompanies the last two—is to involve more of your body in what you are saying. This is especially true of your face. We have a strong belief that a person's voice is about as expressive as his face.

CONTROL OF RATE AND RHYTHM. Hardly anyone says that his speech rate is too slow, but many people criticize themselves for talking too fast. Now, there is no one rate that is suitable for all people. However, if the rate is so fast that it prevents the listener's comprehension of the idea, or if it interferes with intelligibility because the articulation suffers, then it is too fast. When we have asked students why they talked fast, the usual answer has been that they want to "get it over with." This indicates that the emotions are not under control. If you have this difficulty, find ways of handling your emotions first.

Some people have developed the habit of rapid speech because earlier in life they were apprehensive about being interrupted (as in family conversations), and so they resorted to saying things in a hurried manner. If that is the cause of your rapid speech, it will help you to have practice sessions of discussion in small groups where it is understood that you may have all the time you want to say what you have to say. If you do this, either monitor your own rate or ask someone to signal you when your rate is too fast.

Arhythmical speech is another deficiency in the use of the time factor. The rhythm of your speech is determined by your use of quantity and pause. The stutterer has the most serious problem in this respect; he can control neither the amount of time he gives to a word nor the place and length of his pauses. When other people are arhythmic, we say that their speech is jerky or irregular. Part of the reason may be in the speaker's fluency of thought and language; part of it may be in personality factors; part of it may be his lack of rhythm in everything that he does. Your ability to improve your speech rhythm, then, will depend upon what you can do to eliminate the primary cause(s). However, it will also be helpful to do much oral reading, using materials that have a variety of rhythm; include poetry of different kinds, including blank verse, but also use speeches that have good oral style, and use excerpts from plays.

VOCAL VARIETY. We have found in a study of the speech of teachers that students react more to the lack of variety than to a deficiency in any one of the elements of voice. This is due in part to the fact that change stimulates attention; it is due, also, to the fact that variety in the voice usually results in the content of speech being clear and its impact greater. Good variety means that all of the four elements of the voice change as the ideas of the speaker unfold and as he reveals his feelings about them. But this should not be a patterned variety (repetitious melody)—i.e., the voice changing within a phrase, but the phrases having the same pattern. You hear this when a teacher says in a kind of artificial melody, "And now, boys and girls, I shall read you a story...." You may hear it also when an instructor is going through the same explanation for the third time.

What can you do to achieve meaningful variety? In short, it would be the implementing of what we have said about improving each of the elements of voice. However, let us put it into four main directives. The first of these would be to develop a mind that is sensitive, aware, and discriminating. You need to cultivate an awareness of your world and the people in it. Your imagination should be sharp. Then keep in mind that things become significant to the listener only if they are significant to the speaker; therefore, you need a strong realization of meaning in what you say.

As a specific kind of practice, try saying some ordinary short sentences in as many ways as possible. For example, can you say the sentence "What do you mean by that?" so it will mean each of the following:

1   I know what the others meant.
2   Your words don't make it clear.
3   Are you insulting me?
4   It makes no sense at all.
5   I'm puzzled.

Try this with such sentences as: "I see what you mean"; "We've had a very lovely time"; "That will be your assignment for Monday."

Related to the above is the second directive: Develop your perceptual abilities. This can apply to the use of all of your senses, but it is particularly important in seeing and hearing. Seeing enables you to perceive all of the meaning in printed material, the source of so much of your learning. This is obviously of utmost importance if you read to others. But seeing also enables you to perceive the reactions of others to you and to your ideas. On the other hand, hearing not only can give you meaning from others' voices, but it enables you to give attention to the meaning of your own voice. Do you really hear the quality, the loudness, the pitch changes, and the rhythm of your voice? Do you know how others hear you?

A third directive is to develop controlled emotional response. Note that we have implied that emotional response is desirable; interesting speech is emotionally toned. However, there needs to be control. Often the voice lacks variety because the emotions are inhibiting the full play of the voice. For example, the constant fear of making a mistake or of saying the wrong thing is the worst of demons with respect to interestingness that comes from vocal variety.

Finally, we would say: Develop a responsible vocal mechanism. This means that all the way from breathing to articulation you want a mechanism that will do what you want it to do. This requires physical fitness, ear training, and practice. Much of the practice may have to be with specific exercises; but don't overlook the opportunities you have to be in plays, to read aloud, to give speeches, to be a group chairman, or to contribute to class discussions. If you are perceptive, you will learn from all of these.

To conclude this chapter we want to assure you that we do not believe that voice is an end in itself. Rather, we think of it as being an integral part of your personality in that it reveals your reactions to yourself and others, and it helps to produce reactions in others. It is an intricate mechanism, having almost infinite capacity for communicating your thinking and your feelings. If it is taken for granted and little attention is given to it, it may communicate poorly or falsely what you mean and what you are.

FOR FURTHER READING

Anderson, Virgil A.: *Training the Speaking Voice*, 2d ed., Oxford University Press, New York, 1961.

Bronstein, Arthur and Beatrice Jacoby: *Your Speech and Voice*, Random House, Inc., New York, 1966.

Eisenson, Jon: *The Improvement of Voice and Diction*, 2d ed., The Macmillan Company, New York, 1965.

Fisher, Hilda B.: *Improving Voice and Articulation*, Houghton Mifflin Co., Boston, 1966.

Gray, Giles W. and Claude M. Wise: *The Bases of Speech*, 3d ed., Harper & Row, Publishers, Inc., 1959, chaps, 2 and 3.

Hanley, Theodore D. and Wayne L. Thurman: *Developing Vocal Skills*, Holt, Rinehart and Winston, New York, 1962.

King, Robert G. and Eleanor M. DeMichael: *Improving Articulation and Voice*, The Macmillan Company, New York, 1966.

Van Dusen, C. Raymond: *Training the Voice For Speech*, 2d ed., McGraw-Hill Book Company, New York, 1953.

Van Riper, Charles and John V. Irwin: *Voice and Articulation*, Prentice-Hall, Inc., Englewood Cliffs, N.J., 1958.

CHAPTER EIGHT

ARTICULATION AND PRONUNCIATION

A personnel officer in an elementary school district employed a new teacher for the second grade. She was an attractive young woman, very intelligent, but she had what he described as a "cute lisp." When school began, the second graders liked her very much. In fact they were so influenced by her that before long every one of the children also had a cute lisp, just like hers. This experience has a message for you. As a potential teacher, you can understand the effect of the teacher's behavior upon her pupils. As a student in a speech course, you should now be aware that you cannot afford to have speech that is substandard in any way because of its influence upon your own oral communication.

Research studies show that elementary school teachers in the field place a high premium upon their own speech proficiency as a basis for aiding their own students to develop in oral communication. Lillywhite, Phelps, and Basye,[1] who surveyed 1,004 successful teachers on this point, found that 80.5 percent regarded "speaking with correct articulation and pronunciation" as the most significant aspect of speech ability in influencing their pupils to speak correctly and clearly.

DISTINCT ARTICULATION—A BASIC NEED

But the need for good articulation—the ability to produce speech sounds clearly and accurately according to phonetic standards—is a necessity for a teacher *at any level*. Mumbled, careless, or inarticulate speech not only reduces your teaching efficiency, but makes an unfavorable impression upon your professional colleagues, the parents of your students, and other laymen. One college lecturer in sociology spoke so indistinctly that students could not understand him well enough to take notes. Their attendance at lecture was a waste of time, and certainly their interest in the course was negligible, as a result.

Careless or sloppy habits of articulation also mark a person as uneducated or uncultured. As a teacher you cannot risk presenting such a picture of yourself in a faculty meeting, a professional convention, or a conference

---

[1] Herold Lillywhite, Waldo Phelps, and Granville Basye, "A Study of the Importance of Proficiency in Public School Teaching as Related to the Speech Curricula of Institutions Offering Teacher-training," *Western Speech*, vol. 14, no. 4, pp. 5–14, October, 1950.

with a parent or administrator. Also, speech proficiency is an important factor in being hired and promoted. In the Lillywhite, Phelps, and Basye study, 221 administrators were asked to evaluate the importance of speech in hiring teachers: 84.5 percent regarded it as significant or very significant. In merit ratings and classroom effectiveness, 62.1 percent of administrators considered it significant or very significant in end-of-year ratings; 91.4 percent believed it to be very significant in overall classroom effectiveness.[2]

Thus, it should be clear to you that intelligible speech is an asset to you personally; it increases your classroom effectiveness and is invaluable in professional relationships. Strive to develop speech that marks you as an educated person of high quality. In achieving such a goal, take inventory briefly by asking yourself these questions:

1 What impression does my speech make upon others?
2 Is it clear-cut, distinct, and characteristic of a cultured person?
3 How often do my listeners ask me to repeat what I say because they did not understand me the first time?
4 Do they miss certain parts of my sentences? The beginning? The middle? The ending?
5 Do they fail to understand certain words?
6 Am I guilty of omitting sounds? Slurring sounds? Substituting one sound for another?

The answers you give will indicate how well you have mastered articulation—the key to intelligibility in speech. Ask your speech teacher to assist you in making an accurate appraisal of your needs. If you cannot be understood easily, you should do something about it.

CAUSES OF FAULTY ARTICULATION AND INDISTINCT SPEECH

The first thing you can do to improve your articulation is to recognize the causes of your difficulties. Then work to remove them. *Carelessness, lack of pride in acceptable standards for good speech, and laziness* indicate an attitude that invites poor articulation. As a natural result of such an attitude, incorrect habits of speech develop. The overcasual campus attitude, popular indifference to certain traditional aspects of culture, current slang, or beatnik talk are some of the common outcroppings of these causes. You may find

[2] *Ibid.*, p. 6.

yourself in a conflict between the articulation which will "pass" in your campus group and acceptable performance for your student teaching situation.

Imitation of poor models goes hand in hand with undesirable attitude. Sometimes parents, companions, television idols, etc., greatly influence the habits you develop, as well as the standards of speech you accept. Vulgar speech, lisping associated with a baby-talk philosophy, or foreign dialect may result from imitating unsuitable models.

Chronic hearing losses may also cause omitting and distorting of sounds because one has never *heard* them well. Similarly, *disease or illness* which has affected the proper functioning of muscles, tongue, jaws, palates, lips, etc., may cause serious impairment of articulation. *Abnormal formation of the structures* or parts of the mechanism may also interfere with intelligible speech. Crooked teeth, a short tongue, or a cleft palate are some examples of such causes.

Most articulatory defects are caused by carelessness, laziness, or lack of pride. If you desire, you can remedy these most easily.

KINDS OF ARTICULATORY ERRORS

From the causes above, three main types of errors result. First are *omissions*, in which you leave out sounds. Younger children and high school students are more guilty of such errors than college students, but you do make them. Sometimes they result from carelessness, but there is also a chance that you may have habituated an omission because the sound was difficult to produce, or because of foreign dialect. One high school teacher habitually said *dint* for *didn't*. College students who say *reconize* for *recognize* or *goverment* for *government* are omitting sounds.

Next are *substitutions,* in which you replace a correct sound with an incorrect one. The *dis, dat, dese,* and *dose* boys are all substituting the *d* sound for the *th* sound. The college freshman who wants to be a *th*peech teacher because she *loveth to put on playth* is asking for trouble because of her substitution. The Puerto Rican student who likes *thees ahppy* country has substituted his native sounds for those of English. Then, there is the all too familiar trio of *git, jist,* and *becuz.*

Finally, there are *distortions* in which you approximate the correct sound but fail to produce it exactly. The boy who was *goingk* to California and the exchange student who was *shtuck* in the revolving door were both distorting speech sounds.

HOW TO IMPROVE YOUR ARTICULATION

You can improve your articulation in a number of ways:

1 *Be aware of your mistakes.* With the help of your speech instructor you can learn quickly of the mistakes you make. Careful listening to your own speech, either live or on tape, will aid you in such an analysis. In this process be sure that you can discriminate between the correct sound and the incorrect one.

2 *Learn to produce the correct sound alone.* Knowing your mistake, proceed to learn to produce the new sound correctly in isolation. Practice this until you never make the old mistake. You need to "set" the new habit and never permit the incorrect sound to occur.

3 *Practice the correct sound in syllables and words.* After successfully setting the correct sound in isolation, practice it in syllables and words. Use it to start a word (initially), in the middle of a word (medially), and to end a word (finally). Also, employ it in various blends and combinations so that you have control of it in every possible situation.

4 *Employ the correct sound in sentences.* Since most of your speech is in phrases, clauses, and sentences, you must use the correct sound in your normal speaking pattern, in sentences. Practice it aloud in drills from speech texts, in original sentences you devise, and in selections of literature containing it. They are excellent materials.

5 *Utilize the correct sound in your continuous speech.* The final test is to use the sound in all everyday speech situations you meet—social conversation, discussion, public speaking, oral reading, etc. In this way you establish the correct sound in your daily communication. If you employ it in such situations naturally and correctly, the new sound becomes "a part of you."

The suggestions above are basic ways in which you can improve your articulation. Try them on any problems you may have.

KINDS OF SPEECH SOUNDS

VOWELS. The sounds or tones produced in the larynx by the vibration of the vocal folds are called vowels. Contrary to the old schoolbook statement that there are five vowels, *a,e,ı,o,u,* there are in most classifications of vowels in speech fourteen such sounds. In producing vowel sounds, although there is vibration of the vocal folds, there is not much narrowing of the vocal passage. The throat is kept open. Vowels are shaped by movements of the tongue, lips, and jaws. A classification of vowel sounds is possible accord-

Vowels

DICTIONARY SYMBOLS	PHONETIC SYMBOLS	KEY WORDS	
ē	i	be*a*d	f*ee*t
i	ɪ	b*i*ll,	*i*nk
ā	e	st*a*y,	r*ai*n
e	ɛ	h*e*lp,	l*e*t
a	æ	*a*dd,	c*a*tch
ä	ɑ	p*a*lm,	f*a*rm
ô	ɔ	s*aw*,	s*ou*ght
ō	o	sh*o*w,	*o*bey
o͝o	ʊ	sh*oo*k,	p*u*t
o͞o	u	m*oo*n,	r*u*le
ŭ	ʌ	*o*ther	c*u*t
ȧ	ə	*a*bove,	mic*a*
ur	ɝ	h*ea*rd,	b*i*rd
er	ɚ	act*o*r,	persu*a*de

ing to the action of the tongue in shaping them. The list of the vowels appears above with symbols and markings found in the dictionary and in the International Phonetic Alphabet. Observe that spelling in English does not accurately determine the way vowels are spoken. The symbols of the phonetic alphabet are consistent with the way sounds are uttered. The key words will help you to recall the particular vowels used in each word.

Vowel Classification and Exercises

The following words, shown in the classification, contain the various vowel sounds. Practice them, noting *where* they are produced. High, middle or central, and low describe the tongue position. Try to keep an open throat, and learn the precise tongue and lip positions needed. Add other words to those given to increase your practice.

FRONT VOWELS	MIDDLE	BACK
High i (ē)		u (o͞o)
(be*a*d, f*ee*t)		(m*oo*n, r*u*le)
I (i)		ʊ (o͝o)
(sl*i*p, bu*i*lt)		(sh*oo*k, p*u*t)

FRONT VOWELS	MIDDLE	BACK
Middle e (ā)		o (ō)
(stay, rain)	ɝ (ur)	(obey, show)
	(bird, heard)	
ε (e)	ɚ (er)	
(help, let)	(actor, persuade)	
	ʌ (ŭ)	
	(cut, other)	
Low æ (ă)	ə (à)	ɔ (a)
(add, catch)	(above, mica)	(saw, sought)
		ɑ (ä)
		(palm, farm)

DIPHTHONGS. In English you combine or blend two vowels to produce diphthongs. They seem to be *one* sound, because you are used to hearing them that way. The common diphthongs are *ou*, as in *show* or *opal*; *ei* as in *pale* or *say*; *au* as in *how* or *out*; *ai* as in *lie* or *guy*; *oi* as in *soil* or *voice;* and *iu* as in *pew* or *cute*. Make a list of words containing diphthongs which are commonly used in our language.

CONSONANTS. Consonants are more likely to be noises, rather than tones, as is the case of the vowels. By narrowing or constricting the vocal passage above the larynx in some way you produce a great number of such sounds. Most classifications include about twenty-five sounds. Different parts of the speech mechanism interrupt, stop, or in some way alter the breath stream as it comes out so that the vowels in speech are combined with the consonants to form syllables and words. The teeth, tongue, jaws, lips, hard and soft palates are the important parts used in shaping consonant sounds. Consonants are classified in terms of the *kind of action* which produces them and the part of, or *place in*, the mechanism which is involved. The third aspect of consonant production deals with the presence or absence of vocal vibration. Consonants having such vibration are *voiced*. Those without it are *voiceless*. In pairs such as *b* and *p*, *z* and *s*—the first sound in each pair is voiced, the second voiceless.

1 *Plosives* or *Stops*. By a momentary and complete *stopping* of the air stream in the vocal tract, pressure is built up and suddenly released. This action causes the sound given this name. There are six such sounds, classified in terms of the organ doing the stopping. For example,

b and *p* are stopped by the lips; *d* and *t* by the tongue against the teeth ridge, just behind the upper teeth; *g* and *k* by the action of the tongue against the soft palate.   Each of the first sounds in these pairs is voiced.

EXERCISES

Speak these words, exaggerating the stop sound at first.   Then produce them in your normal manner, noting and feeling the action which produces them. Be sure that your production is clear and definite with plenty of activity of the articulators involved.

beat-peat	deem-team	ghoul-cool
bar-par	din-tin	gouge-couch
bee-pea	dale-tale	gout-cow
bet-pet	dredge-trudge	grit-kick
bomb-palm	label-lapel	ago-account
about-paper	pardon-party	buggy-yokel
labial-April	body-rotate	organ-local
label-suppose	ready-flutter	stag-took
above-support	cad-cat	egg-seek
hob-hop	bud-but	pig-pluck
sub-cup	had-mat	sprig-hick
hub-lip	lid-light	dug-chuck
rob-pop	seed-seat	flag-walk
	felled-felt	

Note also that in the first few words in each column the stop sound is at the beginning of the word (initial): in the next group it is in the middle (medial); in the last it is at the end (final).

2 *Fricatives.*   These sounds are produced by narrowing the vocal passage so that the air stream is set into vibration by forcing it through a restricted opening.   The sound is the result of friction between the air stream and the structure which is narrowed, hence the name.   Sounds in this group include *v* and *f*, ð *th* (voiced), as in *there*; and θ *th* (voiceless), as in *thick*; ʒ *zh* (voiced), as in *pleasure* and ʃ *sh* (voiceless), as in *ship*. Combinations of *d* with *zh*, as in *fudge*, and *t* with *sh*, as in *lurch*, are called *affricates*—a word derived from a prefix and a root word which mean "to rub against."

3 *Nasals.*   These are sounds in which the air sound stream is diverted through the nasal passages.   The sounds of *m*, *n*, and *ng* are in this group. They are found in such words as: *mad, naughty,* and *ring.*

EXERCISES

Consonants

DICTIONARY SYMBOLS	PHONETIC SYMBOLS	KEY WORDS
p	p	pool, supper, lip
b	b	boot, rabbit, rib
t	t	team, letter, elect
d	d	dog, ready, need
m	m	met, memory, dim
n	n	new, only, lemon
ng	ŋ	sing, longer, finger
f	f	fair, affair, puff
v	v	value, even, salve
k	k	cap, cocoa, neck
g	g	gap, linger, brig
r	r	ran, orange, car
l	l	leaf, hollow, meal
th	θ	think, faithful, oath
th	ð	there, other, wreathe
s	s	set, faster, loss
z	z	zebra, fuzzy, graze
sh	ʃ	shoot, wishing, fish
zh	ʒ	rouge, seizure, mirage
w	w	wit, away, forward
hw	hw	when, wheel, nowhere
y	j	year, loyal, value
ch	tʃ	chin, chew, ratchet
j	dʒ	joy, judge, gauge
h	h	ham, ahoy, rehire

4 *Glides.* There are four of these sounds: *hw, w, j, r.* The characteristic of each is that the articulators are set for one sound, but they move from it to another sound. In the first of the sounds listed above, the position of the articulators is for *h,* but they move to the formation of *w*—as in *what.* (In all words beginning with *wh,* the first sound is *hw.*) In the case of *w,* the articulators are set for the sound, o͞o, but they move to the position for the next vowel—as in *we.* The third glide, *j,* (usually spelled with *y*) is made by the articulators set for ee, but they move to the next sound—as in *you.* (It is interesting to note that *we* and *you* have the same sounds, but one has them coming in the reverse order of the other.) The glide, *r,* is made by the articulators set for the central vowel that is heard in *bird,* but they move to next sound—as in *ride.*

TABLE 8–1. Consonants Classified According to Parts of the Mechanism Used in Articulation

PART OF MECHANISM	Stop-plosive		Fricative		Affricate		Glide		
	VOICED	VOICE-LESS	VOICED	VOICE-LESS	VOICED	VOICE-LESS	NASAL VOICED	VOICED	VOICE-LESS
Lips (Bilabial)	b	p					m	w	hw
Lip-teeth (Labio-dental)			v	f					
Tongue-teeth (Lingua-dental)			ð	θ					
Tongue-gum ridge (Lingua-alveolar)	d	t	z ʒ	s ʃ	dʒ	tʃ	n	l	
Tongue-hard palate (Palatal)								r j	
Tongue-soft palate (Lingua-velar)	g	k					ŋ		
Vocal folds (Glottal)				h					

PRONUNCIATION

As a teacher you not only need to have speech that is *distinct* and meets phonetic standards, but you also should be sure that your *pronunciation* is correct according to *dictionary* standards and those of educated persons in your locality.   Correct pronunciation is one of the refinements of good speech.   It is an index of your cultural background and your educational level.   In teaching, your pronunciation can have an important influence upon the speech of your pupils and your faculty associates.   You cannot afford the bad impression socially or professionally that errors make.   Get rid of them, as well as any unusual or peculiar pronunciations.

When someone tells you that you have mispronounced a word, these are the mistakes you may have made: (1) You have stressed the wrong syllable; (2) you have placed the sounds in the wrong syllable; (3) you have misused one or more consonant sounds; (4) you have misused one or more vowel sounds.   Such misuses of speech sounds in pronunciation are the same as those in articulation—by omission, substitution, or distortion.   Thus, *soph-more* is a mispronunciation of *sophomore*, as *athelete* is of *athlete*; also, *prefer'able* is incorrect for *pref'erable*, and *theay'ter* for *thēa'tre*.

THINGS TO KNOW ABOUT PRONUNCIATION

AMERICAN PRONUNCIATION IS CONFUSING.   It is easy to make such mistakes because of the confusion caused when the same letters have no consistency in the way they are sounded in different words.   For example, the letter *i* is pronounced one way in *hit*, another in *kite*, and still differently in *machine*.   In this series the letter *a* has five different sounds—*cat, father, place, half*, and *call*.   It is no wonder that one of your pupils, a recent immigrant from another country, might be confused.   Some letters may have ten different sounds; some sounds may be represented by fifteen different spellings!

REGIONAL PRONUNCIATIONS DIFFER.   In addition to the inconsistency of the sounds of individual letters, further problems come from differences in regional pronunciation.   For example, the word *data* may be pronounced *dayta, datta,* or *dahta.*   All three of these are used acceptably in certain parts of the country, yet they can cause difficulty for one hoping to find any standardized pronunciation in the United States.

GENERAL AMERICAN PRONUNCIATION. Outside New England and north of the Ohio River, over 125 million persons living in the Midwest and West use general American pronunciation. The *o* in their speech is a conventional *o,* as in *hope.* They sound the *r* before consonants and at the end of words. This pronunciation is used generally over radio and television and is the basic type developed in James F. Bender's *NBC Handbook of Pronunciation,* a very useful volume for the teacher, published by Thomas Y. Crowell Company (New York). It gives only one pronunciation each for over 15,000 names, places, and common words frequently mispronounced.

EASTERN PRONUNCIATION. Persons living in New England and those native born in New York City total about 20 million who use this pronunciation. They do not sound the *r* before a consonant (as in *port*) or when it is a final sound (as in *player* or *waiver*). They typically use *a* as pronounced in *farm,* before *f, s, th,* and *ns.* They also make some variations in the *o* sound.

SOUTHERN PRONUNCIATION. Nearly 30 million persons in the Old South use this pronunciation. It is characterized by not pronouncing *r* before consonants (as in *port*) or when it is a final sound (as in *player*). The *a* is pronounced as in *hat* before *s, f, th* (as in *affirm, ask, wrath*).

PRONUNCIATION IS BASED UPON THE ACTUAL SPEECH OF THE PEOPLE

Although books on speech and voice and diction are helpful to you, the best printed sources are dictionaries. If you consult them, you will find that their editors confirm the principle that acceptable pronunciation rests upon the actual speech of effective citizens in whatever localities they live. This basis is found in Webster's *New World Dictionary of the American Language, The American College Dictionary,* Webster's *New International Dictionary,* and Kenyon and Knott's *Pronouncing Dictionary of American English.*

To determine standards, questionnaires are sent in a continuous process to various cultured professional people, authorities on language, and occupational groups to find preferred pronunciations. The dictionary reports these findings in listing under each word with preferred pronunciation given first and others following.

IMPROVE YOUR PRONUNCIATION

You can improve your pronunciation by your own efforts if you follow certain systematic methods.

FAMILIARIZE YOURSELF WITH SOUNDS OF ENGLISH. Study the books suggested earlier, noting very carefully the introductory parts of the dictionaries and the guide to diacritical marks that appears on each page.

LEARN HOW WORDS LOOK IN PRINT. Become familiar with the appearance of words in print, as well as how they are spelled, and how they are pronounced. If you say *heighth* or *excape* or *libary*, it may be the result of your not knowing how the words look as much as your not knowing how they should sound.

LISTEN ACCURATELY TO YOUR PRONUNCIATION. You should know how you pronounce words. Make a list of the words you mispronounce. Note what you do incorrectly. Is it accent, syllabification, incorrect production of vowel sounds? Of consonant sounds? Be sure you know the *kind* of error you make.

ADOPT THE PRONUNCIATION OF CULTURED PERSONS IN YOUR REGION. Whether you live in the Midwestern, Eastern, or Southern regions, find the best pronunciation for that region. Listen to good speakers on radio, television, or in person. Check your pronunciation in relation to theirs, and maintain such standards as long as you live in the region.

CORRECT YOUR PRONUNCIATION ERRORS. Use any of the good dictionaries mentioned earlier, and with the help of good models, eliminate your mistakes. Do not permit yourself to slide back into the old habits, once you have discovered your errors and corrected them.

USE THE CORRECTED PRONUNCIATION IN YOUR SPEECH EACH DAY. Having mastered the new pronunciations, use them freely, in your conversation at home, in school, or in your work. Soon they will be a part of your everday speech.

A List of Words Commonly Mispronounced by College Students

abandon	adapt	alumni	athletics
absurd	adult	another	attacked
accept	almond	armistice	because

bona fide	escape	longevity	resonant
bronchial	evidently	long-lived	Roosevelt
burial	experiment	maintenance	route
caramel	facetious	menu	sacrilegious
cavalry	genuine	naphtha	schism
civilization	gesture	often	similar
clique	giblets	pantomime	sophomore
comparable	height	particular	spontaneity
corps	heinous	partition	status
coupon	hospitable	pathos	stomach
culinary	inaugural	pectoral	subtle
diphthong	inherent	penalize	superfluous
drama	insurance	perform	sword
dramatist	interesting	pharynx	tarpaulin
draught	intramural	precedence	theater
drowned	introduction	preferable	tremendous
eczema	irrelevant	probably	undoubtedly
education	Italian	pronunciation	vaudeville
electoral	lamentable	quay	viscount
eminent	larynx	realize	wash
English	library	recipe	won't
epitome	literature	recognize	your

FOR FURTHER READING

Fairbanks, Grant: *Voice and Articulation Drillbook,* 2d ed., Harper & Row, Publishers, Inc., New York, 1960.

Fisher, Hilda B.: *Improving Voice and Articulation*, Houghton Mifflin Co., Boston, 1966.

Hahn, Elise, Charles W. Lomas, Donald E. Hargis, and Daniel Vandraegen: *Basic Voice Training For Speech*, 2d ed., McGraw-Hill Book Company, New York, 1957.

Hanley, Theodore D. and Wayne L. Thurman: *Developing Vocal Skills*, Holt, Rinehart and Winston, Inc., New York, 1962.

King, Robert G. and Eleanor M. DeMichael: *Improving Articulation and Voice,* The Macmillan Company, New York, 1966.

CHAPTER NINE

PHYSICAL BEHAVIOR

Every teacher has at his disposal two symbol systems for oral communication—a *visible* system involving his actions and appearance, and an *audible* system including all speech sounds that he employs. Most of his acts in speaking—lecturing, discussion, oral reading or interpretation—use both systems. He needs to be successful in using both if he is to be effective as a teacher. For this reason it is important that you make considerable effort to improve your visible as well as your audible communication.

PHYSICAL BEHAVIOR IS UNIVERSALLY UNDERSTOOD

As you contemplate such improvement, recall your response to the actions of teachers you have known. The messages they conveyed were *conspicuous and universally understood.* They also caused you to make certain judgments about the teachers—judgments regarding their motivation, competence, personality, and mental attitude. Some judgments were favorable; they helped your approach to learning. Others were not, often becoming distinct barriers to your interest, attention, and desire to learn.

Consider the nervous, new teacher who drops his note cards and is too confused to reorganize them; the sloppy character with uncut hair, a scrawny beard, and an overcasual approach; the prima donna type whose affected manner calls more attention to her than to her material; the key jangler who continually distracts you. How would such teachers affect you in a classroom? Obviously, they would not be particularly helpful to learning.

In contrast, visualize a poised, mature teacher. His lecture is well organized and interesting. His bearing and manner convey an enthusiasm for teaching his subject. He is also skilled in using physical activity to hold interest and to reinforce each point so that it lives for you. He has few, if any, aimless or distracting mannerisms. You find that you are eager to go to his class. Learning is enjoyable and easy because of him.

TWO KINDS OF PHYSICAL ACTION

In face-to-face talking you cannot escape the fact that the listener is observing your behavior. He is trying to gain meaning from what he sees you do, as well as from your language and voice. He expects a consistency among all three. But he notices two kinds of actions—your *intended* actions and your *unintended* actions. Let us look at both of these, considering the latter one first.

UNINTENDED ACTION.   This is the kind of action that you use because you are you. It will reflect such things as your age, sex, body build, and health. But it will also reveal your reactions to these factors. For example, it will indicate either your acceptance of your age or your effort to deny it; it will suggest your own satisfaction with your own sex role or your inclination to adopt behavior of the opposite sex; it will show your adaptation to the size and shape of your body or it will show your self-consciousness or preoccupation with it; it will assert your feeling of good health or it will communicate your lack of it.

Your unintended action, like your voice, also reveals certain personality characteristics. The fearful person may have a posture (standing or sitting) that appears "frozen"; he may suggest by restless movements and gestures that he would like to escape; but he may also feel like a cornered animal, and he therefore has to fight his way out. The emotionally unstable person finds it difficult to maintain physical poise—whether it be in his posture, his facial expression, or his use of his hands. The aggressive person is inclined to stand with feet firmly planted; he uses vigorous, decisive gestures; he seldom takes his eyes off his listener. The confident person seems to be all-of-one-piece. He is alert in a relaxed sort of way and reacts spontaneously and naturally to his thoughts and feelings as he speaks.

A broad principle governs the effect of physical behavior in human relationships. This is the principle of *empathy*. Stated simply, it is the tendency individuals have to reflect or adopt the muscle tone and actions of persons they observe, or with whom they are closely associated. A classroom has a certain intimacy because students and teacher are in close proximity. At times they work in small groups in a conference or in a seminar situation. Even in the usual class situation, teacher actions are the center of classroom procedure. As students watch the teacher, they have an *empathic* response to everything he does. They reflect his whole attitude toward his ideas and his listeners.

In a schoolroom there is also an imaginal or mental counterpart. As students learn their teacher's ideas, they project themselves into his mental state, also. Thus their attention is gained, held, and responses developed through empathy, which involves them mentally and physically.

INTENDED ACTION.   This is the kind of action that is determined by a speaker's purpose in talking. It is a part of his conscious expression, but that does not necesarily mean that it is planned in advance. It may be total bodily movement, but usually it consists of those gestures which emphasize, describe, or suggest idea. Thus, they help to clarify or to reinforce what the speaker is trying to communicate by language and voice. It is primarily with this kind of action that this chapter is concerned.

EFFECTIVE ACTION AIDS THE TEACHER

Numerous specific uses of action help the teacher in his job.

SUITABLE ACTION AIDS RELAXATION AND CONTROL OF TENSION

New speakers tend to "tighten up" before they talk to a group. Even experienced lecturers or discussion leaders have this reaction. It is the body's way of anticipating a critical situation. Actually, tension results from a surge of energy produced in the body by the secretion of adrenalin into the blood stream. Thus, the body supplies "drive" for the anticipated need. Muscular activity is an outlet for this energy. By using action, the speaker is able to reduce tension, to relax, and to feel more at ease *physically*. This activity aids *emotional* relaxation because of the close relationship between glands, muscles, and the nervous system. As a person becomes less emotionally stirred up, he also begins a *conscious effort* to relax. As the cycle continues, he brings tension under greater control because he uses action to help him.

ACTION HELPS THINKING AND FLUENCY

Since a speaker uses his muscles and nervous system in thinking, his control of physical behavior helps him in thinking. A teacher conducting a discussion or talking to a class can often take advantage of this relationship by using his arms or hands freely, by moving from one location to another, or by shifting his posture. Such activities stimulate thinking. When thinking is aided, a teacher can usually verbalize more effectively and choose language more appropriate for expressing his ideas. A teacher who is active *physically* is usually *mentally* alive.

ACTION AIDS VOCAL PRODUCTION

Speech production uses the same muscles employed in basic bodily functions. Muscular action affects the breathing patterns, the operation of the vocal mechanism, and the parts of the body that articulate or shape speech sounds. *A controlled body is essential to a controlled voice.* As a teacher develops muscular control, his vocal quality improves, his pitch and melody are more suitable, his tempo is better, and his expressiveness is greater. Thus, proper muscle control aids him to use and to coordinate the many muscles involved in speech.

ACTION IMPROVES DIRECTNESS AND
AUDIENCE CONTACT

To be an effective speaker, a teacher must talk *to* his listeners; he must be direct. One of his best specific means of establishing and maintaining audience contact is through action. By holding the eyes of his audience with his eyes, he helps to ensure their attention and gain from them the response he seeks. But there is an even greater value in this awareness of the listeners; this is the speaker's opportunity to use feedback. Listeners' reactions can indicate eagerness, surprise, satisfaction, doubt, perplexity, hostility, rejection, indifference, or boredom. Most of these reactions can be *seen* by the speaker. If he is then flexible and willing, he can make the desired adjustments to what he sees. He may capitalize on positive feedback; but if the feedback is negative, he can review, paraphrase what he has said, ask direct questions of certain listeners, or open the subject up for questions. Since so much of teaching is interaction, it hardly seems possible that a teacher could be effective without the closest eye-contact and other evidences of directness.

EFFECTIVE ACTION BENEFITS THE AUDIENCE

Good physical behavior by the teacher has specific benefits to his students. Everything he does is instantly perceived and is extremely visible to them. His actions are even more important to his listeners than they are to him.

ACTION AROUSES ATTENTION AND HOLDS
LISTENER INTEREST

Students will not listen voluntarily to a teacher for a long period of time. Their attention span is limited. They stay with him for a while, and then slip away, sometimes never to return unless he *does* something. This happens with older or trained listeners, also. Action provides a vivid means for him to capture and hold their interest—a change of posture, gestures involving any part of the body, suitable facial response—all keep the listeners interested. A stimulating classroom teacher is one who is enthusiastic and animated in physical behavior. Students like a vital, energetic teacher who has plenty of variety in his presentation. They listen to what he says, and remember it.

ACTION CONVEYS SPECIFIC MEANINGS TO LISTENERS

Action itself is communication. Many of the specific ideas and feelings of the teacher reach his students through his use of action. Elementary school children, for example, respond eagerly to the extensive physical behavior of the teacher as he tells a story. Every description, characterization, and explanation becomes more vivid through that action. Through empathy, children participate in the story. A high school social studies teacher employs action to dramatize an incident; a science instructor describes an important process. They can readily establish important relationships through action.

ACTION REINFORCES VOCAL MEANINGS
FOR LISTENERS

Oral language and vocal expressiveness in themselves are effective audible means of communication. However, they often require support or reinforcement by the teacher's action if they are to gain maximum emphasis. General physical vigor usually requires *specific* gestures or *appropriate* facial expression to gain effectiveness. When a teacher concentrates strongly upon ideas or has a deep purpose in what he says, suitable action may develop spontaneously to aid the students.

SUGGESTIONS FOR USING ACTION EFFECTIVELY

Although a teacher's action may be developed spontaneously or unconsciously, it needs appropriate control. Such control depends upon his own personality, the content of his talk, the audience, and the occasion. He learns such control by developing action that is "right for him" in the communication situations he faces in his daily school routine or outside it. Affectation or mechanical action is unsuitable. Self-motivated behavior, spontaneously employed and *appropriate to him*, is best.

To improve your use of action, realize its function as a basic means of communication. Then learn to relax and free yourself from tensions. Use abundant action first. Then develop control, making action specific and purposeful in your teaching. With time, you can add special techniques and polish them.

The kinds of action you employ can be studied individually.   They include posture, movement, and gestures.

POSTURE

Posture is the way you hold your body in sitting, standing, or walking. It communicates a message to an audience as soon as they observe you. As a professional person and a community leader, you should have a posture that makes a good impression.   Put aside the casual carelessness of an undergraduate.   Your principal, members of the school board, townspeople, and students respect teachers who have physical poise.   They expect them to *look* like mature persons with some dignity.   Stand, sit, and move with the bearing of a leader.

Poor posture, particularly among women, is very noticeable and makes a bad impression.   No teacher can afford to be careless about posture.

Before a class or public audience every aspect of your posture (and appearance) is visible.   Some teachers try to achieve informality in a classroom by sitting on the edge of a desk, by leaning on a lectern, or by putting one foot upon a front seat.   In general, and especially among men, this behavior is not undesirable.   However, among women it would not be appropriate. Usually more formalized situations outlaw the overcasual manner and require action suitable to them.

Occasionally a speaker or teacher succeeds although he seems to defy good taste in posture.   However such a person generally has other attributes— brilliant ideas, unusual humor, a reputation as a scholar—all strong enough to compensate for erratic physical behavior.   Thus, Will Rogers, the famous cowboy humorist, would lie down on the floor and tell some of his stories. Billy Sunday, the great evangelist, would climb all over the furniture, or even smash it.   Audiences accepted these actions because of the reputations of these speakers as "showmen."   An ordinary teacher cannot afford these eccentricities. It is better for him (or her) to defer any acting until sure of the effects.

HOW TO IMPROVE YOUR POSTURE

Posture should tell the audience the *right* things about the mental attitude of the speaker.

DEVELOP POSTURE THAT SUGGESTS VITALITY

To keep students on their toes your posture should reveal you as an energetic, intellectually alive, sincere, enthusiastic teacher with respect to your purpose, your materials, and your job. Students can very quickly spot pompous, bored, or disinterested attitudes when the teacher's physical manner communicates them. Similarly, they respond "in kind" when he reveals favorable, positive things about his alertness, interest, or intelligence.

HABITUATE POSTURE THAT SUGGESTS POISE

One does not automatically have an erect posture. He does have all of the basic structures—skeleton, muscles, tissue, tendons and ligaments—but he must *want* to have good posture and do something about it. He must *control* the structures and *habituate* his physical attitude.

This necessitates basic control of the head and upper part of the body so that by lifting the chest one pulls the spinal column into better line. This influences the whole skeleton: the shoulders are pulled back somewhat; the hips and other parts of the lower body fall into the natural line established by the spine. Such a posture can be habituated.

MAINTAIN A POSTURE THAT INCREASES YOUR EFFICIENCY AS A SPEAKER

Our suggestions for improving posture can help to make you more efficient as a speaker. By "standing tall," maintaining proper control of your weight, and being mentally alert, your body can perform speech functions more easily. The breathing mechanism operates freely; the muscles of the neck, throat and larynx function more readily; the lips, jaws, and tongue can shape speech sounds more easily. Good posture is the obvious starting point in control over the muscles that produce visible symbols in speaking, and closely affects the production of the audible symbols, also. Well established habits of good posture ensure the body's ability always to serve speech purposes more efficiently.

Professional speakers, actors, and models spend many hours to develop posture that is comfortable and suggests strength, poise, and naturalness in the performance. As a teacher, you will need the same qualities to have maximum impact upon your students.

MOVEMENT

If a speaker changes his posture, he has used *movement*. To some persons, it is synonymous with walking. Movement, like posture, begins the visible process of communication before one utters a spoken syllable. A teacher often begins his talk as he *moves* to his desk, *walks* to the door and closes it, or *steps* to the chalkboard to write instructions upon it.

INITIAL MOVEMENT—TO A BASIC LOCATION

When a teacher walks with assurance and vitality to his desk or to his place before the class, he suggests by this manner that he means business and expects students to listen. However, if he tiptoes hesitantly to his desk or moves uncertainly into his place before speaking, his listeners may say to themselves, "Oh, oh—a new teacher; and is he scared!" The chances are that they will give such a person a run for his money, or they may need to be shown who is in charge. If the teacher's approach is awkward or clumsy, it may provoke laughter or a breakdown in his acceptance by the group. A poor beginning because of inappropriate movement puts an obstacle in the teacher's way. He should therefore make his first impression a strong one.

Beginning teachers sometimes start speaking too soon, while they are still moving, or before they reach a suitable location before the class. The students, watching the movement, are not ready to listen and therefore miss the opening comments. In your initial movement, proceed with confidence to your place before the group. Lay out your notes, get set, look briefly at the audience, and *then* begin to speak. Audience attention and general results will then be much better.

MOVEMENT DURING YOUR TALK

Movement during your speaking has certain important functions. It helps you relax, it arouses and holds attention, it is a form of visible punctuation for the listener.

Certain meanings are associated with certain types of movement. Moving *toward the audience* usually indicates appeal or presentation. Moving *away from the audience* signifies withdrawal or concession. Moving *to the right or to the left* is used to punctuate, denote a transition, or a change in content from one idea to another. Movement on the platform should always be integrated with what the speaker is saying; visible and audible meanings should be closely and smoothly linked. It should have a purpose, and not be aimless platform "pacing." It should also be smooth and well coordinated. Do not think that the problem of action can be solved by doing nothing. Absence of *any* movement, without some compensating expressiveness in voice, variation in speech materials, or vitality in other kinds of action, can easily cost a speaker the attention of his audience. Teachers, especially, should be aware of the necessity for some "change of pace" in their activity. Actually, they have many opportunities for such contrast by using movement to the chalkboard, changing location from one side of the desk to another, or by supplementary action used in pointing out or showing things.

MOVEMENT AT THE END OF YOUR TALK

Beginning teachers are often eager to "escape" quickly from an audience situation. As a result, they start to leave their place in front of the class before they have finished the audible portion—they are still talking. Such premature physical communication usually ruins the audience's attention to the closing remarks. The action says to them, It's all over; you can stop listening now. *It is important to finish the visible and audible messages at the same time.* By keeping your physical location and poise until the end, you sustain the whole effect of your talk. Restrain the impulse to "get out of there." Finish your remarks; pause briefly, and then move.

GESTURES

Gestures include any actions of the head, face, hands, and arms that are used for communicating meaning. In fact almost any part of the body may be employed to make a gesture. Gestures convey specific ideas and emotions, and also emphasize and support vocal meaning. Fidgeting describes the whole range of aimless actions a teacher might make—jingling the change in one's pocket, playing with a string of beads, fumbling with a bracelet, twisting a wrist watchband, adjusting glasses, or scratching one's head. These are really unintended actions that tell something about the speaker, but they detract from what the speaker is saying. If they are not habituated, they usually disappear as he learns to use gestures *constructively* to communicate ideas.

Good gestures help a teacher: (1) to secure confidence; (2) to relax and break muscle tensions; (3) to convey definite meanings; (4) to secure and maintain the attention of the listeners.

USE OF ARMS AND HANDS.   In conversation, a person uses the hands, arms, shoulders, and torso both naturally and abundantly.   There are no restraints as he tells a good story, graphically describing the disappointing conclusion of a fish story in which the big one got away.   Similarly, the modern version of charades involves a whole system of such gestures to help watchers discover the title of a play or a recent motion picture.   Speakers in a classroom or outside it ought to feel free to reinforce speech with gestures.

FACIAL EXPRESSION AND THE HEAD.   Of all kinds of action, the face is most expressive.   Audiences in a schoolroom, an assembly, or a discussion invariably look at the face of the speaker.   It reveals the speaker's sincerity, conviction, annoyance, fear, anger, good humor, enthusiasm, and many subtle shades of mood or emotion.   A wonderful smile, a serious frown, a determined set of the lips or jaw—all convey more to the listeners than numerous gestures of the hand or arm.   They notice facial expression quickly and respond to it because it is so highly visible.   They are often frustrated by the poker face of a speaker which reveals little.   Responsive facial expression, so important to any speaker, is one of the teacher's most valuable assets.

The head is also an expressive agent in gesture.   More often than one realizes, he uses a nod or shake of the head almost unconsciously to give approval or denial of an idea.   He may also emphasize a point by vigorous head action, reinforcing such a statement as, "I'm sure I am right about that!"   Head and facial expression usually coincide in vivid physical communication.

BASIC PRINCIPLES OF EFFECTIVE GESTURES

ORIGINATE WITHIN THE SPEAKER

Gestures are not something that one superimposes or merely adds to embellish his speech.   They spring from a genuine desire within him to communicate certain *meanings* to his audience.   The gesture which is "overlaid" or "pasted on" to what he is saying calls attention to itself because it is not properly motivated. Inner purpose touches off the action used by the speaker. He then develops it into the *form* suitable to his particular meaning.

A PART OF THE WHOLE BODY

If a gesture is to be effective, it must be made in relationship to the whole body. It is not made with one finger, the hand, or arm alone. The speaker needs physical unity in producing effective gestures. His face, stance, and hands must all say the same thing at the same time. The meaning dominates the *whole* physical response of the speaker; therefore, when he gestures, he presents a *complete* and convincing effect. Thus, he shows by his action that he really *means* what he says!

SMOOTH AND WELL COORDINATED

Sometimes well motivated gestures may be awkward or jerky. Thus the attention of an audience is called to the gesture rather than to what it means. To be most effective, gestures should have ease and smoothness that come from suitable muscular coordination. With such qualities they will be a part of the total act of speaking. Practice and experience, plus the knowledge of technique, help the speaker to achieve such coordination.

STRENGTH AND RELAXATION

Lifeless, weak gestures do not convince an audience. They do not carry the speaker's meaning properly because they are half-formed and lack definiteness. Some relaxation is also needed so that flexibility and *control* of the muscles of the arms, hands, wrists, and fingers will be possible. Control allows the speaker to use muscles he needs to obtain vigor without calling attention to the gesture itself.

PROPERLY TIMED

The listener is aware of gestures very quickly. To allow him to relate gesture to voice correctly and clearly, gestures should usually slightly precede the words to which they refer. The finishing action of the gestures thus is exactly timed to hit the word stressed or the phrase to be supported by the action.

GESTURES SHOULD BE VARIED

Anything that is repeated regularly either calls the attention of the observer to its recurrence or else it loses its effect. So it is with gestures. The speaker who uses only one or two different gestures—such as bringing the edge of the hand down to the lectern or using the index finger in one certain way—is only communicating his ineptness. If one observes a skillful speaker, he notices that there is a wide range of gestures—with either hand or with both. To detail all of the kinds of gestures would suggest an elocutionary approach. However, each person can find a repertoire of gestures that are compatible with his own personality. What one does naturally in conversation will indicate these.

In summary, it is important that potential teachers recall the basic facts regarding the use of action to make delivery more convincing. A teacher should know that action is a universal means of communicating ideas and emotions; he should understand that it helps both the speaker and the audience; he should have learned that posture, movement, gesture, and facial expression are the basic kinds of action; he should understand also the uses and principles for effective use of action. It is only necessary to apply this knowledge to increase his success in delivering his ideas in the classroom and in professional situations which await him.

FOR FURTHER READING

Allport, Gordon W.: *Personality, a Psychological Interpretation*, Holt, Rinehart and Winston, Inc., New York, 1949.

Black, John W. and Wilbur E. Moore: *Speech: Code, Meaning, and Communication*, McGraw-Hill Book Company, New York, 1955, chap. 11.

Mehrabian, Albert: "Communication Without Words," *Psychology Today*, September, 1968, pp. 53–55.

Oliver, Robert T. and Rupert Cortright: *Effective Speech*, 4th ed., Holt, Rinehart and Winston, Inc., New York, 1961, chap. 13.

Rahskopf, Horace G.: *Basic Speech Improvement*, Harper & Row, Publishers, Inc., New York, 1965, chap. 15.

Sorrenson, Fred S.: *Speech For the Teacher*, The Ronald Press Company, New York, 1952, chap. 3.

White, Eugene E.: *Practical Public Speaking*, 2d ed., The Macmillan Company, New York, 1964, chap. 12.

PART THREE

IMPROVING
THE USE OF SPEECH

CHAPTER TEN

CONVERSATION AND PERSONAL CONFERENCE

Every teacher is going to be confronted with a variety of conversational situations. Even though you may not have taught school for a day, you could name many of these. As a person, at least 75 percent of your speaking is conversation.

"GOOD" CONVERSATION

What is conversation? It is a spontaneous interchange of ideas between two persons, or among several. But the etymology of the word *converse* is interesting, too. It is derived from the Latin verb *conversari* which means "dwell, or associate with." Thus, conversation is the essential element in our human associations. As such, it is central in family life, dormitory life, religious expression, civic relationships, occupational success, and even international politics.

But why do people converse? If you were to answer that question now, one of the first reasons you would probably give would be "to get information." Yet the "information" you were thinking of would include such things as: when your mother is coming home; what weather is forecast for tomorrow; where Joe is stationed now; when the Christmas vacation begins. The next questions are: Why did you *want* the information? Why did you talk about so many other things in the same conversation?

It is obvious that we converse chiefly for social pleasure. We are naturally gregarious, and enjoy the companionship of others; but this association is more satisfying when we stimulate each other with symbolic expression—our language, our voices, our gestures. It is true that other purposes may be involved in this process. For example, we want to achieve social acceptance; we wish to disarm hostility or determine whether or not there is hostility toward us; we try to reveal our good will or our need to the other person; we may simply want to study the personality or reactions of a certain individual for either selfish or altruistic reasons; we may want to influence his acts. It may be that we feel the need for self-expression or emotional release; or are trying to understand ourselves by clarifying our ideas, revising our values, or searching for satisfying goals.

Whatever may be our reason for conversing, we can say it was a good one if it had these results: (1) It was a satisfying experience in that the participants improved their human relationships; (2) it was mutual in that it was reciprocal—each speaking, each listening, each thinking, each reacting.

In his study to discover which are the factors which differentiate effective and ineffective conversation, David C. Phillips found that among women college students, "having an interesting topic" was the most frequently mentioned factor in good conversation. However, other factors often mentioned were: the student herself was in a good mood, the other participants had something worthwhile to say, the group was friendly, the group was frank and sincere.[1] It would seem that all of these indicate the *desire* to commune with others—through contributing or through listening, or both. In other words, the attitudes of the conversers were positive, and there was some purpose, subject, or idea that they had in common. Given those two basic factors, it is quite likely that the two results mentioned in the paragraph above will follow.

Perhaps this could be made more specific if we were to look at "the good conversationalist" and at "the poor conversationalist." In the study by Phillips, he found the following: (1) The eldest child was a good conversationalist significantly more times than she was a poor conversationalist; (2) poor conversationalists often did not recognize their deficiency, while good conversationalists were conscious that their conversation was satisfactory; (3) good conversationalists were rated significantly higher in physical beauty and neatness than were poor conversationalists; (4) little or no relationship existed between conversational ability and (a) section of the country from which the student came; (b) the amount of travel done by the student; (c) the number of brothers and sisters; (d) the previous speech training of the student (humiliating for us to report!). He concludes that the chief requirements for the conversationalist are: *a broad background, a good voice, an adequate vocabulary, sociability, and self-confidence.*[2]

Now what about the poor conversationalist? If your honest and considered answer to the following ten questions results in more than three of them being answered with yes, you would do well to read and apply the remainder of this chapter.

1   Do I get a secret pleasure from listening to the misfortune of others?
2   Do I resent disagreement with my statements?
3   Do I avoid stating my opinion, preference, or wish?

[1] David C. Phillips, "Some Factors That Make for Effective and Ineffective Conversation," unpublished doctoral dissertation, University of Wisconsin, December, 1946.
[2] *Ibid.*, p. 180.

4   Do I tend to find fault more than I praise?

5   Do I tend to make one-syllable responses?

6   Do I have the habit of getting "stirred up" by an excitable question or remark?

7   Do people avoid kidding me?

8   Do I talk more than my share of the time?

9   Does my voice sound harsh or final?

10   Does my mind drift off to other subjects when people talk to me?

CONVERSATION AS SOCIAL ADJUSTMENT

Conversation plays a leading role in the way in which people live together. As such, it also reveals the personality, while at the same time it helps to shape the personality. A "person," says the *American College Dictionary*, is "a human being who is conscious of his social relations to other human beings toward whom he acts." Having the means of expressing himself through language, a person is able to use conversation as his chief means of revealing his consciousness of his social relations and to act toward other human beings. Thus, conversation is both a sociological and psychological trait. It helps us to understand others and to establish a relationship with them; it helps us to understand ourselves and to express that self to others. And since our personalities are not "skin enclosed," but are a part of our whole social environment, conversation becomes the medium for the influence (inflowing) of our society and culture upon us.

Conversation exists because of the human need for social adaptation. When someone asks, "Has your mother recovered from her operation?" the information that the question would elicit is relatively unimportant. What the question probably means is:

I want to talk with you further; I feel kindly toward you, and so I am concerned with what might affect your happiness. I know your mother has been ill and that you have her much on your mind. It may give you some feeling of release to talk about her, and it will bring us closer.

On other occasions, we "talk with" a person to clear up a misunderstanding; we talk with a student in order to find out what's bothering him; and a wise school administrator *talks*, face-to-face, with a teacher in a helpful way instead of deducting a half-day's pay from his check because of a slip in observing school regulations.

An important factor in using conversation successfully for social adaptation is the role we take.   Recently our daughter's teacher and her husband were guests in our home.   Since we knew them also through church, social, and civic activities, it might have posed a problem for the teacher as to her role in our home.   Our daughter, of course, thought of her as "teacher"; but the teacher took the role of simply "friend"—friend of our family, even though she was aware of the special contacts she had with the daughter at school. Often people have difficulty in conversation because they are not clear about their role.   Sometimes, because their status changes, they fail to change their role along with it.   The host forgets that he is expected to take more initiative than his guest; the clergyman forgets to avoid preaching at the dinner table; the teacher is still lecturing or otherwise maintaining the teacher status at the bowling alley; the lieutenant still feels his bars when playing softball.

This is related to another factor, that of the self-image (self-concept).   Much has been written recently about this in relation to mental health.   Our self-image largely determines the way we see other people and how we respond to them.   In *The Great Enterprise*, Harry Overstreet points out the two general ways in which people misconceive themselves: overestimating oneself, and underestimating oneself.   He says:

> *In both cases, the individual remains unaware of the fact that the estimate he places upon himself does not comport with reality.   Therefore, he acts as if he were what he really is not.*[3]

In conversation, people making either of these mistakes tend to be left alone.   If they overestimate, they become a "pain"; if they underestimate, they may be deserted for someone more real and interesting.   They are both viewed somewhat with suspicion because they do not "ring true."   The conclusion is, then, that the closer our self-image comports with reality, the more "natural" we are, the more we shall be accepted socially and the more we shall converse with zest and pleasure.

At times it may seem to be difficult to *be* natural.   For those situations we would suggest that, first of all, you be unaffected in voice and manner. Keep your attention on listening to and communicating ideas rather than trying to make any kind of impression.   Along with this, be in earnest and give your undivided attention to the other person(s) in the conversation.

---

[3] Harry Overstreet, *The Great Enterprise*, W. W. Norton & Company, Inc., New York, 1952, pp. 43–44.

Try to feel at home and be your most spontaneous and interesting self. This will help you to be also simple, rather than pompous or exaggerated, and it will give your speech a note of candor and forthrightness.

As social adjustment, conversation is naturally interpersonal, and so it is interaction. Words, smiles, gestures are stimuli which affect us; therefore, after every conversation we are not quite the same again. But to be *inter*action, it must be reciprocal. Is it too much, then, to ask that a teacher's conversation with a pupil result in changes in both teacher and pupil? This was probably not the case in the instance where a little girl reported to her mother: "Mama, I had the most interesting conversation with my teacher after school today!" The mother replied, "Well, I'm glad to hear that. And what did you say?" The little girl answered, "I said 'm-m—hm' three times!"

Our interactions, of course, become the hub of human relations. We said in the early part of this chapter that one of the conditions for a satisfying conversation was improved human relationships. How does this come about? The answer is through our attitude as both listener and speaker. Failure in this is sharply put by Harry and Bonaro Overstreet in the chapter entitled, "Talking It Out" in *The Mind Alive*:

> *Portraying the loneliness of a marriage that has failed, Edwin Arlington Robinson speaks of the estranged husband and wife as "two who have no longer much of anything to tell." It would be hard to describe more concisely the final stage of break-up in a once intimate relationship. Back of this stage, we know, there must have been many words that sought somehow to induce understanding; and also probably, many angry and reproachful words. The ultimate sign, however, that the relationship is not to be redeemed is that a kind of wordlessness takes over: neither party any longer tries to articulate his feelings, even in anger. Husband and wife, in such a case, may maintain a stony silence; or they may achieve a tired courtesy on the level of small talk, thereby tacitly admitting that they are again strangers.[4]*

The basic ingredient for human relations is understanding. This means that we are more concerned about finding the *cause* of another's behavior in conversation than we are about resenting it or condemning. Ashley Montagu illustrates it this way:

[4] Harry Overstreet and Bonaro Overstreet, *The Mind Alive*. Copyright, 1954, by W. W. Norton & Company, Inc., New York, 1954, pp. 42–43, and used with the permission of the publisher.

Suppose someone you know fails to respond to your "good morning." That immediately arouses antagonism. Yet it is quite possible that this "rude" person simply did not see you or was so preoccupied that he didn't realize what was happening. As a human being you ought to be aware of the possibility of such states of mind. It is far better to assume their existence as the explanation of such apparently boorish behavior than aggressively to write it off as bad manners.[5]

Our attitude in listening is important for human relations. So often we do not really listen to people. Oh yes, we hear what they say, but we do not hear why they say it, or why they say it as they do. We do not listen "with people"; we listen "about people." We need to follow the injunction *"listen with understanding."* This needs to be applied not only to conference tables, but to our social conversations, to parent-and-child talk, and to teacher-pupil communication. For example, when the third-grade girl reported to her teacher after the Christmas vacation, "My dad and mother got drunk on New Year's Eve," the important thing was not what the child said, but how she *felt* when she said it. The sympathetic listener, the listener who understands, becomes an objective person and so does not have himself on his hands; instead, he has become an asset to the conversation.

THE ELEMENTS OF SPEECH IN CONVERSATION

CONTENT

Since conversation is the basis or norm for all speech, it would be profitable to look at the elements of speech as they apply there. The first of these is the content of our speech: our thoughts, the topics of conversation, what we think about them. Here, we would do well to observe as the first principle the advice of Seneca, "Let thy speech be better than silence." But if we do speak, it is necessary that we should take our audience into consideration first. Is what you are about to say of interest to the listener? Is there anything in it that would be embarrassing to him or would hurt his feelings? Is it appropriate to say at this time or among those present? Will it give someone else an opportunity to carry on the conversation? Often, of course, we show good sense in *not* talking about a subject. As someone has well

---

[5] Ashley Montagu, *On Being Intelligent*, Abelard-Schuman, Limited, New York, 1951, p. 182.

said, "The real proof of courtesy and restraint is to have the same ailment the other person is describing and not mention it."

Along with the choice of what to say is the development of it. We need to monitor ourselves a bit to make sure that we are not talking too much about "*my* score," "*my* son," "*my* job," etc. And if there is humor, much better that it be at the expense of the speaker than at the expense of any one in the group. Do not *over*develop an idea, either. There is a limit to the listener's attention span. Most of us know the person in conversation who has an incident to relate; but before he can tell it, he says, "Perhaps I had better go back a bit and explain the circumstances." Often we know more facts pertaining to an incident than we think it wise to tell simply because they are not essential to the main story or because they might be undesirable for other reasons. Voltaire put it well when he said, "The secret of being tiresome is to tell everything."

LANGUAGE

A few years ago we received a Christmas card from a retired professor, an author of several historical novels. It carried an original poem, a part of which follows:

Of all the glimpses we have caught
Of all the worth our time has bought,
Of all the profits we have earned,
Of all the lessons we have learned,
Our minds and hearts can never reach
Beyond the scope of daily speech.

For words enable us to live
With others and to get and give
The glowing truths that words impart
To mold the mind and warm the heart.
Without them we should quickly be
Turned back to dismal savagery.

How lovely speech when used by friends
To serve the best of human ends;
It makes of life a gracious whole;
It finds for life its ordained goal.
For basic truths are measured by
The words that sink or soar on high.

For thoughts unformed are often stirred
To fullness by our common word;
And deeds themselves ne'er come to birth
Till words have shaped them to their worth.
For symbols do the substance find,
And form the outlines of the mind.

This certainly highlights the significance of language in our daily lives, and, therefore, in our conversation.

Basically, in conversation, as elsewhere, we want our words to be well chosen. Mentor Graham, the teacher of Abraham Lincoln, is quoted as telling Lincoln never to forget that "the right words will guide the world." What, then, are the "right words"?

First of all, they are the acceptable words. That means that they are in current usage by the present company. This does not mean that a teacher deliberately makes grammatical errors or mispronunciations just because they are made by those present; that is hypocrisy. Words are acceptable, also, when they are in good taste. Most people know enough to avoid vulgarities in polite society; but some do not realize that a grownup does not use "teenese," nor do we expect a woman to use men's vocabulary or vice versa. Finally, words are acceptable if they are tactful. A writer on etiquette says, for example: "*Tact* says, 'How well you look!' *Thoughtlessness* says, 'How much better you look!' "

The right word is not only the acceptable word, it is the apt word. It is the word which, better than any other word, conveys to the listener what you are thinking or feeling. The old, worn-out words should not be called upon unless we can do no better. They are words such as *wonderful, grand, awful, cute, OK, darling, nice.* They are phrases such as *that's the way it goes; oh, really; I know; you see; as far as that goes.* It might "perk up" your conversational language to read occasionally the "Picturesque Speech" page of the *Reader's Digest.* We recall one item which read, "When the conversation fainted, he leapt forward with restoratives."

One final suggestion for the use of language in conversation: Use the promotional word. We use that term for lack of a better one to refer to the beginning and the ending of a remark. At the beginning of a remark in conversation we reveal our reaction to what has just been said. There we can hurt the previous speaker or we can dull the edge of the conversation by the words we use. At that point our language should frequently contain phrases such as: "I'm glad to hear you say that . . ."; "I've often wondered why . . ."; "I feel, too, that . . ."; etc. They suggest that the speaker was interested in what had been said and sought further ideas for carrying the conversation along. The language at the end of a contribution can help, too, by suggesting that the other person (or another person) can pick it up from there. If you end a remark with "But that's the way it goes" or "It sure is a funny world" or "I'm glad you like it," there is little to stimulate a thought in another converser. However, you do give him a chance if you throw out such a cue as, "But didn't you make your own?" or "I've been wondering what you thought of it" or "Your children must be getting excited." Notice how the promotional language is almost sure to have the word *you* in it. You can't avoid using the *I*, but if *you* is kept in the forefront, conversation will probably neither lag nor become fruitless.

VOICE

The effectiveness of language in conversation depends in part upon the voice that utters it. This means that the voice ought, first of all, to be intelligible. That includes both audibility and distinctness; otherwise, you will have straining, tense listeners and you will hear in tiring frequency the words, "I'm sorry, but I didn't hear . . ."; "Did you say . . .?"; or "Whom did you say she was with?" Listening to a tape recording of your conversation, taken when you were unaware of it, might sensitize you to the intelligibility of your voice.

Such a recording might reveal some other things about your use of voice. You might find that it is drab, unstimulating, and tiring. This might be due to its normal quality; it is even more likely to be caused by your voice habits. You have heard the voice that sounds so tired it even wearies you; or you have heard the voice that seems to be always slightly caustic or has a drop of venom in it; or you have heard the voice that is always so final and ungracious as to freeze any timid ones in the group. These voices contribute to neither of the two basic conditions we set up for satisfying conversation.

MANNER

By "manner" we refer here to your appearance and actions. These, we believe are less important than the other elements of speech; however, they should not be neglected. Since conversation is for pleasure, others can enjoy it more if they get a pleasurable response just from looking at you. An unshaven face, dandruff on the collar, clashing colors, and hair that is obviously "rinsed" with an unnatural color—any of these can be distractions to the conversation.

In your actions, posture is relative to the formality of the situation.   In sitting, women can be annoying by either of two tendencies: One is to be constantly making sure that too much of their legs is not visible; the other is to be completely oblivious of their exposure.   Your actions can be distracting, too, by continually turning away from a speaker.   You can be aggravating to the person with whom you are talking if you try to speak to or keep tab on everyone else in the room.   You owe it to the speaker to give him your full attention; at that moment he should feel that he is the most important person in your consciousness.

IMPROVING YOUR CONVERSATION

Throughout this chapter we have been implying various means by which you might improve your conversational ability.   At this point, we should like to offer some specific techniques.

The first of these is the use of observation.   Observe the conversations of others—even those in plays, movies, and radio or television shows.   Observe the good listener.   Notice the physical evidences of his attentiveness; be alert to how he encourages the speaker by his reactions and how he stimulates the speaker by throwing in an occasional phrase or short sentence to "draw him out" further.   Notice how he seems to bring out the best in the other person.   Then notice how the skillful speaker "takes the ball" from another with appreciation, and after he has concluded, he tosses it for someone else to take.   Above all, don't neglect to observe the kind of personality that is friendly, gracious, and stimulating.

If you can do it, there is no substitute for an examination of your own attitudes in conversation.   Of course, this includes the role that you play in conversational situations and the self-image you have.   You could ask yourself: Do I feel that others are always more important or more informed than I?   Do I feel that I must be the dominant person?   Can I change my role in different situations?   You need to examine your attitudes toward others, also.   You could ask yourself some of the questions listed earlier in the chapter under the heading of "Good Conversation."

Another device is to rethink a conversation shortly after you participated in it.   Ask yourself in what ways it gave a satisfied feeling, and what ways you felt dissatisfied.   Was it an unfortunate word or comment or question?   Was it the apparent reactions of the other person?   Was it poor listening?   Was it any cockiness or showing off on your part?   These and other questions might lead you to modify your next participation.

If you feel that language is your primary problem in conversation, you might do any of the following. Get a book on etiquette to familiarize yourself with the niceties of introductions, dinners, receptions, etc. Study books on English usage and pronunciation. Be an alert and sensitive listener to instructors, clergymen, and others who you believe have effective language usage. Use the material and suggestions in Chapter 6.

Using a tape recorder can be of great help. Of course, you will know that you are being recorded, but soon you will be able to be quite natural while it is running, especially if you place the microphone where it is not conspicuous. Use it when you are making a telephone conversation. Use it to record your dinner table talk. When you play it back, notice your voice, keeping in mind what was said earlier about voice. Then, notice, too, the attitudes of the other person(s) in responding to you—as shown in *their* voices. Note how well you modify your speaking according to the feedback you get from them. With a recording, it is possible for you, also, to make a written transcription of the conversation. Study it to notice the proportion of your participation and the length of each contribution. Observe the language—not only the correctness, but also the fluency, the conciseness, the vividness, and the "I's" and "you's."

You can make little conversational games, also. Imagine yourself in a given social situation and decide what you would say under various circumstances; do this with different personalities that you know. It might be helpful to record this or to write down what you would say. Another way is to have a friend play the role of someone you would like to be able to converse with, and the two of you stage a conversation. Recording it and listening to the playback would be not only helpful but probably entertaining.

One final suggestion: Use your own initiative to devise a method for improvement!

PERSONAL CONFERENCE

An interview is conversation for specific purposes, but possibly less informal and spontaneous. As a teacher, you will have three chief kinds of interviews: with school administrators, with parents, with pupils. In addition, you may occasionally have interviews with custodians, salesmen, businessmen, clergymen, etc., but the principles we shall deal with in the professional interviews will also apply in those situations.

FOR EMPLOYMENT

Your first professional interview with a school administrator has been or will be in connection with securing a job. Your placement office, if you are in college, very probably has some printed suggestions on such topics as: "Arranging the Interview," "Preparing for the Interview," "Your Appearance," as well as on "The Interview Itself." Here we are concerned chiefly with the last item.

The person interviewing you undoubtedly has had more experience in interviewing people than you have had being interviewed. Therefore, he can detect a "phony." Above all, then, be your natural best self. Be genuine; be frank. When questions are asked, give a considered, but forthright answer—avoid indecision and hedging.

Secondly, show a real interest in what the interviewer says. If it is possible, you should have obtained some information about the job, the school, the administrator, and the community. This not only suggests alertness on your part, but it enables you to listen with more understanding. Don't forget that as you listen, you have a good opportunity to learn something about the personality, interests, and values of the interviewer. This is important if he is the superintendent or principal; for you want to work with a person with whom you would be free to communicate, whose standards you could work under, and whom you could trust. Therefore, be interested in him as well as in the position. If he chooses to talk about his family, his hobbies, and other interests, carry on a friendly conversation with him.

Finally, be ready to ask questions. A pamphlet put out by the Iowa Association of School Boards, the Iowa Institutional Teacher Placement Association, and the Iowa Association of School Administrators contains this sentence: "Most employers are impressed more by the candidate who asks a few good questions than by those who merely answer the questions of the interviewer."[6] The one question you should avoid, however,—unless the interview comes to a close without its being raised—is that of salary. The interviewer will probably bring that up. The questions you do ask should be intelligent ones concerning the philosophy of education that prevails in the school, the kind of community it is, the age, turnover, professional growth, and extracurricular interests of the staff, etc. But, again, listen closely to the answers to your questions, and follow a question up with one or two more questions if necessary.

[6] Clifford E. Erickson, *A Practical Handbook for School Counselors,* The Ronald Press Company, New York, 1949, p. 55.

At the beginning of the interview you would have presented yourself promptly and graciously.   At the close, do not linger, express your appreciation for the interview, be sure you understand what the next step will be, and then leave.

It is interesting to know why candidates are rejected because of an interview. Dr. Frank S. Endicott, the director of placement at Northwestern University, surveyed 153 companies to find the reasons in the business world for rejection.   Out of the fifty reasons he found, we are listing below those which we think would be pertinent to teachers:

1 Overbearing, overaggressive, conceited, superiority complex, know-it-all
2 Lack of confidence and poise, nervous, ill-at-ease
3 Lack of tact
4 Lack of courtesy, ill-mannered
5 Lack of social understanding
6 Little sense of humor
7 Intolerant, strong prejudices
8 No interest in community activities
9 Inability to take criticism
10 Condemnation of past employers
11 Indecision
12 Narrow interests
13 Radical ideas
14 Failure to express appreciation for interviewer's time
15 Asks no questions about the job
16 Indefinite response to questions
17 Inability to express himself clearly, poor voice, diction, and grammar
18 Poor personal appearance
19 Lack of vitality
20 Failed to look interviewer in the eye
21 Limp, fishy handshake

WITH A PARENT

In some people's minds an interview or conference with a parent means some sort of a crisis.   That is usually not true, however.   A parent-teacher conference *may* be required to resolve a conflict or some other critical situation.   However, it may be desirable for purposes of getting acquainted, for exchanging information regarding a pupil, for discussing the pupil's progress, for room-mothers' activities, etc.   Any such conference should be looked upon more as an opportunity than as a crisis and should be approached by the teacher without a feeling of defensiveness or worry. Her expectation should be that it will be mutually beneficial.

Of course, it is more desirable to have the interview at the school than any other place. Better, also, to have it in the room where the parent's child spends its time, rather than in the corridor, in the principal's office, or in the teachers' lounge. However, there are times when a more casual chat between a parent and the teacher will accomplish more.

The interview can usually be opened in much the same way that a conversation would begin. This will help the parent to feel that he is on an equal level with the teacher. The opening comment or question, therefore, need not be on the main subject of the interview. It is important that a feeling of mutual acceptance and mutual interest be established.

As the conference proceeds, you will have questions to ask, but avoid suggesting that this is a cross-examination. There should be a real attempt to understand each other. This means that the answers to questions should be clear before any new questions are asked. As the questions are answered, it is important here, just as in conversation, that you listen with understanding. If the parent should want to "get something off his chest," listen to him— calmly. Show that you appreciate his point of view and his feelings, and then quietly get him to understand how it looks from your point of view. If a difference needs to be resolved, let the parent feel that you need his help in working it out.

If you feel that the parent does not come in just to be critical, and if the parent feels that your first concern in your job is to help the child, the conference can be friendly and useful. If the unusual case arises, however, where the parent is angry or obdurate, and remains so, then you are justified in calling in the assistance of an administrator. In nearly all cases the interview can be closed with graciousness and a friendly spirit, leaving the means of communication open for further cooperation.

WITH A PUPIL

In the interview or conference with a pupil, your role changes again. Pupils sometimes interview teachers, but generally the teacher is the interviewer. However, the basic principles of all interviews still apply. Interviews of this kind do not have to be "scheduled"; often the time is a minute or two before or after a period or during moments of contact elsewhere in the school.

However, when a conference is planned, the specific suggestions given by Clifford E. Erickson might serve as a guide. They are as follows:

1 Gather some information in advance and study the data before the interview.
2 Use a warming up period to get acquainted.
3 Study counselee to determine your starting techniques.
4 Follow counselee's lead before moving from the general into the specific, from the obvious to the less apparent.
5 Use an exploratory period to learn a little about all aspects of the counselee and to locate general areas of possible importance.
6 Try to locate some achievements, strengths, prides, or drives of counselee to use if necessary.
7 Show a *direct* interest in the counselee.
8 Accept his statements and attitudes as *facts* (as a starting relationship)
9 Don't argue, try to persuade, or coerce.
10 Don't gossip about others or show any tendency to reveal confidence:
11 Use "conversational hooks"—end with a question or pick up some thing he has already said.
12 Answer his questions in a frank, straightforward way.
13 Avoid a patronizing or sympathetic manner. Don't cry on his shoulde
14 Encourage comments by counselee but *do not probe.*
15 Don't reveal your attitudes or you will condition the rest of the inte view. Don't imply, suggest, or indicate your reactions.
16 Begin with the most important thing on his mind. How did it begir When did he first notice it?
17 A discussion of a test result is often a good place to start an intervie
18 Be sure the counselee has a chance to release his tensions.
19 Encourage counselee to carry his own responsibility for his problen
20 Permit him to tell his own story in his own way. Don't interrupt.
21 The interviewee should be considered as a conversational equal.
22 The interviewer makes clear the client's responsibility for planning a action.[7]

Modifications of the above may be made according to who asked for t conference, the purpose of it, and the circumstances under which it is he In any case, it should be conversational in nature but should hold to its limit

[7] *Ibid.,* p. 55.

purposes. A good conference with a pupil is often worth more than two or three class periods.

Practice to become a stimulating and respected conversationalist in all of your informal interpersonal relationships. You will find it rewarding for your personal life; but you will also find that it is a sound basis for improving your speech and that it will pay dividends in your growth as a teacher.

FOR FURTHER READING

Eisenson, Jon and Paul H. Boase: *Basic Speech*, 2d ed., The Macmillan Company, New York, 1964, chap. 10.

Erickson, Clifford E.: *A Practical Handbook For School Counselors,* The Ronald Press Company, New York, 1949.

Fessenden, Seth A., Roy I. Johnson, and P. Merville Larson: *The Teacher Speaks,* Prentice-Hall, Inc., Englewood Cliffs, N.J., 1954, chap. 7.

Nichols, Ralph G. and Thomas R. Lewis: *Listening and Speaking,* William C. Brown Company, Publishers, Dubuque, 1954, chap. 12.

Smith, T. V.: "The Art of Conversation," *House Beautiful*, March, 1959, pp. 124, 127, 151–152.

Sorrenson, Fred S.: *Speech For the Teacher*, The Ronald Press Company, New York, 1952, chaps. 9 and 10.

CHAPTER ELEVEN

GROUP DISCUSSION

Our democratic society rests upon the right and the ability of its citizens to assemble and discuss the problems that face them. The cracker-barrel session is a typical American institution. In the town meeting, one of the earliest of such organized groups, Americans have faced and solved problems for over 300 years. In education, discussion also plays a part of great importance.

The classroom is often a discussion group, led either by the teacher or a designated student. Committee meetings in classes, clubs, or professional organizations are discussions. They are organized and conducted to find facts, to evaluate policies, to solve problems, and to recommend action. Participation or supervision—in meetings of student councils, faculties, PTA groups, or school boards—necessitates a teacher's knowing *how* to take part in discussion. A basic philosophy, familiarity with discussion types, mastery of preparation methods, organization, and procedure are of distinctive value to a teacher.

THE NATURE OF DISCUSSION

Group discussion is a means of cooperatively exchanging ideas, information, and opinions for the purpose of learning, and of thinking together to solve problems. It takes place under the direction of a leader, either previously appointed or indicated during the discussion. It may occur before an audience or in a closed session, with only the members in attendance. To understand the nature of discussion, you must understand its characteristics.

DISCUSSION IS GROUP THINKING OR INQUIRY
The most important use of discussion is probably its value in employing group thinking to solve problems. Many school and classroom problems can be resolved by this method.

In a consolidated secondary school a very capable speech teacher had developed much interest in individual speech activities, debating, and theatre. The school was active in the program of the state association. On weekends, many festivals and tournaments were available to the group. Administration, faculty, parents, and students were all eager to have the pupils enjoy the advantages of these events. Because of the location of the school, as well as that of the scheduled tournaments, transportation was a major problem.

In most cases the traveling group was between fifteen and twenty students. Trips averaged fifty miles one way. The schedule called for early Saturday departure with return in the late afternoon. The school budget was modest.

First attempts to solve the transportation problem made use of family cars with parents as drivers. This solution, however, was not wholly satisfactory. The cars were needed for other purposes on weekends. Frequently parents could not contribute a whole day to serve as chauffeurs. The questions of liability and insurance entered the picture. The results of this plan were far from the best. Too few cars, changes in family schedules, variety in driving ability, and unwillingness of some parents to take responsibility— these were some of the disadvantages. ¡

Faced with a baffling problem, the teacher asked the principal to organize a committee to try to arrive at a practical solution. This he did, appointing the teacher, two parents, the school business manager, two students, and himself as members.

They held several meetings in which they employed these standard steps in discussion:

1 Statement and definition of the problem
2 Analysis and exploration of the problem
3 Suggestion of solutions and their evaluation
4 Selection of the best solution (or solutions)
5 Suggestions for putting solutions into action or trying them out

Applied to the situation facing them, the developments were as follows:

Statement and definition of the problem. After some comments about the experiences on their first trip, one of the students suggested this question as the best statement of their problem: "How can we transport our students safely, conveniently, and economically to the speech events we wish to attend?" There was general agreement upon this wording. Next came observations that "safely" meant that drivers should be competent, careful persons, and that insurance protection as provided by state law should cover all students. "Conveniently" was easily defined to mean "on a schedule suited to the time and place of the events to be attended." The word "economically" was clearly set forth by the business manager who stated "all trips must be within the budget available for this activity."

Analysis and exploration of the problem. The first part of the analysis was the observation that the present method of using individual cars driven by parents was not satisfactory to students, the parents, or the school. The *effects* noted were these: not enough cars, uncertainty in procuring cars, wide variation in the ability of parent drivers, failure to provide complete insurance protection, inability to maintain a satisfactory time schedule on trips, impossibility to take all students. The basic *cause* producing these effects was the use of individual cars owned and driven by different parents. The *values* or *criteria* set up for any transportation system to be used were those originally included in the problem: safety, convenience, and economy.

Suggestion of solutions and their evaluation. To solve the problem by removing the causes mentioned, and thereby eliminating the effects, the group advanced a number of solutions. They attempted to check all of these in relation to the values they wished such proposals to have. Solutions proposed were: (1) the railroad, which had a main line connecting several of the towns to be visited; (2) a commercial bus line with connections to many smaller communities in the area; (3) chartered bus, by means of which a standard commercial vehicle could be hired for the day's trip; (4) purchase of a school bus for use not only in transporting students on speech trips, but also athletic events, music festivals, 4-H club meetings, etc. All these solutions were evaluated and discussed pro and con in terms of their suitability in handling the problem.

Selection of the best solution (or solutions). Following careful consideration of the four proposals, the committee decided to use the third for the duration of the school year. A chartered bus provided space enough to carry all students. It was driven by a licensed bus driver. It was completely covered by insurance. It could be engaged for whatever schedule was established. It was within the expenditures budgeted for the program for that year. An added recommendation was made for the following year, with the support of the principal, business manager, and parents. This involved the purchase of a school bus with a regular driver employed by the school. The estimated expense for all transportation for school activities was thought sufficient to make such a step advisable, both financially and in terms of practical needs of the school.

Suggestions for putting solutions into action. Because the committee recommendations were supported by the administrative officers, the new program was announced to the faculty and the students. The necessary bus transportation was arranged for the remaining events of the year, and the transportation problem was solved.

DISCUSSION IS COOPERATIVE NOT COMPETITIVE

In a discussion all members are working together. They are "cooperatively exchanging ideas, information, and opinions." They are thinking together. In such a relationship they are trying to help each other to learn or to solve a problem. They are *not* attempting to win an argument or to compete with each other to gain a decision.

DISCUSSION IS A DIRECTED ACTIVITY

Discussion must have some direction to be effective. In this particular case, the chairman of the committee (who was the speech teacher) conducted the committee meetings. Such leadership does not indicate domination of the discussion. The leader acts as a guide to promote discussion; he keeps it moving according to a certain pattern in order to obtain results in trying to solve the problem. The five steps above provide the pattern for such an approach. Some discussions are not so definitely structured, nor is a leader appointed in advance. Under such conditions, it is the belief that the group will choose its own leader, or one will assume a function of leadership during discussion. Persons inexperienced in discussion method ordinarily have greater success with a preappointed leader who is well qualified. With good leadership they also become more efficient, as well as more democratic, in their procedure. Teachers need training in leadership of such situations before they enter student teaching or before they are regularly employed in a school system. Otherwise, their efforts in discussion may well become confused, aimless operations that seem to get nowhere.

As thought is stimulated and comments from the group are offered, the leader learns to direct or indicate lines of participation by his questions and comments, which will keep things moving toward the goals of the discussion. Such leadership draws out ideas, and provides stimulation for the thinking of all members of the group.

DISCUSSION IS DYNAMIC

This means that the thinking and conclusions of the members of the group are not *set* or *static*. They develop and change as the discussion proceeds. "Thought in process" best describes this characteristic. When new, challenging information is introduced, any member may change his opinion, if he desires. This process of inner stimulation is an important attribute of the process.

DISCUSSION IS DEMOCRATIC

Every person in a discussion has an equal right to think and express himself as he pleases. With a cooperative attitude underlying the process and skillful leadership operating, discussion is the most democratic of all forms of speech activity. However, because all viewpoints should be heard in such a situation, discussion often requires more time than other forms of deliberation.

DISCUSSION IS BASED UPON SOUND INFORMATION
AND GOOD PREPARATION

Because it is a group activity and a specific time and place to speak is not assigned to each member of the group, some persons have the mistaken idea "that you don't have to prepare for discussion." As one opportunistic individual expressed it, "All you do is talk off the top of your head." Nothing could be more incorrect. Discussion is not merely pooled ignorance. Effective discussion rests upon a thorough knowledge of the problem, good analysis, a careful search for solutions, and profound thought about one's conclusions. Many opportunities appear for the development of new, freshly stimulated ideas in a discussion. However, a grasp of fundamental information underlies them, and is the basis for creative thinking.

DISCUSSION REQUIRES ORAL SKILL

In discussion, each speaker is a member of a group in which he "talks over" the problem at hand. *Within* the group he shares what he knows and believes. Unlike the situation in lecturing or in other forms of individual speaking *before* an audience, he does not present a speech. He participates in the process of discussion, employing the various qualities of effective oral communication as he does so. His contributions as a speaker in the discussion have effect in the group product that is evolved.

DISCUSSION IS DONE BEFORE AN AUDIENCE
OR IN A CLOSED SESSION

In order to use discussion to serve greater numbers, the actual process of discussion may be conducted before an audience. Thus everyone is able to hear the original analyses and suggestions, which may "stir up" the thinking of listeners in the audience, as well as that of the discussion group. The panel discussion, for example, is effective as such a method. In other instances, discussion is confined to members of the group. Committee meetings, such as those in the example cited earlier, operate in closed session. In the example, the group reported their findings to the faculty and the students *after* they had held their deliberations. Certain forms of discussion are particularly adapted for such purposes.

SUBJECTS AND PROBLEMS FOR DISCUSSION

Three kinds of problems (or subjects) are used in discussion. A problem concerned with the truth or falsity of a matter is called a question of *fact*. Does the United States have a rocket capable of reaching the moon? is a question of fact. The answer to the question can be obtained from the scientists in our space program who have been studying, building, and experimenting with various types of space machines. A problem that asks whether something is good or bad, or attempts to explore the worth of a matter, is a question of *value*. Is the Russian system of education superior to that of the United States for training citizens in a democracy? is a question of value. If the problem states that something should or should not be done, it is a question of *policy*. Should private schools be subsidized by the federal government? is question of policy. Any kind of question is usable in discussion. However, the question of policy is most adaptable in the five-step pattern of discussion which has been discussed previously.

TYPES OF DISCUSSION

Each of the various types of discussion has its own particular characteristics, which teachers will find helpful as they select a discussion form for their use. Part of the success in using discussion depends upon the choice of the best type for the occasion. The types include (1) informal discussion, (2) round table or small conference, (3) panel discussion, (4) the dialogue, (5) the symposium, (6) the lecture-forum, (7) the forum, (8) the Phillips 66 or buzz session, (9) the film forum.

INFORMAL DISCUSSION

Often discussion emerges from a situation which is basically a conversational one, in which the purposes are sociability or entertainment. When the persons speaking turn to serious purposes such as learning or solving problems, they enter the area of discussion. Discussion may be carried on very informally, and yet follow a pattern like the one noted earlier. Students and teachers often exchange ideas and opinions in informal situations which move into other discussion types at a later time.

ROUND TABLE OR SMALL CONFERENCE

In a committee meeting various degrees of formality may be present. In reality it is a small conference group. A round table discussion is very similar. The table (as a prop) may be present, serving to aid face-to-face procedure. However, the same attitude may be developed if the members are seated in a small circle, and talk things over in the same cooperative manner. The thing that characterizes this type, in addition to its purpose and pattern, is the "closed session" kind of inquiry. Under such circumstances the leader and group members proceed to share ideas, analyze, and propose solutions to the problem at hand.

PANEL DISCUSSION

In a panel discussion, the small group is merely placed before an audience. As a rule, four to eight persons make a good size for a panel. Arranged in a semicircle or hollow square, the members of the group not only can see and hear each other, but they communicate so that the members of the audience can see and hear them, also. A real panel is a spontaneous discussion, usually directed by a leader. It is not a series of prepared speeches. The leader keeps the discussion moving and allows free participation among the members of the group. Long speeches are not encouraged. The pattern usually follows the steps in group thinking or some systematic plan agreed upon, which will cover the problem for the audience and the members. It is traditional to follow the panel with a question period or *forum*, which is discussed below. The panel is frequently used in radio or television broadcasting.

THE DIALOGUE

In the dialogue, two persons participate, one asking questions, and the other answering them. The questioner acts as the discussion leader. His partner is usually an expert on the problem under consideration or one whose opinions and knowledge are respected. A skilled questioner asks prepared questions in such a way that the audience will feel that he represents them. The basic information revealed in the answers of the expert becomes the principal content of the discussion. The dialogue, like the panel, is often used in radio and television.

THE SYMPOSIUM

A symposium is a series of prepared speeches presented on a single subject. A leader or chairman presides, introduces the speakers, who talk directly to the audience. Generally a forum follows a symposium. There are two ways of planning and presenting the symposium. In the first, the problem is divided, and each speaker handles his particular section of it. A question of policy such as: Should private schools be subsidized by the federal government? can readily be divided into three sections. One speaker can develop the problem and possible need for support; a second can discuss the various plans for subsidization; a third can evaluate the plans. A second method is to allow each speaker to present his views on the problem as a whole, presenting his analysis and solution in each case. Under this plan speakers may be chosen to represent various points of view. The audience would benefit from this breadth and variety of discussion. In either plan speakers have the responsibility to prepare fully and with sufficient adaptability to meet the conditions and essential points as they arise in the meeting.

The symposium has the definite advantage of allowing greater control over the nature and amount of material to be presented. Also, speakers can anticipate questions by the audience and prepare accordingly to meet them, as well as stimulate further inquiry from the floor. Its chief disadvantage is that it is not as flexible as the panel discussion.

The leader not only introduces the speakers, but also opens the discussion and provides relevant comments to connect the talks given. If he thinks it wise, he summarizes the contributions made. He also presides over the forum if one follows.

THE LECTURE-FORUM

A lecture-forum includes a speech followed by a question and discussion period. The chairman, who presides, introduces the speaker and the subject for the occasion. The speaker is selected because he is an authority on the question. Two possible types of speeches are used in the lecture-forum. One is an informative talk with considerable depth in which the speaker presents background, facts, and arguments, but does not give his conclusions.

The audience uses the discussion period to explore the subject further by asking questions, expressing its opinions, and reaching certain conclusions. In the second type of speech, the speaker presents his views, his supporting reasons, and leaves the question open for the audience to explore. He usually finds his views challenged, and is given an interesting test in defending them.

THE FORUM

As indicated above, the forum is an audience questioning and discussion period that may follow a panel, dialogue, symposium, or a lecture. Forum discussion is a useful method, but varies in the way it may be conducted, depending upon the subject, chairman, and the size or kind of audience. The leader may conduct the questioning period in a small, informal group with considerable ease. However, in a larger meeting he cannot use the same techniques which will succeed in a panel situation. Frequently he will find a larger audience has more inertia. It may not respond readily, or on the contrary, many in the group may wish to talk. For such occasions he will need to develop suitable techniques to keep the situation in hand, yet retain liveliness and spontaneity.

THE PHILLIPS 66 OR BUZZ SESSION

This form of discussion, devised by J. Donald Phillips, is used principally to help a *large* group in preparing questions for use in a forum situation. A lecture or speech usually precedes the discussion, and opens up the problem. The pattern used is as follows: (1) The chairman constitutes small groups of six persons, or six pairs each, who simply move their chairs and face each other to confer; (2) each group discusses the problem for a short time (six minutes is a common length of time); (3) each group selects a representative to present one question to the whole audience for consideration in the forum; (4) the chairman calls for these questions, which are presented by each group representative *very briefly*; (5) the chairman summarizes these recommendations, indicating how they relate to the whole question; (6) the chairman then leads the discussion of these questions by the whole group, making sure that each recommendation is considered, and that decisions on each are the result of group thinking.

This method allows a quick coverage of group reactions and fixes attention on particular questions considered important to the individual groups. As a rule, the buzz session allows key points to be discussed and is a short method of involving the entire group in considering the problem. Such a method is not ordinarily needed in a small group which can use the other discussion methods.

THE FILM-FORUM

Today many excellent films are available so that the problem for discussion can be presented by first showing a film. A 16-mm sound film or a 35-mm filmstrip will do the job effectively in setting the background or foundation for the discussion which follows. Full-length feature films and short subjects are now available on 16-mm through Films Incorporated, a division of Encyclopaedia Britannica Films. Other companies have a great variety of titles in every subject field. Certain relevant suggestions may prove useful: (1) Be sure that physical facilities are arranged to permit showing and suitable viewing of the film; (2) be sure to preview the film for content, length, and critical points which it presents; (3) plan the questions to be used in starting the forum, moving from general to specific points; (4) allow everyone an opportunity to ask questions and make comments about the film; (5) before showing the film, list on a chalkboard or chart the key points to look for in viewing; (6) conclude the forum while it is still alive, and summarize the contributions of the group.

PREPARATION FOR DISCUSSION

THE PARTICIPANT

The effectiveness of discussion is directly related to the knowledge and thinking of the participants. Whenever you take part in discussion, you have an obligation to prepare as fully as possible. Your preparation can be of two types: (1) *broad* or *general*, from your experience and previous reading. Thus, you bring your entire general education into the discussion. (2) *specific*, through your investigation of the immediate discussion problem. Use both of these types in preparing to take part. Specific research methods are similar to those you employ to get materials for an individual speech. Sources on contemporary affairs include such weekly magazines as *Time*, *Newsweek*, *U.S. News and World Report*; newspapers such as *Christian Science Monitor* and *The New York Times*; periodicals such as *The Atlantic Monthly*, *Saturday Review*, *Harpers*, *The New Republic*, and others. All of these may serve your broad, and at times, your specific preparation. Specialized pamphlets and books also supply needed information to enrich your specific preparation of discussion subjects.

Selection and arrangement of your materials is essential as you gather information. As a participant, you will find it helpful to make an inventory of your ideas and information in a systematic sentence outline with the steps in discussion as your principal headings. This will be an effective guide for your contributions during the discussion.

THE LEADER

Each leader also has the responsibility of making a paper plan of his preparation. If you are to lead a discussion, prepare carefully and fully upon the subject. In addition, develop your outline to meet the specific needs and responsibilities of your job:

1 Plan your opening remarks: refer to the occasion and the reason for the discussion; introduce the topic and state any limitations or definitions already agreed upon; introduce the speakers, giving relevant information.
2 Develop your "kick-off" questions to ensure an interesting, positive lead-in to the body of the discussion.
3 Plan series of questions introducing and following up main issues in the discussion; arrange them under the main heads or basic steps.
4 Anticipate needs for transitions and internal summaries to point up progress and relate the various steps in the discussion.
5 Plan tentatively and generally your final summary and your concluding remarks; these may have to be adapted later.

Your leader's outline provides a guide for your procedure. If necessary, write out your introductory comments and the details of your speaker introductions. Follow these with your outline for the main part of the discussion, using the basic steps as your principal heads. Because a leader's job is to stimulate others to talk, you plan "push button" questions to ensure participation. Such questions must cover critical points in the basic content of the subject. Develop them for each point your group explores. Your major challenge is to prepare such provocative questions that speakers will respond relevantly and effectively. One question under each point is usually not enough. Plan a series that has a follow-up sequence, anticipating participation that may develop. Such planning helps you to keep the discussion going. Flexibility is another important part of your outline. Be ready to modify and adapt your scheme on the spot, if necessary, to follow changes in ideas or new information as soon as they are contributed. This method keeps your content alive and holds interest.

Another part of your preparation is to know and study group members. Some have interesting ideas, wide experience, or a wealth of information.

Include questions in your outline so that you can utilize their abilities and backgrounds. Similarly, you can employ them to present particular positions or points of view on the problem or solutions you are considering.

Plan your summary and concluding remarks in advance even though they may be general or tentative. You may have to change or add, but this preparation helps you to avoid last minute organization of the product of the discussion. By employing a skeleton or fill-in form you can easily adapt it on the spot to your needs.

THE BRIEFING SESSION

Although you know that discussions are not "scripted" or rehearsed line by line, it is excellent insurance for you as a leader and for the members of your group to hold a briefing session several days in advance. As the person in charge of such a meeting, you explain your ideas for opening and closing the discussion, describe the mechanical arrangements, get information about your speakers, and come to some understanding on definitions and limitations of the question to be discussed. Further, you can learn the limits and the nature of the information, as well as the positions held by your speakers on the subject. You may suggest further investigation. You can probably agree upon a basic sequence and the major issues to be discussed so that you will know points of conflict and agreement among the group members.

Such preplanning ordinarily aids in developing a smoother, clearer discussion progression, and provides definite goals for preparation by the leader and the speakers. Remember, however, that your briefing session should not attempt to "set" the participations or rehearse lines or speeches to be given. It merely clears up beforehand certain details so that the actual discussion time may be used to concentrate upon the vital issues of the problem and their development during the discussion.

PHYSICAL ARRANGEMENTS

Local conditions affect the amount of control you will have in making such plans. Obtain chairs, tables, and other necessary furniture. Arrange the chairs so that members of the group can see each other. For a very small group, seating the members around a table is best. Thus you have a face-to-face situation which will build a "group feeling" and will encourage shy or inexperienced persons to take part. Often, in a panel of six or more members, you will find a semicircle or hollow square desirable. Here are examples of such seating:

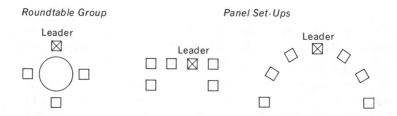

In each case your arrangement will depend upon its suitability for the type of discussion and occasion. Also, the use of visual aids, displays, or chalk-boards will affect the arrangement. Chairs should be placed so that such items are clearly visible to the audience, and can be used easily by group members.

Other physical arrangements which you need to consider in advance are name cards for participants, ventilation, paper or writing materials, lighting, noise conditions, an easel for charts, and ashtrays.

SUGGESTIONS FOR PROCEDURE IN DISCUSSION

A GENERAL APPROACH TO PARTICIPATION

You will increase your effectiveness in discussion if you know (1) desirable attitudes, (2) appropriate procedure, and (3) techniques of participation. Attitude rests upon applying the philosophy of cooperation in the group. All are working together to solve a problem. The situation is flexible and dynamic. Expect change, differences in opinion, and an effort by all to seek causes for such differences. Be tolerant and helpful. Maintain an objective, though inquiring mind. Be willing to go more than halfway to meet other speakers. Control your emotions, yet be enthusiastic as you learn, and with your knowledge and thinking try to help solve the problem under consideration.

Procedure varies greatly in formality. The panel is less formalized than the symposium. A committee meeting, usually very informal, proceeds at a conversational level. In small groups you rarely need to obtain leave to speak, but talk at the appropriate moment. You are the judge of the appropriate time and manner for your contribution. Do not try to dominate, and do not interrupt others. Observe and think before you speak. You can then do a good job as a participant.   Should several persons appear eager to speak at once, let the leader know in some way that you wish permission to speak.

Technique in participation best follows a simple formula.   State your opinion first.   Then present your reasons and facts to support it.   Last, indicate how you arrived at this conclusion and why it is important to this discussion. Thus, your position will be relevant, clear, and substantial.   Furthermore, you will not give the impression that it is personal or hastily conceived.

SPECIFIC SUGGESTIONS ON PARTICIPATION

The general approach to participation sets a pattern to aid your conduct as a member of any discussion group.   Below are further specific helps for you.

MAINTAIN A GENUINE COOPERATIVE ATTITUDE.   It is essential that every member have such an attitude.   Do not show off or try to win an argument.   Contribute seriously to a clear analysis of the problem and aid in getting the best solution to it.   Place the good of the group and the progress of the discussion ahead of your personal desires.   Share your knowledge with the group.   Be willing to listen carefully to other members.   If they present new information and sound thinking, be willing to consider changing your position accordingly.   Make a careful study of your own opinions and prejudices.   Be sure that you understand the bases for them. Then consider the problem and possible solutions apart from your feelings. Maintain an attitude of scientific inquiry and objectivity.   Evaluate pros and cons of a policy impartially and apart from your economic background, political affiliations, or religious beliefs.

STAY ON THE SUBJECT.   An objective approach is of little value unless your comments are *relevant* to the particular issue at hand.   Your contributions become really significant if you are cooperative, if what you say is on the subject, and applies specifically to the point under consideration.

PARTICIPATE VOLUNTARILY AND ENTHUSIASTICALLY.   Teamwork in a discussion depends upon the desire of all to do well.   By positive, voluntary comments you make your knowledge, good thinking, and reactions a part of the group process.   The leader will appreciate enthusiastic participation.   He knows that the discussion cannot move ahead if persons sit back and say nothing.   Do not contribute just for the sake of contributing. Rather, make your remarks meaningful and helpful to the discussion, without any attempt to monopolize it.

LISTEN EFFECTIVELY AND COURTEOUSLY.   To be a successful participant, you need to know everything that takes place in a discussion. Effective, courteous listening ensures this.   It also guarantees that what you say is relevant and appropriate to the pattern of discussion as it proceeds.

USE TACT IN HUMAN RELATIONS.   Because group thinking depends upon the combined effort of a *number of people*, remember that tact and consideration for their feelings gain best results.   Shun the ever-positive, dogmatic comment.   When you disagree, do so politely.   Say: "Your point is clear; however it seems to me, etc.," or "You have interesting evidence, but the conclusion I draw is different from yours."   Prefer "This appears to be true" to "I've got the stuff and I *know* I'm right!"

BE AN EFFECTIVE SPEAKER.   A group situation is no excuse for individuals to speak badly.   Apply effectively the fundamentals of speech you know.   Good oral communication is essential in discussion.   Sound ideas and information, clear organization, and appropriate language, with physical vitality and sufficient vocal projection in delivery, help to make discussion interesting and successful.

LEADERSHIP DURING DISCUSSION

You have observed that careful preparation is absolutely necessary for the leader.   Following are numerous practical suggestions to help you during the discussion:

MAKE AN EFFECTIVE START.   The leader has important duties in opening the discussion.   He needs to carry them out positively and effectively.

Perform routine essentials first: state the subject and the reasons for discussing it; introduce the speakers, giving their qualifications; indicate the time allowed for the panel and the nature of the forum period, if one is to follow; ask the opening question of the group, but follow it up to particular persons. This sequence or lead-in is direct and effective; it also avoids the hazard of "dead-air" or silence, an awkward condition at the start.   Certain other planned openings are usable: (1) develop a vivid case or example of the problem; (2) state the major points of conflict; (3) use an appropriate quotation; (4) set forth various positions on the problem.

Having made a strong start, proceed to use questions developed in your preparation outline and others evolved during the course of the discussion to meet the need for following up lines of participation.   These ways of using questions are practical: (1) Prepare and plant starter questions to ensure quick replies and to keep things moving; (2) Use "What" questions to get personal reactions: "What are the facts on this issue?" or "What solutions are proposed?" or "What is your stand on this matter?" (3) Use "Why" questions to find *reasons, causes,* and *justifications* for opinions. (4) Use "Who" and "Where" questions to check authorities and sources of evidence.

KEEP THE DISCUSSION MOVING AHEAD IN AN ORDERLY MAN-NER. Your preparation outline is your means of planning a sequence and a procedure for you to follow. Using it, you must keep the discussion alive and on the track. Make clear the basic positions and opinions that develop. Relate parts of the discussion to your total job or analysis and the finding of solutions. Certain specific methods can help:

1 *Follow your planned steps in group thinking.* This action uses your prepared outline, yet allows for adjustment to new developments. The basic steps in group thinking are your foundation. They ensure an orderly development following your introduction and a conclusion that is appropriate. Inexperienced leaders find a maximum of security and success with this method.
2 *Discuss key issues and then tie them in.* Experienced leaders may find this method more interesting and exciting. Start the discussion at the point where you can develop the greatest interest; build the discussion around this and move to other significant issues. These points are the focus of your discussion rather than the five basic steps. As they develop, tie in the contributions of the speakers to them and to the total problem. Interest is the key value utilized by a skillful leader employing this method. His ability to link up vital points to the key issues provides an orderly progression. Although some material may be left out, current interest is served strongly and logically.
3 *Make relationships clear by your comments.* Every leader needs to help members of his group and the audience follow clearly and understand relationships of parts of the discussion as it progresses. Your comments are the most effective means of linking new to old materials, or the part to the whole. Develop the use of good transitions for this purpose as you move from one part of the discussion to another. Skill in clarifying such relationships as you proceed is valuable.
4 *Employ summaries wisely.* Closely related to your skill in linking parts of the discussion is the ability to help your participants be certain of what they have covered, as well as what they still must do. Summaries,

suitably placed, accomplish this purpose. Learn to take stock of the achievements of the group, and combine this awareness with accurate perception of areas yet to be discussed. A clear-cut tersely worded summary crystallizes the sometimes confused mass of content so that it becomes apparent to all. Develop the ability to grasp the core of an issue and word it simply and clearly. This is a great asset in discussion leadership.

5   *Learn methods of developing important material.* A leader needs to be able to cover the important areas of the discussion efficiently, yet with suitable detail and specificity. Be sure that you do not permit useless or unproductive talk to waste your time. Tactfully move the discussion to another point or speaker by your observations that "Your point seems quite clear, Tom. Shall we hear what Jane has to say on the next point?" Such a progression usually helps. Then check your techniques on types of questions you use to evoke desired responses. Review the use of who, what, why, when, where, and how questions. Each has a specific purpose and value in gaining ideas and information.

Further, follow up statements by members to get specific examples, illustrations, statistics, and quotations to prove arguments and make positions vivid or clear. You may be able to provide appropriate items, or better tap the reservoir of knowledge of your participants to enrich their contributions.

LEARN TO KNOW PEOPLE AND HOW TO HANDLE THEM IN DISCUSSION. Human beings are fascinating yet complex individuals. As a leader much of your success depends upon your knowledge of how to deal with them in discussion. Here are some suggestions for working with certain individuals.

1   Evoke contributions from the person who is reticent to speak: "Sue, how does that fit in with your experience last summer?"
2   Curb the tendency of one person to talk too much: "Now Jeff has given us several ideas; does someone see this in a different way?"
3   Intervene when one person holds forth too long (When he stops for breath) : "Pardon the interruption, George, but I think we should go back to that point you made earlier . . . "
4   Call the generalizer back to specifics: "That's quite an assertion; do you think we can support it with specific instances? Where would it apply on our campus?"
5   Hold in check the impatient member: "I know we would like to move

on this, but hadn't we better look at some of the possible results? Would it work in all cases? Who has an idea on that?

6 Bring a member back to the point of discussion: "It would be interesting to follow that line of thought, but I think we'll have to agree that it doesn't bear directly enough on our problem."

7 Restrain a person from dealing in personalities: "I wonder if we could avoid making this a personal attack; don't you think it diverts us from the question before us?"

8 Cool off the person who becomes too emotional: "We can appreciate how you feel, Nancy, but how would we want to word this in our report? Who has a suggestion?"

9 Open the mind of the biased or prejudiced person: "That sounds like a good argument for debate. However, let's see if there are some other angles from which we might view this."

10 Get the joker to be more helpful: "I'm glad we can see the humorous side of this, but seriously, Jim, would you accept the idea that . . .?"

CONCLUDE THE DISCUSSION BRIEFLY AND CLEARLY. Your preparation outline gave you a basic plan for your conclusion. Your product in discussion may or may not have followed your plan. The chances are that you will have to adapt or even modify decidedly the conclusions you prepared. Your notes, taken during the discussion, will be the source of those changes. Make your adjustments, following these possibilities for a clear-cut, brief summary that will state accurately what the speakers achieved: (1) a summary organized around the conclusions and recommendations of the group; (2) a summary organized upon the principal issues in the discussion; (3) a summary organized around the steps in the group-thinking process.

EVALUATING DISCUSSION

Discussion may be evaluated by oral critiques of expert or lay observers upon the techniques and results of the discussion. It may be evaluated in terms of its effects upon the opinions of the participants and listeners in the audience regarding the question explored. It may be evaluated as an experience in learning the methods and procedures of discussion. Various rating sheets and blanks are available to assist in evaluation and in constructively criticizing your discussion (see Figures 11-1 and 11-2).

Analysis Form 17

REACTION TO GROUP DISCUSSION

(Please check the point on the scale that represents your considered opinion. If you wish to clarify or explain your decision, please do so on the reverse side of this sheet. *Do not sign your name.*)

1. Are you satisfied with the conclusions (if any) reached in the discussion?

Very much so	Moderately	Not at all

2. Were the attitudes of the discussants conducive to cooperative action?

Very	Moderately	Not at all

3. Did the group adopt and follow an orderly or systematic approach toward the solving of the problem confronting it?

Very much so	Somewhat	Not at all

4. As a consequence of the discussion, have you gained any new insights or new and useful information and understanding?

A great deal	Some	Very little

5. Were you given opportunities to express your opinions and present facts?

Often	Occasionally	Infrequently

6. Would you suggest any changes in the leadership of the discussion?

Many	A few	None at all

7. Could the members have contributed more effectively to the group's leadership?

Very much more	Slightly	Not at all

(OVER)

FIGURE 11-1   Rating sheet for a member's reaction to a group discussion.   Source: David Potter and Martin P. Anderson, *Discussion: A Guide to Effective Practice,* Wadsworth Publishing Company, Inc., Belmont, Calif., 1963, pp. 221–222.

8. Which of the following changes would benefit the group? (Check as many as you wish.)

___ a . Better definition of problems discussed.
___ b . Better individual preparation.
___ c . More responsible leadership.
___ d . More carefully planned agenda.
___ e . More democratic leadership.
___ f . More consideration for members of the group.
___ g . Greater sharing of leadership responsibilities.
___ h . More orderly procedure.
___ i . Friendlier atmosphere.
___ j . Wider spread of participation.
___ k . Greater adherence to the discussion topic.
___ l . Greater concern for the feelings of the discussants.
___ m. More effective presentation of facts and opinions.

Analysis Form 18   Name_____

SELF-ANALYSIS FORM

(The effective discussion participant is one who recognizes his defects, does not feel defensive about them, and is willing to do something about them. How do you score on the following items?)

(Check one) YES   NO

CRITERIA FOR DETERMINING INDIVIDUAL GROWTH:

1. Have you substituted adequate practices for inadequate ones?

2. Do you try to understand and accept others' viewpoints?

3. Do you have few feelings of inferiority and superiority to-ward others in the group?

4. Are your feelings of resistance to disagreement relatively infrequent?

5. Can you express your convictions without excessive emotional involvement?

6. Can you work harmoniously with others who differ with you?

7. Are you interested in assuming leadership functions as well as being a follower?

8. Do you try to support others in discussion?

9. Do you internalize private concerns in discussion?

10. Do you try to be cooperative rather than competitive in discussion?

CRITERIA REFLECTING PROPER ATTITUDES AND PROCEDURES:

1. Do you make thorough preparation for each discussion?

2. Do you try to be a good team member?

3. Do you make maximum use of your own experience and knowledge in discussion?

4. Do you concentrate on the group's goal above your own ego needs?

5. Do you make flexible adaptations to the needs of the dis-cussion situation?

6. Do you have few feelings of defensiveness?

7. Do you try to complete as best you can all tasks that may be assigned to you?

8. Do you know what your faults are and do you do something about them?

9. Do you try to focus on issues rather than on personalities in discussion?

10. Do you try to provide opportunities for others to participate effectively in discussion?

11. Do you assume responsibility for your actions?

12. Are you more concerned about getting a job done than about getting credit for it?

FIGURE 11-2. Self-analysis form for a discussion participant. Source: David Potter and Martin P. Anderson, *Discussion: A Guide to Effective Practice*, Wadsworth Publishing Company, Inc., Belmont, Calif., 1963, p. 223.

FOR FURTHER READING

Barnlund, Dean C. and Franklyn S. Haiman: *The Dynamics of Discussion,* Houghton Mifflin Company, Boston, 1960.

Borman, Ernest G.: *Discussion and Group Methods,* Harper & Row, Publishers, Inc., New York, 1969.

Crowell, Laura: *Discussion: Method of Democracy,* Scott, Foresman and Company, Chicago, 1963.

Fessenden, Seth A., Roy I. Johnson, P. Merville Larson, and Kaye M. Good: *Speech For the Creative Teacher,* William C. Brown Company, Publishers, Dubuque, 1968, chap. 18.

Gulley, Halbert E.: *Discussion, Conference, and Group Process,* 2d ed., Holt, Rinehart and Winston, Inc., New York, 1968.

Lee, Irving J.: *How To Talk With People,* Harper & Row, Publishers, Inc., New York, 1952.

Wagner, Russell H. and Carroll C. Arnold: *Handbook of Group Discussion,* 2d ed., Houghton Mifflin Company, Boston, 1965.

CHAPTER TWELVE

BUSINESS MEETINGS

Within a period of two days, a teacher supervised a class business meeting, gave a report to a faculty meeting, participated in the election of officers for a teachers club, and presided at the business meeting of his section of the State Teachers Association. In all these activities he used directly his knowledge of parliamentary procedure.

In addition, during the same two days, he served as adviser to the Student Council and answered numerous questions about the handling of club meetings in his own school. His knowledge served indirectly to aid his students in a multitude of situations that faced them.

From this person's experience you can anticipate that you, as a teacher, will draw frequently upon your knowledge and skill in using parliamentary procedure. It is, therefore, important that you learn now as much as you can to help you in presiding and taking part in meetings.

PURPOSES AND PRINCIPLES

Parliamentary procedure is a fundamental democratic method. Its first uses among English-speaking people date from the reign of Edward I in England, when in 1295 he called the Model Parliament to consider measures for the common defense. This group of knights and burgesses was a conference, expected to decide upon action to meet the "common dangers" facing the country. No group such as this can discuss or debate questions without some guiding rules. Since that time and for nearly 700 years, our current parliamentary rules and procedures have developed. They now have become so complete and detailed that teachers and students need to take time to study and practice their various forms.

In using them, you will find that they (1) provide an efficient, orderly way of handling business meetings, and (2) ensure that every person in an assembly has a voice and a vote in proposing business, debating it, and deciding what should be done about it. You will discover also that skilled, unscrupulous persons can use their abilities to dominate or destroy the very rights the rules were designed to protect. You will find that your only defense is thorough knowledge and intelligent use of parliamentary procedure in all meetings where it is employed.

There are certain underlying principles you should know. The first is the acceptance of *the rule of the majority*. In any body that guarantees your participation as a member, you agree to accept the decision of the majority. You also understand, however, that in the various deliberations of the assembly *the minority must be heard and represented*. In debate, especially, the rule requiring a two-thirds vote to limit or stop debate protects the minority. Other rules establish the rights and privileges of individuals as minority groups.

A second principle is that of *responsibility to serve or to do your share*. Your right to vote and to discuss questions before the assembly includes your obligation to "do the chores" in your organization. You are expected to serve on committees, pay dues, hold office, take part in programs—to *work* for and with the group. This is a fundamental concept you should always remember in a school or in your role as a citizen.

A third principle is that of *equality and respect for the rights of the individual and for the group*. As a member, you receive the same courteous treatment as everyone else. However, you in turn recognize that the assembly is greater than any single member; you are therefore committed to accept its goals and policies. You respect its authority.

A fourth principle is *the right of full and free debate* on all matters before the assembly. As Voltaire is reported to have said, "I may disagree with what you say, but I will defend to the death, your right to say it."

These basic principles underlie parliamentary procedure and should help you to understand it more clearly.

ORGANIZING A GROUP OR MEETING

There are two types of organized meetings—*permanent* ones, such as a student council or club, and *temporary* ones, such as a pep meeting, a political rally, or an alumni reunion. In a permanent organization you elect officers, and have a constitution, bylaws, and a regularly scheduled time and place to meet. In a temporary meeting you do not elect officers, but usually designate or appoint someone to preside.

To form a permanent organization, first invite those interested to attend an opening meeting. Elect a temporary chairman and secretary and discuss the purposes of the organization—its nature and importance in your school or community. Clear your plans with the school activities office so that you follow the rules for new organizations. With the advice of the persons present at the initial meeting, the chairman should appoint a committee to draft a constitution for the club.

The constitution should contain the name of the group, its purposes, the time and place of meetings, officers, and qualifications for membership. Bylaws should include dues, size of a quorum, a list of standing committees, and the order of business.

To complete the organization, the constitution is discussed paragraph by paragraph, changed where necessary, and approved by a vote of the members. Finally, the permanent officers are chosen, and any relevant business taken care of in a session guided by parliamentary procedure.

ELECTIONS

A permanent organization can follow certain effective, tried methods in electing its officers. The most efficient means is to appoint a nominating committee in advance of the election so that it can prepare a list of candidates. A teachers club or a professional organization ordinarily uses this method. After the committee reports, the chairman is obligated to call for further nominations from the floor.

To nominate from the floor, you say, "Mr. Chairman, I nominate Ted Weeks." The chairman repeats the name and directs the secretary to record it. There is no need to call for a second, since nominations do not require one, unless specified in the constitution or rules of the meeting. Nominations may be made until all are satisfied or until a motion to close them is made from the floor, seconded, discussed, and passed.

If there is no nominating committee, all officers are nominated from the floor. The chairman calls for them in order, one office at a time—president, vice-president, and so on.

Voting on candidates follows, usually by secret ballot. Tellers appointed by the chairman distribute, collect, and count the ballots. They then report the results in writing to the chairman, who announces them.

VOTING

There are six methods of voting on motions or in elections. In a small business meeting you generally vote by voice because this is most practical for motions requiring a majority vote. It is obviously not usable on motions taking a two-thirds vote, when votes must be counted exactly. In taking a voice vote, the correct form for the chairman is "All in favor of the motion say 'Aye.' " As soon as the vote is noted, he says, "All opposed say 'No.' " Do *not* use the *incorrect* form in taking the negative vote: "All opposed same sign." Remember "No" is the opposite of "Aye."

A second method used when votes must be counted is a show of hands. It is a sensible precaution, if you are presiding, to ask the secretary to help you count and tabulate negative and affirmative votes. Another similar method for use in obtaining an exact count is a standing vote. This method takes more time, but it is desirable in a close vote. With the help of the secretary you can be sure of accuracy.

A timesaving method is the use of "unanimous consent." If you are presiding, and a motion is strongly supported, you may ask, "Are there any who object to this motion?" If none respond, you conclude that the motion is passed and announce that result. If there is an objection, put the motion to a vote, using a standard method.

In elections or on any question requiring secrecy, employ a vote by ballot. Any member can so move if he desires. As chairman you handle his motion as any other principal motion, being sure it is seconded and has a majority vote.

If a record of each vote is required as in a large assembly, a roll-call vote is necessary. As the secretary calls the roll, he records the vote of each member. This is not done in ordinary, small meetings.

VOTING TERMINOLOGY.   In addition to methods of voting you should be familiar with terms and their application. *Majority* means one more than half of all the votes cast. *Plurality* means the highest number of votes cast. In an election with candidate A receiving fourteen votes, B thirteen, and C ten, A has a plurality, but not a majority of votes.

The term *state* means to repeat the wording of the motion; however, the word *put* means to *restate* the motion so that it can be voted upon.

Knowledge of voting methods and terms increases your confidence in using parliamentary procedure.

OFFICERS AND THEIR DUTIES

The elected officers perform certain specific tasks. There is little overlapping of duties. In the case of absence of an officer, another may be asked to assume added responsibilities.

Chairman. The president or chairman presides at all meetings, conducts business, helps to determine policies, provides leadership, and makes committee appointments.

Secretary. An important officer, the secretary keeps the records, writes minutes of the meetings, maintains a roster or list of members, calls roll at meetings, and tabulates roll-call votes. In most school organizations one person does all secretarial duties.

Treasurer. All financial business is done by the treasurer. He collects dues, receives and pays bills, and reports the financial condition of the organization.

Committees. Two kinds of committees serve in organizations: *special* committees and *standing* committees. A special committee is appointed for a particular function or occasion and serves for a short time only. As soon as its job is completed, it is dissolved. It might plan a dinner, party, or school open house.

Standing committees are appointed by the chairman or president of the club.

On-the-spot, hasty appointments are not best. The chairman can select a stronger committee if he takes time to check personal qualifications and announces members later. Groups of three, five, seven, or any odd number are the rule. The person initiating a project is usually named chairman; of course, he can decline if he does not have time to serve.

The committee chairman calls meetings, conducts sessions, and reports results of the work of the group. Members are responsible for doing their share at all times and not leave the job to the chairman to complete alone.

PARTICIPATING IN THE MEETING

The rules of parliamentary procedure should bring order and fairness in dealing with problems in a meeting. They should help speed the handling of business and cause meetings to operate more efficiently. Some small and informal groups, however, may not need parliamentary procedure, but only ordinary discussion. Do not insist upon it unless it is appropriate and really helps.

PROCEDURE AND THE ORDER OF BUSINESS

Every meeting follows a certain order in handling business. This varies with the organization, club, class, or group. The basic steps are these:

1   The chairman calls the meeting to order.
2   The secretary calls the roll.   (This may be omitted if a count of attendance is not required.)
3   Reading of the minutes (by the secretary) and their approval.
4   Reports of officers.
5   Reports of boards and standing committees.
6   Reports of special committees.
7   Unfinished business.
8   New business.
9   Adjournment.

These suggestions will help you to learn this procedure. To call the meeting to order, the chairman says, "The meeting will please come to order," or "The meeting is called to order." Next he asks the secretary to call the roll. He then calls upon the secretary to read the minutes of the last meeting. As soon as the minutes have been read, he asks, "Are there any additions or corrections to the minutes?" If there are none, he says, "If not, the minutes stand approved as read." If members make corrections, he tells the secretary to make the corrections indicated. Then he states, "The minutes stand approved as corrected."

The next essential item is the treasurer's report. It includes a statement of money received and money spent, and contains the balance on hand in the club's treasury.

The chairman next asks for reports of boards and standing committees. In some organizations they report orally at each meeting to the whole group. In others they may report only when they have important matters to present. Usually, written reports of standing committees are also given to the secretary.

Reports of special committees are next called for. The chairman should know which committees will have reports and who will make the report for each committee. The order for these should be determined in advance.

Unfinished business comes next. The chairman asks the meeting, "Is there any unfinished business?" He usually directs this question primarily to the secretary because that officer will have a record of such matters in the minutes of the last meeting. Business is considered in the order it is brought up by the members. Following unfinished business, questions of new business are considered. These are introduced by members when the chairman inquires, "Is there any new business?"

After all new business is disposed of, a proposal to adjourn is in order.

PARTICIPATING IN DEBATE

As a member of the organization, you have the right to speak your ideas on any debatable motions considered. Most main or principal motions, many subsidiary motions, and numerous others are debatable.

To take part in debate, first obtain the floor by addressing the chairman as "Madam Chairman," or if a man is presiding, as "Mr. Chairman." The chairman will nod to you or call you by name if he grants you permission to speak. There are certain courtesies generally observed in debate. If two members stand at the same time, the floor is usually given to the one who has not spoken previously. In the same situation, the member representing a point of view not yet expressed is ordinarily recognized first. If a woman and a man rise simultaneously, the floor is usually given to the woman.

When you participate in debate, do not mention the names of persons. This allows reasoning and evidence rather than personalities to influence decisions. Say, "The previous speaker" or "The person who introduced the motion," instead of using names.

Time limits have an important role in debate. A club may have only a total time of fifty minutes for a meeting in a school situation, but even an after-school meeting must have limits. To ensure the completion of business on time, organizations often restrict debate in certain ways. This is done by (1) limiting the length of time each person may speak on a motion— for example, two minutes per member; (2) limiting the total time for debate on each motion—for example, ten minutes per motion.

Although such limitations interfere with "the right of full and free debate," they are for the welfare of the group. Some organizations include such a standing rule in their bylaws. In any meeting, however, you as a member can move to change any restrictions. If more time is needed for full discussion and deliberation, important business can be referred to a committee. Its proposal can then be reported for consideration at a later meeting.

KINDS OF MOTIONS AND THEIR USE

The main goal of parliamentary procedure is to facilitate the business of the meeting. Business is introduced by a motion—*a proposal for action by the group.* You will need to know certain basic facts about motions.

MOTIONS. There are four kinds: main, subsidiary, incidental, and privileged.

Main motions are used to bring original business before the house. They propose action by the assembly.

Subsidiary motions are those applied to main motions or others in order to dispose of them in some way. Subsidiary motions must be discussed and voted upon before the motions to which they are applied can be voted upon.

Incidental motions arise out of the business at hand. They concern matters that must be settled before the motions out of which they arise can be voted upon.

Privileged motions deal with needs, rights, and privileges of the members of the assembly. Because of their nature, they take *precedence* over other motions and may be presented while other motions are under consideration.

All these types of motions will be explained and considered individually later in this chapter.

Every motion has definite qualifications that determine its use. These questions establish them: (1) What is the purpose of the motion? (2) Does it take a second? (3) Is it debatable? (4) Can it be amended? (5) What vote does it require? (6) May it interrupt the speaker? All these questions are vital in your use of motions, and they are answered for you in the Table of Parliamentary Motions, pages 208 and 209.

PRECEDENCE OF MOTIONS. You probably noted the italicized word *precedence* in the earlier section, describing the importance of privileged motions. This indicates that certain motions are more important than others. They are, therefore, given a higher rank, i.e., they take precedence over those that are less important. Therefore, in a meeting, higher ranking motions are considered ahead of those of lower rank. In Table 12-1, all parliamentary motions are listed by type and are numbered according to their precedence. *Higher numbered motions take precedence over those which have smaller numbers in the table.* Thus privileged motion number 22, To Adjourn, takes precedence over number 21, To Take a Recess. All privileged motions take precedence over subsidiary motions. However, in the list of subsidiary motions number 8, To Lay on the Table, is of higher rank than number 4, To Refer to a Committee, etc.

HANDLING MOTIONS—A BASIC PROCEDURE

To guide your use of specific motions, you must first learn a basic procedure for handling *any* motion. These steps are essential:

1 Recognize the person who rises to make a motion.
2 Listen to the motion.

3 Secure a second for the motion.
4 State the motion or have the secretary read it.
5 Open the motion for discussion.
6 Close the discussion.
7 Put the motion to a vote; be sure to state the motion exactly.
8 Vote on the motion (voice vote, show of hands, etc.).
9 Announce the result of the vote (the motion is lost, the motion is carried).

MAIN MOTIONS

There are two types of main motions—*original and incidental.*

An *original main motion* introduces any matter of new business for consideration of the assembly. For example, "I move that we send one delegate to the meeting of the Michigan Education Association" is such a motion. It must be seconded, debated, and voted upon unless it is disposed of by applying to it a subsidiary motion. A main motion takes a majority vote.

An *incidental main motion* does not present new projects for consideration of the group, but rather deals in certain ways with the work of carrying out the business of the assembly or with its future or past action on such matters. Examples of such motions, treated essentially in the same way as original main motions, are the motion to rescind, to reconsider, and to take from the table.

Rescind. There are times when an action of a group is hasty, undesirable, or ill-advised because of conditions that have changed. Therefore, the assembly wishes to revoke it, and would use the motion to rescind to achieve this end. If notice has been given of such intent, at an earlier meeting, a majority vote is needed. However, if the action is desired immediately without notice, a two-thirds vote is required. The motion takes a second, is debatable, and may be amended. The effect of its action is to "wipe out" or remove from the record.

The usual wording is "I move to rescind the vote on _____." If desired, the words "and to expunge it from the record" may be added.

Reconsider. When the assembly has passed a motion and at a later time members desire to bring it up again, they may move to reconsider. It requires a second, takes a majority vote, is debatable if the motion to which it is applied is debatable, and is in order if someone has the floor.

The wording is "I move to reconsider the vote on _____."

TABLE 12–1.   A Table of Parliamentary Motions

MOTION	PURPOSE	NEEDS SECOND	DEBATABLE	AMENDABLE	VOTE	MAY INTERRUPT SPEAKER	SUBSIDIARY MOTION APPLIED
I *Original or principal motion*							
1 Main motion (general) Main motions (specific)	To introduce business	Yes	Yes	Yes	Majority	No	Yes
a To take from the table	To consider motion tabled	Yes	No	No	Majority	No	No
b To reconsider	To consider defeated motion	Yes	When orig. motion is	No	Majority	No	No
c To rescind	To nullify or wipe out previous motion	Yes	Yes	Yes	Majority or 2/3	No	No
II *Subsidiary motions*							
2 To postpone indefinitely	To suppress action	Yes	Yes	No	Majority	No	Yes
3 To amend	To modify a motion	Yes	Yes	Yes (once only)	Majority	No	Yes
4 To refer to a committee	To modify a motion	Yes	Yes	Yes	Majority	No	Yes
5 To postpone to a certain time	To defer action	Yes	Yes	Yes	Majority	No	Yes
6 To limit or extend limits of debate	To restrict debate	Yes	No	Yes	2/3	No	Yes
7 To call for previous question	To close debate and force vote	Yes	No	No	2/3	No	Yes
8 To lay on the table	To defer action	Yes	No	No	Majority	No	No
III *Incidental motions*							
9 To suspend rules	To change existing rules and order of business	Yes	No	No	2/3	No	No
10 To close nominations	To stop nominating officers, etc.	Yes	No	Yes	2/3	No	Yes
11 To reopen nominations	To permit additional nominations	Yes	No	Yes	Majority	No	Yes
12 To withdraw a motion	To modify a motion	Yes	No	No	Majority	No	No
13 To rise to point of order	To correct error in procedure	No	No	No	Decision of chair	Yes	No

No.	Motion	Purpose						
14	To appeal from decision of chair	To correct decision on procedure	Yes	If motion debatable	No	Majority	Yes	No
15	To divide motion	To modify motion	Yes	Yes	No	Majority	No	Yes
16	To object to consideration	To suppress action	No	No	No	2/3	Yes	No
17	To call for division of house	To secure a countable vote	No	No	No	Majority if chair desires	No	Yes
IV	***Privileged Motions***							
18	To call for orders of the day	To keep assembly to order of business	No	No	No	None un-less objection	Yes	No
19	To make matter a special order	To insure consideration at specified time	Yes	Yes	Yes	2/3	No	Yes
20	To raise question of privilege	To make a request during debate	No	No	No	Decision of chair	Yes	No
21	To take a recess	To dismiss meeting for specific time	Yes	No	Yes	Majority	No	Yes
22	To adjourn	To dismiss meeting	Yes	No	Yes	Majority	No	No
23	To fix time of next meeting	To set time of next meeting	Yes	No	Yes	Majority	No	Yes

If the motion is passed, debate on the original motion is reopened (if it was debatable), and another vote is taken upon it.   If the vote reverses the earlier action, the last vote stands.

To take from the table.   If a motion has been deferred by laying it on the table, either at a previous session or at the same meeting, it may be considered again if a motion to take it from the table is passed.   This motion takes a second, is undebatable, and requires a majority vote.

The correct wording is "I move to take from the table the motion to _____."

By passing the motion, debate on the original motion is reopened, and another vote made possible.

SUBSIDIARY MOTIONS

Used to dispose of main or principal motions, the following subsidiary motions delay action, affect debate, change wording, and either defer action or speed up voting.   They are made, discussed, and voted upon during the time for debate on main motions, to which they apply.   They are listed in the order of their rank or precedence.

1   Lay on the table
2   Call for previous question
3   Limit or extend the limits of debate
4   Postpone to a definite time
5   Refer to a committee
6   Amend
7   Postpone indefinitely

Lay on the table.   When the assembly cannot settle a question quickly and wishes to dispose of it in order to deal with more urgent business, this motion is an effective one.   It is quick to administer because after being seconded, it is undebatable and takes only a majority vote.

The wording of the motion is "I move to lay the question on the table." If this motion carried, the question is "tabled" or suppressed, and cannot be considered unless someone moves *to take it from the table.*

Call for previous question. To stop debate, one calls for this motion. Its name indicates the purpose of the motion—terminate the discussion and *vote upon the motion under consideration.*   At any time during debate, a member may call for the previous question.   It requires a second and takes a two-thirds vote.   It is undebatable.   If it carries, the chairman immediately puts to a vote the motion to which it applies.

The wording of the motion is "I call for (or move) the previous question."

Limit or extend the limits of debate. To restrict the debate upon a motion or set specifically the amount of time for debate, this motion is employed. It may be made at any time during debate. It takes a second and a two-thirds vote.

Two wordings are possible: "I move that the total debate upon the motion be limited to ten minutes." "I move that debate be limited to three minutes per person."

Postpone to a definite time. To defer action to a certain time, indicating a particular date and/or hour, employ this motion. It requires a second, is debatable, and takes a majority vote.

Refer to a committee. Often a proposal should be studied by a committee before action is taken by the main body. Best wording is "I move to refer the matter to a committee of three, appointed by the chairman, to report at the next meeting."

Amend. To change the wording of a motion, one moves to amend it. These changes can be made by inserting or adding words, by striking out words, or by combining such methods. Amendments must be made before the motion to which they apply is voted upon.

After amendments are approved, the main motion is next voted upon, as amended. If they fail, the main motion may be debated further and voted on.

The proper wording is "I move to amend the motion by adding the words _____ so that the motion will read: _____."

Postpone indefinitely. To suppress a motion a member may say, "I move to postpone the question indefinitely." This is a method of rejecting the main motion without putting it to a direct vote. It is debatable and opens the main question to debate. If it is passed, the main motion is not really postponed, but rather disposed of.

INCIDENTAL MOTIONS[1]

Certain questions and problems arise out of the consideration of other motions or the business at hand. These incidental motions are the most common:

1 Point of order
2 Appeal from the decision of the chair

---

[1] Do not confuse with *incidental main motion.*

3 Suspension of the rules
4 Objection to consideration
5 Division of the question
6 Division of the assembly
7 Make, close, or reopen nominations
8 Leave to withdraw a motion
9 Request for information; parliamentary inquiry

Point of order. Errors in procedure on the part of the chairman or the assembly are not uncommon. Whenever a member notices such an error, he may rise and without recognition say, "Mr. Chairman, I rise to a point of order." The chairman then asks him to state his point of order. The member then states why the action being taken is in question. The chairman either sustains or denies the point. If he supports it, he immediately corrects the procedure involved.

Appeal from the decision of the chair. When the chairman makes a ruling in a parliamentary matter, any member may appeal from the decision of the chair if he believes an error has been made. If his appeal is seconded, the chairman must put the appeal to a vote of the members. If a majority votes in favor, the appeal is sustained.

Suspension of the rules. Under certain conditions discussion or business may be expedited if regular parliamentary rules are not in effect. To accomplish this purpose, a member moves to suspend the rules; a two-thirds vote is required to carry such a proposal.

Objection to consideration. To suppress a motion quickly and to save time, a member may object to the consideration of a *main* motion. To be in order, such an objection must be made after a second has been heard, but before the motion has been opened to debate by the chairman, or any subsidiary motion proposed.

The wording is "Mr. Chairman, I object to consideration of this motion." The motion takes no second and is undebatable. The chairman immediately puts the objection to a vote (by a countable vote). If two-thirds support the objection, the main motion is killed. If the objection fails, the main motion is then debated.

Division of the question. Some motions may contain more than one proposal for action by the assembly. To make consideration easier under such conditions, a member may move to divide the question so that the matters are dealt with separately. A majority vote sustains such action.

Division of the assembly. If the chairman calls for a voice vote, and it is impossible accurately to determine whether "Ayes" or "Noes" prevail, a member may call for a division of the assembly. The chairman must then put the question a second time, using a method of voting that can be counted (show of hands, standing vote, etc.).

Make, close, or reopen nominations. These matters are covered in the section on Elections.

Leave to withdraw a motion. If a motion has been made and seconded and the member making it then feels consideration of it inadvisable, he can ask leave to withdraw it. The chairman asks if there is any objection to the withdrawal. If there is no objection, the chairman may rule that the motion is withdrawn.

Request for information. A member may make a request for information or a parliamentary inquiry at any time. To do this, he rises and states, "Mr. Chairman, I rise to a question of information." When the chairman asks, "What is your question?" the member asks it. The chairman, through whom all such questions must pass, either answers it himself or directs it to someone who can answer the question.

PRIVILEGED MOTIONS

Such motions, relating to needs of the assembly, arise independently of any other motions, and are of such importance that they may be presented in most cases when main motions or subsidiary motions are pending. In the order of their rank they include:

1   To fix the time to which to adjourn (time of next meeting)
2   To adjourn
3   To take a recess
4   To raise a question of privilege
5   To call for the orders of the day

Three of these motions, to fix the time to which to adjourn, to adjourn, and to take a recess, need no explanation except to observe that if there is another motion before the assembly they are undebatable. A question of privilege deals with the comforts of the assembly—heating, inability to hear speakers, ventilation, and similar matters. It may interrupt a speaker and must be decided immediately. The wording is "Mr. Chairman, I rise to a question of privilege. The room is too warm; may we have a window opened?" The chairman rules on such a question.

If the order of business is not being followed, a member may rise and state, "Mr. Chairman, I call for the orders of the day." If the error has been accurately noted, the chairman will make the necessary correction immediately.

FOR FURTHER READING

Auer, J. Jeffery: *Essentials of Parliamentary Procedure*, 3d ed., Appleton-Century-Crofts, Inc., New York, 1959.

Gray, John W.: *Parliamentary Procedure: A Programmed Introduction*, Scott, Foresman and Company, Chicago, 1963.

Sponberg, Harold: *The Meeting Will Come to Order* (booklet), Michigan State University Cooperative Extension Service, East Lansing, 1951.

Sturgis, Alice F.: *Learning Parliamentary Procedure*, McGraw-Hill Book Company, New York, 1953.

CHAPTER THIRTEEN

CLASSROOM SPEAKING

Edgar Dale, the noted writer on audiovisual methods, observes that good teaching is essentially good communication. It requires sympathetic sharing of experiences as well as clear expression of ideas. He adds that "good explaining is the service that students expect of a good teacher."[1] Becker also found that high school students ranked "clear explanations based upon sound organization" highest in a list of ten most significant components of the speech characteristics of superior teachers.[2]

It should be obvious, then, that your oral communication in the classroom requires *effective instructional speaking*—you provide facts and knowledge (inform), and interpret or clarify knowledge (explain) for your students. These functions are basic in your teaching. In your efforts to explain, you will do everything possible to ensure clarity by using the chalkboard, charts, graphs, still pictures, motion pictures, models, objects, and similar materials.

The *general* principles of preparation and presentation in instructional speaking are not different from those in Chapter 5, but the specific elements, many of them closely related to materials and aids in making explanations clear, are different and require careful study.

EFFECTIVE INSTRUCTIONAL SPEAKING

PREPARING CLASSROOM SPEAKING

The practical thing to do is to adapt the general steps in preparation to the special conditions and methods in the teaching situation.

THE SUBJECT. If you are a secondary school teacher, your subjects will be determined by the content of the courses you teach. For example, in United States history even the short talks you give will probably be from that field. Major classroom lectures will be developed in your lesson plans, and will be influenced by the length of the period and the units you teach.

If you are an elementary school teacher, you will have much greater variety because you are responsible for almost the entire daily program of your pupils. In a single morning you might talk about safety rules at school

---

[1] Edgar Dale, *Audio-Visual Methods of Teaching,* rev. ed., Holt, Rinehart and Winston, Inc., New York, 1954, p. 7.

[2] Albert Becker, "The Speech Characteristics of Superior and Inferior High School Teachers, as Revealed by Student Reaction," unpublished doctoral dissertation, Northwestern University, 1949.

crossings, health, reading and spelling, number skills, and geography. Your schedule usually consists of periods ranging from five minutes to half an hour, and greatly affects the scope of subjects for oral communication.

ANALYZE THE AUDIENCE AND THE OCCASION. Every class audience has certain characteristics. As a high school teacher you have a normal expectancy of five such groups each day. They may vary considerably in age, class in school, interests, religion, political beliefs, social experience, and nationality. You will learn to analyze these factors, and in a given class hour, adjust your subject and teaching methods to them. If you remain in the same room throughout the day, the physical conditions will be very much the same for each class. However, if you move from room to room, you may have to adjust to new conditions every period.

In an elementary classroom, you have what might be called a relatively "permanent" audience. As the room teacher, you have the same pupils for the whole day, and usually for an entire school year or term. You retain your own classroom and can build a physical and intellectual atmosphere with some certainty, fitted to your grade and pupils. As you come to know each pupil, you develop a specific analysis of your audience—its limitations and potentialities; its interests; its tastes; its social, economic, family, and religious backgrounds. This great amount of detailed information will enable you to make specific adaptations in your instructional talks to fit the individuals and the group. In some instances, your subject, its organization, and content may be directly planned in relation to specific pupils or small groups *within* your entire room audience. This adaptation to individual needs and interests might be of considerable importance in fire drill instructions, talks about crossing safety, and explanations of particular problems in spelling, reading, and number skills. The presence of any children with speech, hearing, visual, or other physical handicaps definitely affects content and presentation in oral communication by the teacher. Particular types of demonstrations may demand even more adaptation if children cannot see or hear well.

DETERMINE THE PURPOSE AND ADJUST IT TO YOUR ANALYSIS. As we noted earlier, classroom speaking has two important basic purposes— to inform and to explain. Any restriction and specific adjustment of them will be influenced by such factors as the content aims for the day, the time limits, the pupils involved, and the conditions in the room. Thus a talk with an original, general purpose to explain "Colonial Life in New England" might be restricted further to inform the class regarding the "Plymouth Colony." With a pressure of time limits or special interests of the students, this subject could become "Leaders in the Plymouth Colony." Finally, with further restriction a *single* leader might be used as representative, when the teacher discussed "William Bradford." Such adjustment is typical of the need to adapt instructional speaking to classroom conditions.

INVESTIGATE AND GATHER NECESSARY MATERIAL. A fundamental part of your preparation as a teacher is to get the necessary knowledge to teach your subject field at the grade level you have selected. All of the courses in major and minor fields have, or will contribute, rich materials for the instructional talks you will give. Your supplementary readings, observations, trips and travel, film and television viewing, and conversations with stimulating people you meet continually add ideas and information to your reservoir of materials. As you proceed through student teaching and then to a regular position, you will find that your motivation to *know* and your efforts to *enrich* your background become daily, natural parts of your teaching career. Your zeal to be well prepared to teach your pupils will plunge you into reading numerous books and professional journals, viewing films and slides, listening to recordings, attending art exhibits and concerts— all in the enthusiasm of having up-to-the-minute, stimulating content for your daily communication (teaching) for your classes. In other words, your education never stops—because you wish to share what you know with your students.

It is not too early to begin such a quest for knowledge as it relates to your opportunity to teach. The thrill in undergraduate study comes through *learning.* It becomes more exciting when *you* initiate it and follow it through *yourself.* Do not wait for your instructors to pull you through the text, assign bibliographies to read, and force you through examinations to discover whether you have done both. Be a self-starter, and keep your intellectual motor running all of the time. Subscribe to professional journals in your field now. Start to build your own library—books, magazines, pictures, recordings.

Make libraries, museums, and exhibits part of your personal inventory. They are supply lines for knowledge. Familiarize yourself with all of the details of organization, card files, reserve rooms, document and rare book rooms. Make friends with the librarians. They are the teacher's friends; you need them always.

Very early begin to record, organize, and preserve what you learn. Develop a filing system and have places to keep things—notebooks, card boxes, vertical files, clipping folders, picture and print files. These are extremely valuable to you. Mark their content clearly in an orderly, planned indexing system that makes sense to you.   All of these are the intellectual arsenal for your supply of teaching ammunition.

For any given classroom talk you select content from your arsenal.   Your selection fits all of the factors in your analysis, mentioned earlier, that give specificity and definition to your content.

ORGANIZE THE CONTENT INTO A USABLE, WRITTEN OUTLINE. With many, many talks to give in every class you teach, you need a system of notes or outlining that works for you.   The various types of outlines explained in an earlier chapter are all practical—*simple list of words, key phrase*, and *complete sentence.* You need to select one or perhaps combine two or more to evolve a format for notes that is suited to you personally and is effective when you use it in a *classroom communication situation.*

Sometimes you will be influenced by the lesson plan organization and outline suggested in some books on teaching; basic headings include such items as Day and Length of Period, Teaching Material, Knowledge to be Taught, Procedure, Evaluation, and Assignment.   While this scheme provides a topical organization for the day's work, it is not necessarily functional in terms of developing content through a lecture method or a talk by a teacher. It is primarily a guide for broad headings to be covered in a lesson for the day.

One of the most usable types of outline is the content-support-method outline. This permits you to plan your opening or introductory remarks and your conclusion—summary, application, or link to your next day's work—but it stresses and amplifies the body of your talk.   After planning your basic arrangement of ideas, you write your outline.   In the left-hand column marked "Content," list your points in order with the appropriate outline symbol to show suitable relationships.   In the second column marked "Support," opposite each point in content list the supporting example, fact, illustration, or quotation that is relevant.   In the third column marked "Method," include any suggestions or items related to your technique in developing the original point and its support.   You can make such a plan for an entire lecture.

Before presenting the talk to your class, practice all aspects; word the talk suitably for the student audience and employ all the supporting materials, audiovisual aids, and visible aspects of delivery that are necessary.

The following sample outline shows the possibilities of this method.

Outline for Class Lecture

Content	Support	Method
Introduction A. Opening statement: (attention, audience contact) B. Specific subject and purpose: Beautiful mountains of the United States; To inform and describe to the class outstanding scenic mountains.		

Body
I. The South Dakota mountains are distinctive.
	A. The Black Hills
	B. The Needles
	C. Mount Rushmore
	  1. Location
	  2. The four figures
	  3. The sculptor
	  4. Views—side, from base, from top
		Transparency #1: map of South Dakota
		Color slides #1–10: scenes and views of Mount Rushmore

II. Colorado mountains are rugged and beautiful.	A. Rocky Mountain National Park B. Pike's Peak; Garden of the Gods C. Western Colorado—Cliff Dwellers	Transparency #2: Colorado ranges Color slides #11–30: views of each important peak, lake, formation
(Continue to show Wyoming, Montana, California, Washington mountains.)		
Conclusion Summary stating your position on the most scenic mountains in the United States		

Examples, quotations, and statistics can be placed upon 3- by 5-inch cards, numbered or lettered in the same sequence as the content. The cards permit easy reading, visibility, and flexibility in delivery.

For quick visibility in delivery, colored underscoring is a help for some speakers. Use the same color throughout for coordinate points. This can be done with an ink pencil or a felt marker.

If desired, the content outline can be placed on a transparency for use on an overhead projector, on a chart, on a chalkboard, or on slap-on cards for a feltboard. Each point can be revealed as needed and supporting materials developed, numbered, or coded to fit the content outline. If an overhead projector is used, graphs, tables, outline drawings, or diagrams may be placed upon smaller transparencies or "lay-ons" to support points.

Prepare very well the introduction and conclusion of your instructional talk. Before you can teach anyone you must gain his attention, hold it, and be sure that your specific purpose and central idea are clear to him. Your introduction must achieve these purposes. Use your conclusion to review and summarize, apply, or relate your basic content to your next day's work.

PRACTICE THE SPEECH AND WORD IT, USING THE OUTLINE. After careful preparation, nothing is more important than your practice session or "run-through." You invite tension, ineffective presentation in the use of voice and action, and inevitable flubs in language, not to mention possible failures in equipment or audiovisual materials—if your FIRST trip through your talk is the critical one—before your class audience.

Allow enough time in your preparation to have at least one, or perhaps more, dress rehearsals, depending upon how complicated your presentation is. During this practice you actually *do* the job. You become familiar with your content sequence as you verbalize it aloud—not silently. You work out transitions and relationships between main points and the evidence, quotes, and examples, as well as specific actions in your explanation. You check all equipment by using it—projector, film, slides, feltboard, tape recorder, Bunsen burner, solutions—whatever you must use in teaching performance. You select your language and formulate sentences. You correlate and tie together the whole communicative act so that it will move clearly, smoothly, and interestingly for your listeners. You can time it to fit your class situation.

With this experience *previous* to classroom presentation, you are able to edit or change content, check errors if any exist, and be sure of successful functioning of all aids and equipment. It is quite possible that you may want to run through the talk a second time before you are satisfied. In any event, you have invested wisely of your time and energy to ensure a strong presentation.

DEMONSTRATIONS WITH SPECIFIC TYPES OF TEACHING AIDS

The general adaptations of preparation methods to classroom speaking are helpful, but do not include needed suggestions for specific types of demonstrations. These follow with more detailed treatment of each kind of talk related to the particular kind of audiovisual aids that are used.

OBJECTS AND EQUIPMENT

In using objects or equipment in a demonstration, you should remember that a demonstration of this type is a dramatic performance in which you play the principal role. If you play that part effectively, your class will remain interested throughout; they will learn, and they will probably be surging with questions and impulses to do other things based upon what they have learned. You should do everything in preparation and in the critical performance to guarantee a successful educational venture.

PREPARING THE DEMONSTRATION. Plan every step with care. Be sure that your content-method outline is well organized and complete. Select your equipment with care. Check it to see that it is in working order, and is exactly where you want it to be when you need it. Be sure that every step is absolutely clear.

Rehearse your demonstration with everything at hand. Be sure that each step develops smoothly and clearly; relate your use of objects and equipment to your oral development of the content you have planned.

To be doubly sure that the outline steps are clear and *known* by each student, place them on the chalkboard, indicating main and subpoints by appropriate symbols. Keep the outline short. Word it in simple language. Be sure that students correctly record these items in their notes. Cover the outline with strips so you can reveal the outline step by step, pulling off the strips as you proceed.

Set up your objects and equipment on a laboratory table or desk so that all can see and hear what is going on. If necessary use extra lights or a spotlight to help focus attention and aid visibility. If you have small objects, be prepared to draw a sketch of them on the chalkboard, or pass them around at the conclusion of the demonstration.

Prepare written materials to supplement what you have or to guide the students. Have them dittoed or mimeographed. Hand them out *when you need them*, not necessarily at the beginning of the demonstration or halfway through it. Usually students gain most if these are used in follow-up or as a basis for study.

PRESENTING THE DEMONSTRATION.   The success of this demonstration is based upon good communication. Your planned talk is an insurance policy for you here, as well as your rehearsals, which have integrated and smoothed out the entire communicative process.

Be sure that you do not clutter up the demonstration by departing from your basic, simple plan and development. Resist any temptation to expand or add on the spot. Do not wander from the script, so to speak, but do a concentrated, positive job with your planned outline.

Check your group periodically to be sure that your demonstration is coming through to them clearly. Ask spot questions such as, "Do you understand that, John?" or "Can you all see this?" or "Tommy, am I moving too rapidly on this?"

Keep a satisfactory tempo for good communication and easy audience comprehension. Do not hurry your delivery; do not drag the performance. Watch pupil reactions to help you evaluate your pace in the demonstration.

Use the "point-up" technique and internal summary to tie parts of the talk together. Link new materials smoothly, quickly, and clearly to what has been covered. Relate one section to another by your own comment. Be sure that your demonstration *tells, shows,* and *does* what you planned.

Distribute written materials for study and follow-up at the conclusion of the demonstration.

EVALUATING THE DEMONSTRATION.[3]   These questions will help you to evaluate your demonstration. Try to answer them objectively.

---

[3] Adapted from Edgar Dale, *Audio-Visual Methods of Teaching,* rev. ed., Holt, Rinehart and Winston, Inc., New York, 1954, pp. 148–149.

1   Did you evaluate the students' learning—through questions, written tests, discussions?

2   In evaluating your own performance,

    a   Was the preparation skilled and adequate?

    b   Was it followed step by step?

    c   Did you make adequate use of additional material—appropriate to your purpose—charts, feltboard, etc.?

    d   Was the demonstration itself correct?

    e   Was it simple enough so that most of the students understood it easily?

    f   Did you keep checking student interest and concern throughout?

    g   Could everyone see and hear?

    h   Did you ever ask questions? During? After?

    i   Did you help them to do their own generalizing?

    j   Did you take enough time on *key* points?

    k   Did you review and summarize key points?

    l   Was the demonstration a common undertaking? Did the students participate in what you did? Questions and discussion?

    m   Did your evaluation of the students' learning indicate that the demonstration achieved its purposes?

THE CHALKBOARD

Probably the most frequently given classroom talk is one using the chalkboard. Hundreds of teachers present effective demonstrations every day using this piece of standard classroom equipment.

Its advantages are numerous. It is universally available. It is instantaneous, requiring only a piece of chalk and a board to get you into action. It does not require special talent for drawing or long preparation with complicated equipment. You can instantly correct errors. You can suit the tempo of your talk and use of the board to the class. If you desire, you can immediately use pupil participation at the board.

It can be used for practically every subject taught in the schools, and with various colored chalks can offer great possibilities in vividness and clarity. Of course, certain limitations exist in using drawings on a chalkboard— details and depth are often difficult to picture. However, other aids can effectively supplement its use in these cases. With intelligence you can achieve a wide range of uses in teaching with the chalkboard.

PREPARATION FOR THE DEMONSTRATION.   The outline content and organization and the sketch or diagram should be thoroughly prepared. They should appear in your content-method outline with appropriate numbering and lettering of main and subheads or with full detail in your diagram. Supporting examples should also be noted in your outline. You should be ready to develop these orally in a clear, vivid manner and with any support further notation on the board will give you.

You have certain basic methods you can use in doing chalkboard demonstrations. One is to draw, write, and letter *as you talk*, evolving the sketch and spoken content together or "as you go." Another is to put all materials on the board *in advance*, covering them with a sheet or strips to allow you to reveal them one at a time, or as you need them. A third possibility is to develop skeleton sketch or outline (covered until you use it), and proceed on a "fill-in" basis. All three are usable, but you should practice your entire routine and presentation before you get into the actual class situation. Find the rough spots and eliminate them; this is especially important for beginning teachers.

SUGGESTIONS DURING THE CHALKBOARD TALK. These are practical helps for you while you are at the board:

1   Be sure that the chalkboard is clean.
2   Place the sketch on a portion of the board easily seen by the class.
3   Make your drawing large enough and well spaced so that all may see it. Avoid cramped, small figures.
4   Press down on the chalk hard enough to produce a vivid line.
5   Label key parts clearly.
6   Make your letters large and distinct.
7   Step to one side of your sketch as you draw, and relate your comments accurately to the sketch.
8   Talk to the group as directly as possible.
9   If you cannot talk and draw well *together*, sketch and *then* talk. The visible activity will hold attention until you speak.
10 When you turn your head toward the board, boost your vocal volume level to compensate so that the class can hear you.
11 Use a pointer or yardstick to indicate specific items and to help you retain audience contact.
12 Use colored chalks or broken and dotted lines to indicate different, yet related, items.
13 Handle questions as they come; relating them to your sketch adds to your oral content.
14 Check your tempo periodically by asking questions of the class.

THE FELTBOARD

The feltboard permits you to use "slap-ons" that will adhere to the felt surface of the board for the purpose of visually intensifying your talk as you speak.

The feltboard has certain advantages for use in teaching: (1) you can prepare teaching materials to fit a specific, given situation; (2) they can be prepared in advance, filed, used again and again, augmented or changed as you desire: (3) slap-ons can be transported easily, used one at a time or combined with other items to produce new combinations; (4) they reveal a sequence or story built up one point at a time and without any one element distracting the observers before it has been introduced.   Thus, attention and rapport are held throughout your talk.

PREPARATION.   Be sure to have a feltboard of suitable size.   Organize your talk according to the adapted general content-method outline discussed earlier.   Prepare your slap-ons by cutting them into suitable shapes, lettering, or sketching on them the desired words, captions, or figures.   Be sure they are clear and easy to see.   Label each item on the back, also.   Arrange them in the proper order to fit your outline.   Run through your entire talk, wording it properly to ensure clear, smooth use of materials on the board in relation to your content.

USING THE FELTBOARD IN SPEAKING.   These suggestions are helpful:

1   Place the board at eye level.
2   Be sure lighting is suitable for good visibility of all items.
3   Organize and arrange items in piles in the exact order you will use them. Labels you have placed on the back of each item will guide you in following the correct sequence.
4   Place items on the board one at a time; do not overcrowd your board; keep students focusing on each item as you place it.
5   Be sure that your materials are straight and clearly arranged on the board.
6   Because of its high visibility, in a feltboard presentation you may wish to ask students to take complete notes.
7   Handle questions after each item if you desire, or call for questions at appropriate points you select.

FOLLOW-UP ACTIVITIES.   Discussion and questions are the immediate activities following such a talk.   You and your pupils can also develop numerous other activities, or you can plan and assign tests for information, further readings, trips, interviews, oral or written reports, and exhibits, based upon your feltboard talk.

FILMSTRIPS, SLIDES, AND FLAT PICTURES

In an instructional talk using slides, filmstrips, or flat pictures shown through an opaque projector, you must first realize that you have certain conditions different from those that exist when you display a single picture, chart, or object.

First, you have a psychological change because of darkening the room and turning on the projector. Projection is more dramatic; your pupils expect something unusual. Next, with strips, slides, or still pictures *you* do most of the talking, as the materials are projected. Had you employed a sound film, *it* would do the performing. Your awareness of this difference requires you to do specific, and perhaps, more preparation. Finally, if you employ a filmstrip, it has a fixed order; slides or individual pictures permit you to determine the order. Here are some points to remember:

Before Showing

1 Preview the materials; know them; be sure they are relevant and suitable.
2 Determine the order; number and arrange slides and pictures.
3 Plan your introductory remarks carefully to set the scene.
4 Develop the strip or slide lesson with the class—establish the purposes; relate the projected materials to the other content; prepare the pupils for your teaching.
5 Plan your basic content and transitions for each frame or picture; refer to the content-method outline discussed earlier; develop an appropriate conclusion, also.
6 Structure your questions specifically, and locate them in your outline or in the conclusion of your talk.
7 Anticipate student questions and any interruptions that may occur.
8 Rehearse the whole showing, timing it accurately, before class time; make any changes needed.
9 Plan your follow-up activities—further use of aids or field trips, readings, written reports, discussions, and similar experiences.

During Showing

1 Be sure that everyone can see and hear.
2 Check the darkness of the room for effective projection and enough light for students to take notes.

3 Relate the content of the slides or strips to the knowledge, interests, and experience of the pupils.

4 Tie in the pictures to relevant textbook content.

5 Hold each frame on the screen long enough to allow all students to read and understand it.

6 Permit questions that are relevant and important, but do not allow them to disturb the continuity of the filmstrip or sequence.

7 If a tape or disc accompanies a filmstrip, plan for a second showing if some students have not been able to keep up with the tempo.

After Showing

1 Discuss the filmstrip, slides, or pictures, answering further questions.

2 List new information or ideas on the chalkboard.

3 Announce and explain follow-up activities; welcome further student suggestions.

4 Evaluate the showing in terms of purposes, information as revealed by suitable tests, and effects upon students.

MOTION PICTURES, VIDEOTAPES, AND KINESCOPES

In planning a classroom presentation using this group of projected aids, you should know that they have these things in common: (1) a series of events communicated by the visible (video) portion of the film; (2) a sound track (most films) that ordinarily carries narration related to the events; the actual speaking of persons in the film, noises of animals or things; musical background related to the video portion—or a combination of all three; (3) the use of color and/or art work to add to the vividness of the film; (4) continuous sequence of action through the frames of the film (unlike the slide or filmstrip) that makes it less easy to stop, ask questions, or discuss. However, more and more projectors are now made with devices that permit stopping the film and study of individual frames.

With these kinds of aids, you, as a teacher, have many important things to do as an oral communicator. These include preparation and discussion before showing, suggestions and planned activities during showing, and follow-up experiences. It is assumed that you will have chosen the best film for your purposes, previewed it, become familiar with the teaching guides available, and made the proper physical arrangements for showing it.

PREPARATION AND DISCUSSION BEFORE SHOWING. Having established with your class the purpose for showing the film and its relationship to the course and textbook content, a discussion of important facts about the film is indicated. These include:

1 Things to look for in the film.
2 Situations and problems observed in the film.
3 The vocabulary of the film—new words, phrases, concepts.
4 Areas covered or questions the film answers.

A very practical method is to list these four items on the chalkboard as major headings to be explored. In the discussion, list points that develop under the headings as guides for observation, but avoid "overdissection" of the headings to prevent loss of interest in the film. Your role here as an oral communicator is a combination of explaining and leading discussion, perhaps helping students to develop items you may have anticipated in your content-method outline.

ACTIVITIES DURING SHOWING. There should be less planned or directed activity than during the showing of a filmstrip, because the usual method is to run the entire film first and conduct discussion following it. However, you should urge students to take notes, and follow in their activities the points written on the chalkboard as guides. If your equipment permits and the need is indicated, a film may be stopped, questions asked and answered, and the showing continued.

ACTIVITIES AFTER SHOWING. Evaluation through discussion seems the most sensible first activity. By this means you can discover whether the items listed on the chalkboard have been covered by the film. During this discussion you can discover the effects of the film upon the learning of the students. Was new information obtained? Were problems resolved or questions answered? Were attitudes changed or new points of view established? Did the students believe the film helpful to them? Should a second showing be made to clarify points?

Follow-up activities are equally significant. A film showing can lead to further reading in related books, periodicals, or research studies; to viewing other films; to the preparation of models or bulletin board displays; to participation experiences in further discussion or debate, dramatizations, radio or television programs; to field trips; to the invitation of guest lecturers or performers; or to written reports.

Your planning of all these phases in the showing of a film ensures effective communication throughout a meaningful educational experience for your pupils.

FOR FURTHER READING

Brown, Charles T. and Charles Van Riper: *Speech and Man*, Prentice-Hall, Inc., Englewood Cliffs, N.J., 1966, chap. 4.

Bryant, Donald C. and Karl R. Wallace: *Fundamentals of Public Speaking*, 3d ed., Appleton-Century-Crofts, Inc., New York, 1960, chaps. 7 and 8.

Dale, Edgar: *Audio-Visual Methods of Teaching*, rev. ed., Holt, Rinehart and Winston, Inc., New York, 1954.

Gray, Giles W. and Waldo W. Braden: *Public Speaking: Principles and Practice*, 2d ed., Harper & Row, Publishers, Inc., New York, 1963, chap. 18.

Rahskopf, Horace G.: *Basic Speech Improvement*, Harper & Row, Publishers, Inc., New York, 1965, pp. 229–233.

CHAPTER FOURTEEN

SPEAKING OUTSIDE THE CLASSROOM

A teacher is frequently asked to give a speech outside the classroom. When this occurs, many teachers get "panicky" and either decline the invitation or worry themselves almost sick about it. Perhaps you have the notion that you cannot give a speech. If that is true, this chapter can be of some direct help to you when you have the opportunity to speak before an outside audience. Think of it as a kind of "service chapter" to be used when the need arises.

In an earlier chapter we have discussed general methods of preparing speeches. If you have absorbed the content of that chapter, this one will have more meaning for you. We shall deal here with your effectiveness in handling particular kinds of situations and speeches with which you might be involved. From experience and observation, as well as from talks with many teachers, we are sure that you will have numerous questions after you have accepted a speaking engagement. Among them will probably be these:

> Can I do it?
> What kind of speech should I give in this situation?
> How do I give such a speech?
> What can I talk about?
> Can I make my talk interesting to the audience?
> Can I get it across to the listeners?

What follows is meant to help you answer those questions and some others; but notice that word *help*. In the end, *your* perceptions, imagination, and some resourcefulness will provide the answers for your situation.

Let us dispose of the first question at once. Can you give a speech? The answer is simple—of course you can! Your invitation to speak is evidence that others thought you could do the job. Your education and experience qualify you. Others with less background and training are doing it. You have observed scores of speakers—some good, some not. You have been talking to people all your life, and you are—or will be—talking to groups five days a week. These are reasons enough for you to believe you can do it.

THINKING THROUGH THE SITUATION

We can think of a dozen situations in which a teacher might be asked to speak. However, we shall discuss only six of them here. These will be typical of most of the situations encountered by a teacher. They are:

1 Short occasional speeches, including speeches of introduction, welcoming speeches, and speeches of presentation
2 Assembly speeches
3 Speeches to educational groups
4 Speeches to clubs
5 Speeches to religious groups
6 Banquet speeches

Having decided to speak on an occasion such as those listed above, you will first need to gain some perspective of the situation. You can do this by asking yourself and getting the answers to the following questions:

1 How large will the audience be? In what kind of room will they be? Will a microphone be used?
2 Will it be an all-male, all-female, or mixed audience?
3 What will be the range of ages of the listeners? What is the background of the group—occupational, cultural, religious, etc.?
4 What is my relationship to the group? To what extent do I know them and they, me? What common concerns do I have with them?
5 What is the occasion and the purpose for the meeting?
6 How will my speech be related to previous programs and to the other aspects of this particular meeting?
7 When will I speak? For how long? Who will introduce me?

While writing the above, we received a telephone call from the chairman of the local Lions Club in which he invited one of us to speak this evening at a dinner meeting. Since this is a local group in a small town, the writer knows the answers to most of the above questions. This knowledge, together with the information about the length of talk and the topic assigned, reduces the anxiety about the speech and makes its preparation easier and pertinent.

Once you have a grasp of the situation, it is important that you establish a proper image of yourself in the situation. So often people hesitate to give a speech simply because they conceive of a speaker as a kind of Daniel Webster or a clergyman or a television personality. It is well to keep in mind that if you are asked to speak, it is because *you* are *you*! The audience will not expect you to be like someone else; neither will they expect you to be suddenly a god of wisdom or a fountain of all knowledge. They will simply expect that you have acquired some understanding of certain areas of knowledge and thought and have prepared yourself particularly for the subject at hand. It has been well said that you can communicate only what you understand and accept and believe in yourself. This is reasonable, and it need not be a great strain for you to live up to these expectations. In essence we are saying, understand your significance in the situation and try to live up to it.

WHAT WILL YOU TALK ABOUT?

We have found that the finding of a subject for a speech is a problem which nettles college students; perhaps it does adults also. Sometimes the decision is made for you; you are asked to speak on a specific topic. For example, in the request of the Lions Club, mentioned above, the speaker was asked to explain the new trimester plan for the University. In cases like this you will find that the preparation was good for you, since you extended or sharpened your own knowledge of an area that is pertinent to education.

However, if you were asked to speak at a PTA meeting or a service club, you might have some latitude regarding the choice of subject. What would govern your choice? First of all, you would consider the occasion. A mother-daughter banquet brings to mind such subjects as: Famous Mothers, The Education of a Mother, A Mother's Reward, Mother's Revolt, If Mothers Ran the Country, etc. The occasion of "Student Day" at your church restricts your choices somewhat, but still makes possible such subjects as: Our Church Away from Home, Religion and Learning, Does a Student's Religion Change?, Religious Groups on the Campus, and Inter-faith Marriages. Keep in mind that, even though the occasion does allow for a choice of subject, audiences expect a speech that it is pertinent to the occasion, and they feel a bit disappointed if it is not.

The second factor governing your choice of subject is your audience. You will want to consider its size, what the listeners' interests are, why they are there, their relationship to each other and to you. For instance, if you are an athletic coach who is invited to speak at a men's luncheon club, your understanding of this audience will tell you whether or not to speak about the coming season or the past season of the sport, the educational values of the sport, how you coach the sport, the need for new facilities, or how dads can help their sons in athletics. With any audience, keep in mind what they read about, what they listen to on radio or television, what their conversations are about. Ask yourself: what community projects are in the offing? what institutions are they involved in? what issues in government, education, communication, and morals have to be resolved? what social problems need attention?

But you would not talk on any subject unless you considered the third factor in choosing a subject—your own interests. You can speak best on subjects which command you. What are these subjects? First of all, as a teacher, you are interested in youth, in learning, in the program and needs of your local school system, in broader educational problems. You also have a specialty in the level at which you are teaching or in your subject-matter area. You might be an out-of-doors enthusiast, you may have a special interest in physical fitness, in music, in drama, in flower arranging, in skin diving, in photography. So, utilize your own interests, keeping in mind your probable audience interests. A good rule to follow is this: Wherever your interests overlap those of your audience, there lie some potential subjects.

THINKING ABOUT YOUR SUBJECT

We remind you again of another chapter which deals with the preparation of a speech. At the risk of some repetition we shall indicate some preliminary preparation that the uninitiated speaker is inclined to overlook. Having chosen your subject, your next move is *not* to run to the library to read about it. Instead, start to examine the subject—much as you would do if you had picked up a peculiar-looking stone on a lake shore. Begin asking yourself questions about your subject and what you wish to do with it. In one instance we were asked to talk to a group of teachers as part of a series of meetings for in-service training. Our subject was, Teaching Pupils to Think. Here are some of the questions we raised and tried to answer before doing any further investigation or making an outline:

What mental state do I want to have the audience in when I conclude?
Do they want to know *if* pupils can be taught to think or *how* to teach pupils to think?
Shall I discuss how thinking is done?
What kinds of thinking shall I discuss?
What deficiencies in thinking do pupils seem to have?
Shall I talk about the teacher's thinking?
What methods have I used which seemed to help students to think?
What opportunities do teachers have to teach pupils to think?
Is pupil thinking ever stifled in the schools?
Are administrators and teachers sure they want their pupils to think critically?

Trying to answer those questions helped to determine the scope of the speech and to indicate the direction for further preparation.

KINDS OF SITUATIONS

We stated earlier that we would take up six typical situations in which you might be called upon to speak. Now, let us look at each of those with the intent to find practical means for handling them.

OCCASIONAL SPEECHES

THE SPEECH OF INTRODUCTION.   The speech to introduce a speaker should not be long. Someone has said that a master of ceremonies or the chairman of a meeting is like a gate through which the other speakers enter, and the less it squeaks, the better! The purpose of this speech is to build a bridge between the speaker and his audience. It should promote good listening, opening the way for the reception of the speaker's ideas.

To accomplish the above, you will have three things to talk about—in fact you should try to knit all three together: the audience or the occasion, the speaker, his subject. Another way of putting this is to say that you should answer the question, Why do *we* want to hear *this speaker* talk to us on *this subject*? Your concluding sentence will include the name of the speaker and the title of his speech.

Perhaps some specific suggestions regarding the speech of introduction would be helpful.

1   Get information about the speaker *in advance* of the meeting. Have some conversation with him before the meeting begins.
2   In talking about the speaker, mention his accomplishments and position rather than his virtues or personal characteristics.
3   Do not overpraise the speaker; this may hinder him more than it will help him. Likewise, do not direct attention to *how* he will speak.
4   Let your manner suggest friendliness and your desire to hear the speaker.
5   Be sure you remember his name and that you can pronounce it. He is the best source for this. Give his name and the title of his speech clearly and audibly.
6   After introducing the speaker, show some interest, yourself, in what he says; this acts as a cue for the audience. Do nothing which will take attention away from the speaker.
7   After the speaker has finished, make an appreciative acknowledgment of the speech, but do not moralize on the speech or launch into a speech of your own on the same subject. Let his speech keep its impact.

Below is a speech of introduction which might have been given to introduce a speaker at a banquet attended by about 200 football players and cross-country men, coaches, faculty members, and guests.

I know that the Chairman and members of this banquet committee thought long and seriously about whom they would invite to speak to us tonight. They wanted someone who would not only add dignity to the occasion, but one who would also appreciate what football is all about and who would understand the kind of season we have been through.

They agreed on the man they wanted; and because our Coach Doolittle has had a long and close association with him, they succeeded in getting him to come. He is a former high school and university football player himself; he has had an outstanding record as a high school coach and as a coach in two universities before moving to his present position; he maintained a high scholastic record while a student; he is regarded by his players and friends as a fine gentleman.

He comes to us tonight after a hard-won victory by his team over that of Navy. He will speak to us on the subject, "Being a Champion." I am proud to present the head football coach of the United States Military Academy, Mr. Paul Dietzel. Mr. Dietzel.

THE SPEECH OF WELCOME. Occasionally a teacher or a principal is asked to give a speech of welcome—to guests at a recognition dinner, to debaters before a clinic or a tournament begins, to guests from another school who come for an assembly or a special program, or to teachers at an educational conference. In any case, the purpose of the speech is to show your friendliness toward the person or group and to make them feel at home. The speaker wants to show his interest in the visitors and their purpose in coming. He, therefore, has the role of a congenial host.

The opening of his speech would express the pleasure of the speaker or the entertaining group that the visitors have come. Then three other things would be appropriate: (1) some praise of the person or group that is being welcomed—regarding their purposes, achievements, reputation; (2) some information about the place of meeting or the group that is hosting the meeting; (3) the good wishes of the speaker that the occasion may be successful. The conclusion could repeat the pleasure of the host and his hope that the meeting or conference will be worthwhile. It could also include the offer of the hosts to help in any way possible.

This speech should not be long. It is well done if the ideas are not labored, if the language is apt and appropriate, and if it is delivered with friendliness and sincerity.

THE SPEECH OF PRESENTATION. This kind of speech is usually given when a gift is presented or when an award is made for excellence in competitive activity. In the case of the gift, it may be to a retiring member of an organization, to a coach of a team, to a director or sponsor of a group, to a visitor in the community, etc. The purpose of the speech is to honor the recipient, but it may have a secondary purpose, that of maintaining morale or promoting good relationships. Awards or prizes are presented for distinguished or long service to an organization, for winning contests—athletic or intellectual—for being "the most valuable player," etc. Here, again, the purpose is to speak appropriate words of honor and commendation.

The introductory part may be very brief or omitted entirely—unless it seems appropriate to tell the history, significance, or conditions under which the award is made. The main part of the speech should deal with the qualities or achievements of the person which make him deserving of the gift or award. Following this (or perhaps before it) there may be a brief description of it. In conclusion, the speaker presents the gift, indicating his pleasure in so doing and expressing the hope that the recipient will enjoy it.

The speech of presentation requires tact and some restraint. One should not overpraise the person receiving it; this may be uncomfortable for him. If it is a competitive prize or award, it is gracious to give some recognition to the "also-rans." The speech is successful if all persons present feel good about the presentation. Below is a speech of presentation made in Denver, Colorado, in 1935 by Mr. Willard E. Givens, the National Secretary of the NEA.

> *Dr. Crabtree's record speaks more eloquently than any speaker could. He came to Washington in 1917 and started the office of the National Education Association in one room of his house, with one secretary. On January 1, 1935, when he became secretary-emeritus, he left a modern, seven-story building on "Street of the Presidents," six squares from the White House in our nation's capital, and he left there a loyal office force of one hundred and forty-five people, all of whom love and respect him.*
>
> *He started in 1922 the life membership movement that put up that great building, and that has grown from that time until tonight our great national Association has some 5400 life members scattered throughout this great nation.*
>
> *Miss Hale read you a few of the letters that he has received. It is my pleasure on behalf of his friends throughout the nation to present to him from you a beautiful volume of some seven hundred letters from his friends, bound in a beautiful binding presented by the publishers of our*

Journal as a compliment to Mr. Crabtree. It is a great pleasure to present this volume to Mr. Crabtree tonight and to assure you all that it is a great honor to be the successor to such a man.

ASSEMBLY SPEECHES

Of course, some of the preceding occasional speeches might be given in a school assembly. However, there are other speeches which might be given in an assembly for other purposes. Teachers often avoid giving these, but we recommend taking advantage of such an opportunity for the good you might do the listeners, as well as for your own personal growth.

Often such speeches are in connection with a holiday or the birthday of a famous person or the founding of a great organization or institution. They may also deal with experiences of the teacher or with his interest in books, music, sports, human relations, or world peace. A third area could include community problems, school problems, or problems of students.

In preparing such a speech, it is well to decide first of all what you expect to accomplish by it. For example, you might say to yourself, "I want these students to realize that an education is not a thing given to us, but it is something which we, ourselves, achieve." Then you have also decided on the central idea of your speech. For other aspects of preparation, note the suggestions given at the beginning of this chapter and in Chapter 13.

In giving an assembly speech one is faced with the obligation and desire to have the content of the speech valuable, and with the necessity of talking in terms of the students. Since an assembly is part of the educational offering of the school, the occasion should not be taken lightly. In a sense it is like teaching the largest class you ever had. At the same time, if the language and the manner of speaking do not produce receptive listeners, the content of the speech is of no avail. In this situation you will know your audience pretty well and many of them will know you. So, our best advice would be to talk to them in the same way that you do when you seem to have your class "in the palm of your hand."

SPEECHES TO EDUCATIONAL GROUPS

We realize that many teachers who do an excellent job in the classroom disclaim any ability to talk before a group of their peers. Of course, when you talk with your colleagues in conversation, in committee meetings, or in staff meetings—if they do not feel that your ideas are worth listening to, then don't accept an invitation to speak to a larger group of educators. On the other hand, if you are *asked* to make such a speech, it is pretty likely that one or more people think your ideas *are* worth listening to. If you can find the time and have the energy to do it, we urge you to accept the invitation—in the interests of your profession and for the good it will do you.

If you are permitted to choose your own subject, we would refer you to the earlier part of this chapter for suggestions. When you are requested to speak on a particular subject, your first need will be to determine the purpose of the speech. Is it to be informative, persuasive, stimulating, convincing, or entertaining? Next, decide on the central idea; in one sentence state the essence of the speech. Then, decide on a title (although this might evolve during the preparation of the speech). On one occasion we were asked to talk to a PTA audience on "problems in education." We decided to make it chiefly an informative speech; we used the title, "Investment in Education"; the central idea was: We are not getting good returns on our investment in education if we neglect the problems of the deficient student and the dropout.

In getting material for such a speech, don't start with the library. Instead, use our suggestions for "thinking about the subject"; then talk with people who have interests and information on the subject. Probe their thinking, their experiences, their feelings—keeping your own mind free to be eager and creative. Almost inevitably, talk of this kind brings out the titles of books and journal articles which bear on the subject. While your mind is alive to the subject, it is surprising how many things you hear on the radio or television or things that you read in the newspapers or news magazines seem to be related to your subject. In the printed news media, don't overlook the special columns. Eventually, you may want to use the card catalog and the *Education Index* in your library.

The purpose of the speech will influence your selection of ideas, facts, examples, incidents, quotations, etc. It will also influence the patterning of these. If the purpose is to inform (to increase understanding), you will want to begin with what the audience probably knows, or partially knows, or perhaps misunderstands, and then proceed in such a way that the new information is not only understood, but also seems significant.

If the purpose is persuasive (to get action), it is usually best to indicate at the outset that you understand the present attitude of the audience and that you appreciate why they feel as they do. From there, present the problem (e.g., need for more members, lack of members' concern, need for finances, etc.) in such a way that the listeners will want to do *some*thing. If they are in that state, they will listen to your proposal or solution. Two steps remain:

visualize for them how things would be with your proposal in effect; make them *want* to put it into effect by appealing to their "drives": self-respect, prestige, personal gain, love, altruism, pride, etc.

The above two kinds of speeches are often regarded as the basic ones. However, we mentioned speeches with three other purposes. If your purpose is to stimulate (inspire, impress), your aim is not so much to inform or actuate as it is to reestablish certain attitudes, enhance appreciations, or recapture certain values. In that case, you can make much use of the concrete (persons, experiences, stories, examples). Humor is not out of place. Poetry and other literary material is also effective. The patterning is not so important; but if repetition is used, it should be used knowingly and for a purpose. The conclusion is important, for it will set the final emotional tone. Note the concluding sentences of a good sermon or those of a good pep talk.

Sometimes the purpose of a professional speech is simply to convince— to induce belief in an idea, a philosophy, a program, or a person. Here, again, you begin with what the audience may tend to believe; you try to open the listeners' minds for a change of belief you espouse as valid. The conclusion should review the steps in arriving at the belief.

Occasionally a teacher is asked to speak at a dinner meeting of an educational group, for example, at the close of a conference or at a PTA banquet. Since we shall be dealing with banquet speeches later in this chapter, this kind of speech—usually an entertaining speech—will be covered there.

SPEECHES TO CLUBS

Men's clubs, women's clubs, book clubs, music clubs, camera clubs, luncheon clubs, fraternal groups, and others are always looking for speakers, and it is natural that they should think of teachers. Often you will be asked to speak because of your particular area of teaching; sometimes, because they just want to hear *you* speak. In that case, what we have said earlier about choosing your subject may be of some help. Note, also, our suggestions under "Speeches to Educational Groups."

The type of speech, i.e., your purpose, would also be one of those discussed above, or it would be the entertaining speech (see "Banquet Speeches"). However, unless you are speaking at a club meeting to get support for some project or cause, it is usually expected that you will be speaking primarily to inform.

For this kind of speaking situation it helps greatly if you can learn as much as possible about the prospective audience and situation. Usually it will be composed of one sex; but you will want to know the number of members, their occupations and interests, what other guests will be present, your place on the program, the kind of room in which the meeting is to be held, and whether or not they use a public-address system. It also helps to have a chance to visit with some of the members prior to your speaking and to get the tone of the group from the singing, the announcements, the business meeting, and the "ribbing" that goes on.

Club audiences, perhaps more than any other, prefer the kind of speaker who follows the blunt advice: "Stand up; speak up; shut up." They like clear, forthright speaking—but not partisan ideas. They like some humor, but they also like to feel that they have received some new information or have seen a subject in a new light. It would be a mistake to "talk down" to them. One other suggestion—don't forget the "shut up" part of the speech. Clubs often have rigid times for adjournment; so plan the length of your speech carefully in order to conform to the time you agreed to use. It would be better to end it three minutes early rather than to go three minutes overtime.

SPEECHES TO RELIGIOUS GROUPS

If religion is a part of your life, you may be asked to speak to such groups as a Sunday school class, a youth organization, the congregation during the worship service, or a family-night dinner gathering. If you have read this chapter up to this point, you realize that much that we have said about preparation in other situations applies here.

There is, however, one aspect of this situation which you will want to adjust to: that is the desirability of having your speech fit in with the usual tone of the group's meeting and with the preceding programs or speeches. Often the person who invited you to speak can help you considerably in that respect; the minister, priest, or rabbi also can give you some orientation. They might give you good suggestions, too, in connection with the subject of your speech. This is particularly true when you are asked to speak on a subject of their choosing.

When planning to speak to a religious group, the average person probably is more concerned about his use of language than he would be for other groups. Of course, it will have to be adapted to the age-level of the group; but the level of formality will vary, also, according to the type of meeting and the place of meeting. Beyond this, we would say that the language has to be essentially the language of your subject; but it must be the oral style that you can handle.

The delivery of this kind of speech must be adapted, like the language, to the circumstances. Yet it must be consistent with your own personality. It is essential, therefore, that you perceive your role properly. Since you are not a clergyman, you are not expected to act like one—unless you usually do. Again, our advice is to be your best natural self. If you mean what you say and have a warm desire to contribute something to the lives of those listening, you will lose much of your self-consciousness, and what you say will be appreciated.

BANQUET SPEECHES

The main purpose here is to be entertaining, although some serious ideas are in order, also. The materials for such a speech may include the following: recounting the interesting aspects of a season (football, spring sports, dramatics, competitive speech activities); experiences (perhaps accompanied by pictures); narration of stories pertinent to the occasion; light treatment of a serious subject (raising children, teen-agers, being a teacher, methods of teaching, athletics, "the good old days," etc.).

The pattern or outline of this kind of speech is not so important, as long as there seems to be a plausible continuity of ideas or material. If there is a "message" in the speech, it is usually one similar to those used in the speech to stimulate (inspire, impress). It should be apparent quite early in the speech that you do have a serious thought in mind, and the conclusion should be a final effort to "lift" the audience to a higher level of appreciation or a more firm resolve regarding certain values.

No doubt, you are thinking that there will be jokes in the entertaining speech. There may be jokes in any kind of speech, but it is true that there are usually more in this particular kind. The question is: What kind of joke shall we use? Based on considerable use of them and many years of listening to them we shall rank them—from the most preferred to least preferred.

1 A humorous incident involving the speaker (the joke is on him) which is pertinent to the occasion or to his subject
2 A humorous incident involving a person present—pertinent, but not derogatory
3 A humorous incident involving a person known, but not present, which is pertinent

4   A story about some other person or persons which illustrates an idea or applies to the situation
5   A story told about some other person, but which the speaker tries to "pin" on someone present
6   A story which is relevant to nothing in particular
7   A risqué story which might be acceptable only for the one age-group present or the one sex-group present
8   A risqué story which would be resented by any of those present

You will find that the entertaining speech is most successful when these two qualities are predominant: (1) you, the speaker, are feeling alert and yet relaxed and seem to enjoy the occasion; you have established rapport with the group; (2) the speech moves along so that you are just a half step ahead of your listeners most of the time; you do not go beyond the time limit, and the audience would be willing to hear more.

In summarizing what we have been saying about the teacher's speaking outside the classroom, we would first remind you that this kind of speaking is an opportunity for you. When confronted with it, think through the situation and decide on what subject you wish to speak. Determine the purpose of your speech. Then adapt your materials, your pattern, your language, and your delivery to the purpose and to the audience. When you have finished speaking, you need not thank your listeners; they should feel like thanking you.

FOR FURTHER READING

Bryant, Donald C. and Karl R. Wallace: *Fundamentals of Public Speaking*, 3d ed., Appleton-Century-Crofts, Inc., New York, 1960, chap. 24.

Fessenden, Seth A., Roy I. Johnson, P. Merville Larson, and Kaye M. Good: *Speech For the Creative Teacher*, William C. Brown Company, Publishers, Dubuque, 1968, chaps. 20–22.

Gilman, Wilbur E., Bower Aly, and Hollis L. White: *The Fundamentals of Speaking*, 2d ed., The Macmillan Company, New York, 1964, chaps. 9–11.

Oliver, Robert T. and Rupert L. Cortright: *Effective Speech*, 4th ed., Holt, Rinehart and Winston, Inc., New York, 1961, chaps. 20–23.

White, Eugene E.: *Practical Public Speaking*, 2d ed., The Macmillan Company, New York, 1964, chap. 15.

CHAPTER FIFTEEN

REVEALING THE PRINTED PAGE

The teacher is a dealer in ideas from the printed page. Many of these he has assimilated into his own stock of ideas—and therefore into his own phraseology; others he gives to his pupils verbatim, or nearly so. It is with the latter that we shall concern ourselves here.

During the course of a day, you as a teacher may reveal the printed page to your pupils on different subjects and for varying reasons. It may be an announcement from the principal's office or from the president of the PTA; it may be a paragraph from a pupil's paper; it may be an item from the newspaper; it may be a bit of verse, a story, or a narrative of experience. In all these, you would hope to stimulate the minds of your pupils somewhat as yours was stimulated by the material.

WAYS OF REVEALING THE PRINTED PAGE

ORAL READING

There is no doubt about the surface meaning of this term. However, here we do not want you to assume that "saying the words aloud" is all of it. Teachers are sometimes inclined to think that if the pupil pronounces all of the words in a sentence, he is reading it. Likewise, they may feel that if the pupil could hear all of the words the teacher reads, he should know what message is intended. We hope you will conceive of oral reading as stimulating the listener with all of the ideas that were intended by the writer. As a reader you should assume the role of an intermediator between the writer and the listener ("interpreter," if you like).

STORYTELLING

This kind of interpretation of the printed page brings you closer to the material and to your pupils than does oral readings. It suggests more that you are identifying yourself with the people and events involved, and it puts you in a more conversational relationship with your listeners. It does not require a verbatim memorization of the story, but it does imply a sure recall of it and a strong sense of the images you attempt to re-create. It implies people or other creatures *in action*.

PRINCIPLES WHICH APPLY TO ALL

We have already indicated that the goals in the above two speech activities are similar: the stimulation of the minds of your listeners so that they can re-create something akin to what you perceived.   There is also the possibility of their creating something in their own minds which you should incorporate in your efforts to use either form.

KNOWING WHAT THE AUTHOR MEANT

What the author meant, of course, depends in part upon his purpose.   For example, an announcement may contain merely facts—such as, when the bus will leave and where it will be, or how much money to bring to school and what to do with it.   On the other hand, it may have a persuasive element in it: be sure to have your parents come to the "open house" on Thursday evening; see as many people as you can about collecting their old paper for the new projector fund.

But often the author's purpose will be to give the reader or listener a vicarious experience.   He wants you to share with him a pleasurable, or exciting, or meaningful experience.   So he puts into language (symbols of experience) the kind of people involved, the scenes of the incident, and the action that took place.

In another instance, the writer hopes to have you get new concepts of life, of people, and other aspects of nature—and even of yourself.   That is why *Alice in Wonderland, Winnie the Pooh,* "Little Boy Blue," and hosts of other things were written.   Adults, themselves, keep on reading for this purpose to the ends of their lives.

Of course, the author's purpose is only one clue to what he means.   The form in which he writes is another.   The mood in which he presents his ideas is still another.   But, most of all, we depend upon the sentences, the phrases, the words he uses.   In these we look first for his theme, or central idea.   We ask ourselves, "What one idea or thought is he trying to have me think?"   Is he saying something about beauty, about human nature, about human relationships or animal relationships, about love, about rivers, about happiness, about God?   Can you distill into one sentence what the whole selection is saying?

To know what the author meant, it is necessary, also, for you to ask what each part means—whether it be paragraph or stanza.   If this includes more than one sentence, you need to grasp the meaning of each sentence.   But grasp its meaning, not in isolation, but in relation to what has already been said.   Finally, we come to phrases and words.   It is obvious that if we do not understand these, we cannot understand the whole.   But, since any given word may have a diversity of meanings, you must know its meaning in this particular context.   If you do not appreciate the different meanings of words, open your dictionary and see what *meaning* means—or *turn*, or *dull*, or *nice*!

But—there is another meaning.   What we have said above refers primarily to what is known as the denotative meanings of words.   There is also the *connotative*, or emotional, meaning of the word.   It may be in the word alone or in the phrase, perhaps as a figure of speech.   Wouldn't it be silly to take only the literal meaning of:

"Oh world, I cannot hold thee close enough!"

Think of the added meaning in such words as *mother, cottage, alarm clock,* and *party* as you say them to yourself.   The dictionary cannot tell anyone what they mean to you.   The authors of what you read recognize this, and hope that from the context and from your own life of experiences you will find in the word a richness of meaning that the dictionary does not give.

KNOWING MORE THAN THE AUTHOR MEANT

The last sentence in the paragraph above suggests, again, that you read only with what you bring to the material you read.   This is the reason that you can know more than authors do.   Authors write with their own peculiar experiences and information, with insights that could be only theirs.   But as a reader, you may have lived through significant world events, learned facts not known when a certain author wrote, or had experience not shared by him.   For example, Henry Wadsworth Longfellow once visited the arsenal at Springfield and later wrote a poem in which appear the lines:

Were half the power, that fills the world with terror,
Were half the wealth, bestowed on camps and courts,
Given to redeem the human mind from error,
There were no need of arsenals or forts.

That was in 1843.   We might agree that the basic truth written by Longfellow then is still truth for our times.   However, the supporting facts have changed so alarmingly during a hundred years that the truth of the poem has a compelling urgency today.   To realize this, you need only imagine the clumsy single-shot rifles and the short-range, horse-drawn artillery pieces he saw—and little else, except ammunition—then think of the destructive war material which you know exists in these days of scientific mass-killing. Unless you bring that knowledge to the poem, you are not interpretating to the listener what the poem can mean to you.

RESPONDING TO MOOD, IDEA, AND EMOTION

Reading or retelling the printed page to others is not likely to be either interesting or significant unless the speaker is responding to the mood, the idea, and the emotion of the material. By *respond*, we mean to show some effects of the stimulus in the material you are using. This response will first pervade the whole body; but it will be particularly evident in the face. As a result of general muscular activity, the voice is likely to be affected too.

By responding to the *mood* of the printed page, we mean also, having a frame of mind or state of feeling which seems to be indicated. If you know the writer, especially in a personal way, you are able to predict pretty well what his mood would be in writing on a particular subject. If you do not, you will have to keep in mind the setting in which it was written. Take a simple instance. Suppose that you had been at a teachers' meeting in which the subject of room picnics had been discussed, and then the next day received from the principal a directive regarding room picnics—to be read to your pupils. Knowing the background of the directive would enable you to interpret the tenor or mood of the message more accurately. Often, however, you have only the immediate text as a basis for determining the mood. In that case, you will have to use not only the meanings of words and phrases, but also sentence style, the rhythm, tone value, and other literary devices for conveying mood. Your response to these will be determined by your alertness to them and by your insight into the meaning of the whole.

Responding to *ideas* has to be achieved in a similar way. Here you want to know what the author was *thinking*; what is the intellectual content of the message? Naturally, the central idea is of first importance. Once that has been arrived at, then the next effort must be turned toward relating all of the *parts* to the central idea, as well as relating the parts to each other. You could try this by going back to the first two sentences of this paragraph and reading them aloud. How did you respond to *similar*, *thinking*, and *intellectual content?* Would a listener perceive how the ideas of *this* paragraph affected you in relationship to the effect of the preceding two paragraphs upon you? This concept of relationship is the most important one in dealing with responding to ideas; a word or a phrase by itself may have little significance, but placed in relationship to other words or phrases or to other sentences, it can have a powerful impact. The phrase, "what I think," is a common one; so is "I am"; but if you thoughtfully put those two together into "I am what I think," it could change your whole life. That would be response to an idea.

Often the responses to mood and idea are not so apparent as your response to *emotion*. If "the Adam in us" means anything, it means that we are first creatures of emotion. Since an emotion is a generalized bodily disturbance, you would expect an emotional response to be easily perceived. But, again, there will be no response if you have not caught the emotion in what you read. Where will you find it? Of course, it will be in the situations and events which are related; it may be in the writer's deliberate description of a person's feelings or of a scene; it will be in those connotative meanings of words that we spoke of earlier. One of the things that distinguishes a mere television personality from an artist in the use of the spoken word is the relative ability to make an emotional response that is unmistakable and true.

When you fail to respond to all three of the elements of meaning, what you speak does not seem quite convincing to the discriminating mind. That is why a high school student cannot interpret Patrick Henry's speech to the Virginia Assembly without its sounding a bit corny. It is also the reason that Lincoln's Gettysburg Address in the hands of a novice sounds like so much parroting. If you have neither experience nor imagination, you might as well confine your interpreting to announcements, directions, exposition, and the like. There you can hope that the words, properly grouped, will convey enough of the idea "for practical purposes."

GIVING UNDERSTANDABLE CUES

After you have acquired the full meaning of the printed page and have responded to it, the listener may still not be stimulated as you had intended unless he understands the cues to the meaning that you have thrown out. You give these in either visual or auditory form. In the case of the visual cues, the listener "reads" your posture, your movement, your facial expression, and your gesture. From these he expects to get anticipation, confirmation, or emphasis—but not denial—of what your voice is saying. If the oral communication is psychologically normal, the physical reactions of the speaker or reader precede the vocal reactions.   Thus, they do help us to anticipate what is meant.   If the responses of the head and face are consistent with the voice, there is confirmation of what the ears have heard—or the ears confirm what the eye has seen.   If emphasis is present, it is because the visual and auditory cues reinforce each other.

Actually, the vocal cues are of the greater importance.   The words on the printed page are merely *representations* of sounds which originated orally. Therefore, the reader or speaker is really trying to convert back into sounds what the writer wished he could *say,* but was forced to write in order to distribute his message widely.   It is much like the medium of radio: the sound of the person speaking is converted into electronic impulses so it can be broadcast; at the receiving stations these impulses are converted back into sounds for the benefit of the listener.   Because the voice can vary so greatly in quality, intensity, time, and pitch, the possibilities for meaning in it are almost limitless.   For example, how many meanings might be found in the single syllable, "oh"?   David Garrick, the master of interpretation, once said he would give thirty guineas if he could say "Oh" as George Whitefield, the evangelist, said it.

Try this little device.   Saying the sentence, *That isn't what I meant,* can you make it mean any one of the following?

I meant something different.
I insist that you are wrong about what I meant.
Sue might have meant that, but I didn't.
You misunderstood what I said.
It's preposterous to think I meant that.

IF YOU LACK INTERPRETIVE ABILITY

It would be difficult to imagine a person who could not improve his ability to reveal the printed page to others by practice.   However, given the same amount of practice, two individuals could still differ greatly—probably for one or more of the five following reasons:

1   *Lack of awareness.*   Perhaps this is the equivalent of *lack of experience;* for too many of us have been to enough places, known enough people, witnessed enough events to enable us to know a great deal about life— and yet we do not.   Thoreau reminded us that "Only that day dawns to which we are awake," and at another time asserted that a person

could see as much of the world from his back porch as he could by going to Europe. Experience, therefore, really means *opportunity plus awareness.* One of Miriam Teichner's prayers was, "God let me be aware," and that will have to be your prayer, too, if you are to find meaning in what you read.

2 *Lack of imagination.* What is imagination but making mental images of things which are not present to the senses? A person with imagination says, while looking at an old deserted house, "There are wonderful possibilities in that place." The imaginative person was not at Appomattox, but he knew what the Confederate soldiers felt as they turned their faces to the South. The person without imagination must perceive only with his senses in order to appreciate—forgetting that his senses, themselves, may play him false. However, if he has memory, he can develop his imagination. Can you use your imagination to develop that idea?

3 *Inhibitions.* So often a person is aware and has imagination—in short, he knows and responds to what he reads—but he cannot reveal enough of the meaning to others because of his inhibitions. Perhaps he has been hurt in the past for revealing a unique response to something; or perhaps he has been warned so often by the conservators of his culture that he cannot trust his own individual responses. In either case he fearfully avoids the possible discomfort that would come from being what he is and expressing what he feels in the presence of others. If you are this kind, try to remember what you did in the presence of one or two friends, when unhesitatingly and unashamedly you "let your hair down." Here we would paraphrase the Greek proverb, "Know thyself" by advising you to "Be yourself." Failure for a teacher to be himself results in his pupils either saying "he isn't human" or always wondering what kind of a person he really is. In that case, they will never know what he really means when he tries to interpret to them what is on the printed page.

4 *Lack of appreciating the listener.* Reading or retelling to oneself is one thing, but doing it in terms of the listener is another. You have heard the schoolboy read only to get through the part he was expected to read. Teachers might do that under the pressure of covering a certain amount of material in too short a time. But perhaps in a different sense they do it also when they talk or read chiefly to entertain themselves by the material read or by the "charm" of their own voices. The problem is always, How will this be perceived by the listeners?—or, How will this sound in the ears of the listeners? That means that while you read the material yourself in terms of what you know and are, you must

be sensitive to the fact that the listener is hearing it in terms of what *he* knows and is. We are reminded of this when we hear that a little boy who lived in Connecticut began the Lord's Prayer with "Our Father who art in New Haven, how'd you know my name?" Appreciating the listener will not only help you to select the right material for him, but it will make you a more careful interpreter of what you select.

5   *An Unresponsive Body.* Two paragraphs above we noted that a person may interpret poorly because of his inhibitions. It may also be due to the fact that he has a body which cannot show reactions to intangibles. The person may be able to react to an oncoming tackler in football, or to move swiftly to get to a tennis ball, or to play a musical instrument; but he cannot play a role easily or "emote" a line of poetry. In that case he will have to compensate by using language more skillfully and by using the vocal factors—especially time and pitch—with more sublety. The fact that it *is* done by many people who work from scripts gives you reason to believe that you might do it if necessary.

IMPROVING YOUR READING

Many writers have found that it takes an entire book to cover adequately the subject of reading aloud. College courses in speech devote an entire semester to a beginning course in interpretive reading. It would seem presumptuous, therefore, in the space available here, to attempt to cover all aspects of the problem. We believe, however, that the following suggestions, in addition to what we have already said, can be of some immediate and practical help.

SHARPEN YOUR PERCEPTION

Since you read with what you are, and you have become what you are through your responses to the world around you, it follows that you need to sharpen your perceptions of that world. All of us have five senses—and many more—that tell us what is happening to us and what is in existence around us.

Take, for example, what you *can* see, but possibly have not. Have you seen the succession of colors that pervade nature from January to December? Have you seen the moon, "like a ghostly galleon, sailing upon cloudy seas"? Have you seen the face of a lake as it changes from day to day—or hour to hour? Have you seen the different motions of branches as they wave in the wind, or the delicate quiver of an aspen leaf in an almost imperceptible breeze? Do you perceive that the look on another person's face is not caused by boredom or hostility, but perhaps pain?

Likewise, are you aware of the sounds in a city as described by Carl Sandburg in a walk with a friend? Do you notice the characteristic smell of every store or house or classroom that you enter? Do you really hear the conversation of two children playing together in the next room, or catch the melody in the talk that goes on when a little tot is being bathed? Are you aware of the peculiar spirit that pervades a group of people—whether eating, working, discussing, or just listening? Life "has loveliness to sell" (and, of course, unloveliness, too), but if you haven't seen it, how can you read to others about it?

TRY TO PARAPHRASE

In their discussion of "Thinking Aloud," Van Riper and Butler have a suggestive passage:

> *We tend to consider reading the basic skill. But what happens when we understand the words on the printed page? We have been talking to ourselves. In this silent self-talking only the poorest students echo the words they are reading and then they do not comprehend. Many a student complains, "This stuff is so dry that I read it over and over again and it's just so many words." What he means is that he is unable to translate the printed letters into the language of self-talking.*[1]

Paraphrasing what you intend to read can help you to develop self-talk. In paraphrasing, you are expressing the meaning of the author in language of *your* choosing. For instance, "I am a part of all that I have met" might mean to you, "I am changed by every experience I have." To another person it would mean, "I am a creature of my environment." The effort to paraphrase what you are going to read requires you to read with more penetration, and it clarifies the meaning more than anything else can. Don't excuse yourself from this by saying, "But the author says it so well!" Just answer the question, "*What* does he say so well?"

---

[1] Charles Van Riper and Katharine Butler, *Speech in the Elementary Classroom*, Harper & Row, Publishers, Incorporated, New York, 1955, p. 116.

PRACTICE REPRODUCING THE SOUNDS OF LIFE

It seems a minor tragedy that so often a child can imitate the sound of a frog or an airplane or a bird and yet reads aloud so ineptly. It is our belief that a person whose senses are that sharp and whose vocal apparatus is that flexible has the potential to read orally. Likewise, we believe that you, as an older person, could improve your oral reading if you reactivated your senses and redeveloped your vocal agility through reproducing the sounds around you. The world is full (too full) of sounds—ranging from the rumble and roar of the freight train to the subdued mew of a tiny kitten. Get the use of a tape recorder, use some ingenuity, and see what you can do. Remember, "Except as ye become as little children . . ."!

But the world is full of voices, too. Try copying the voices of people with whom you associate. Catch the pitch level and normal quality of a voice and experiment with your own in trying to duplicate it. Then observe the melody patterns, the time patterns, and the uses of intensity, trying again to use them yourself. This can be done easily with an ordinary radio simply by tuning the volume down while you try to imitate the last sentence or phrase you heard. If you have the use of a tape recorder, you can get other voices on tape and thus be able to replay the voice and then try to reproduce it with *your* voice. This kind of practice sharpens your hearing, but it can also aid in making your voice more flexible, and therefore more capable of varying shades of response when you are reading to others.

READ AS YOU TALK

No doubt you have been either bored or exasperated by some of the so-called "interviews" on radio programs in which the questions and answers are all written out in advance; then the two people involved try to read the script as if they were talking with only one of them knowing how to do it! How does the trained radio speaker do it? We are not speaking from the testimony of those who are in radio, but we are quite sure that, first of all, they have observed the patterns of conversational speech. They know that the rhythm of conversational speech is irregular; thus the pauses occur irregularly because the word groups vary so in length; the syllables vary in length because of the speaker's awareness of the significance of the word in the sentence.

You might approach the problem in this way. After you have gained familiarity with some written material (preferably informal prose), begin talking about the subject that the material deals with, leading up to the first sentence of the material. Then continue "talking" about the subject, but now use the words of the material. If you have listeners, you will find that you may have read two or three sentences before they realize you are reading. If you work alone with a tape recorder, do the same thing and then play it back to see if there was a noticeable difference when you made the transition to the written material.

Part of your problem in reading communicatively lies in grammar and punctuation. When you are speaking, you are aware of the function of each word in the sentence and of the relationship that one part of the sentence has with the other part(s). If you are to read intelligently, you need to know the structure of the sentence before you attack it. The punctuation is put in the sentence to enable you to understand the structure of the sentence and therefore its meaning. In reading it aloud, you will have to use the kind of vocal punctuations that people use when they speak their own thoughts. You may write the following sentence: "And they came and found Mary and Joseph and the babe lying in a manger." But when you read it aloud, if you are as unthinking as many people are who have read it, you will have Mary and Joseph in the manger along with the babe. You will have to punctuate it by your use of word grouping and inflection. This will not be difficult if you understand the structure and meaning of the sentence.

PRACTICE THE TECHNIQUES OF ORAL EXPRESSION

The effective *grouping of words*, referred to above, is one of the techniques involved in oral expression. There are many others, only a few of which we shall refer to here. *Emphasis and subordination* is an important element in reading. After you know what is important and what is less important, how do you reveal this when you read aloud? With multisyllable words, emphasis is generally placed on only one syllable of the word. As a simple example, look at the word, *beau-ti-ful*. We say that the first syllable is stressed; but how? You say that it is given more intensity or force. That is right, but that isn't all you do with it. Say it deliberately and listen carefully. You will notice that you also prolonged that syllable more than the others; you also gave it a rising inflection; your voice quality may have also varied between that syllable and the others. You subordinated the other syllables simply by doing less of these things to them. The same principle can be applied to any parts of the material you read.

Indicating a *change of idea* is another technique that needs to be understood. This usually occurs in the first sentence of a paragraph, as is true in the preceding sentence. But it may occur also within a stanza of poetry or within an ordinary prose sentence. We have always wondered, for example, why a sports announcer would say, "The Tigers won the *first* game, 10 to 4, but lost the second *contest*, 2 to 1." Obviously, the new idea is contained in the word *second* as well as in the word *lost*. But the announcer gives you the impression that a contest is something different from a game. Thus, the change of idea really involves the contrasting of ideas, also. Novice readers so often fail to play one idea against another, even when that is the whole point of the sentence. You might try yourself on the following:

> *The theoretical man knows why; the practical man knows how; but the wise man knows both why and how.*

Handling quotations is always something of a problem, especially in stories. The writer has used punctuation marks to help the reader in this, but how can the reader put quotation marks into his voice? The basic devices are the pause and the change of key. If you are reading, "The time has come," the walrus said, "to speak of many things—" failure to pause before "to" could lead to confusion. But each part of the sentence that is a direct quotation also calls for a raising of the voice. The quotation ought, also, to suggest the character of the one who is speaking. If you have some insight into the character and his present mood, the elements of voice quality, force, and time will reveal your response to him.

Perhaps this brings up the question, Should you act or impersonate the character who is speaking? Generally, you should do neither. Rather, as we mentioned above, your effort should be to *suggest* the character. This means keeping your own personality as you lightly sketch that of the person quoted. Therefore, violent physical reactions and extreme grimaces would be out of place. However, if the situation or the temper of the group is such as to warrant impersonation, it might be more fun to use it. Parents and children in a home might enjoy a bedtime story much more by the reader "going all out."

The last sentence suggests that much of our reading to others is purely for enjoyment. Which leads us to say that better than any one technique is the spirit of the reader. Zest and enthusiasm are contagious; so if the reader likes what he is reading, the odds are much better that the listener will, too.

TELLING THE STORY

Do not assume that what you read here will make you a skilled storyteller. It may serve to introduce you to this speech art and to send you to more complete treatments of the subject. Then if you prepare your stories, practice them, and tell them again and again, you may develop some of the skill of the ancient storytellers, who were welcome in every castle and cottage.

Stories should be told to children (and adults!) simply because they enjoy them. But with that enjoyment come other values: a temporary escape from the present self and environment, an appreciation of cultural values, a better understanding of people and their motives, a deeper sensitivity to all living things, an unconscious absorbing of language qualities.

While libraries, schools, and radio programs may have their "story hour," there is no one time for the telling of a story. It is most appreciated when it is suggested by the events or the discussion of the moment. The group should be in the mood for a story. If it is "story time," this mood will have to be created.

Your preparation for storytelling should, first of all, be a general one. This means that you should not only have a command of language, voice, and body, but also a stock of stories and an alertness as to the right story for the moment.

Preparation for a particular story should be made in the way that is most effective for you. It would probably include a first appreciative reading of the story. If you enjoyed the story, yourself, and if you understood why the story made the impact upon you that it did, you would then go on with further preparation. Your next step might be to read it aloud two or three times; however, it might be to try telling it aloud in your own words after the first reading; it might be to try to write it out as you think you would like to tell it; it might be just sketching the significant aspects of characters and action. If you wish to keep the charm of the author's language, you will probably want to reread it aloud after trying to tell it. In any case, we must realize that children will like the story best if it is "in your head."

Any storyteller likes to have the complete attention of his hearers. But usually it is up to him to get it. It will help if your listeners are seated in a fairly comfortable position and so all of them can see you. How they react to you as a person is the first factor in getting their attention. The next is your opening sentence. Often "once upon a time" will do. A question, such as, How would you like to hear a ghost story? can also be effective. You may want to make a brief statement about the story or why you are going to tell this particular one. Once you have the attention, go on, and don't disappoint them.

Your opening sentences will indicate much of your relationship to the group. You want them to feel that you have something to share with them which you have enjoyed yourself, and are enjoying again in the retelling. Therefore, you are not taking the role of a superior talking down to them; neither should they be aware of any attempt on your part to manipulate characters or language.   Your art must "conceal art."   You cannot be effective with either voice or body until the story has become a part of you.

As you are learning to tell stories, however, it would be well to "listen in" on your voice and have an awareness of your bodily actions occasionally. (If possible, have another adult be your observer.)   Try to detect any tendency for your voice to get on a high, strained, indirect key.   Listen to see if you are making the mistake of using a melody pattern that is artificially varied, with too many long slides and sustained notes.   Observe any tendency to become monotonous in the tempo and stressing of syllables.   Note whether or not your voice quality is becoming flat and colorless, perhaps expressing some state of mind that is unrelated to the mood of the story.   Keep a nice balance of bodily alertness and relaxation, but note whether your listeners are *watching* your actions instead of feeling them as a part of the meaning.   Try to catch any inclination to repeat too often the same facial expression, movement of the head, or gesture.   But above all, let your expressions be *you*!

FOR FURTHER READING

Aggertt, Otis J. and Elbert R. Bowen: *Communicative Reading*, 2d ed., The Macmillan Company, New York, 1963.

Armstrong, Chloe and Paul D. Brandes: *The Oral Interpretation of Literature*, McGraw-Hill Book Company, New York, 1963.

Eisenson, Jon and Paul H. Boase: *Basic Speech*, 2d ed., The Macmillan Company, New York, 1964, chap. 18.

Lee, Charlotte I.: *Oral Interpretation*, 3d ed., Houghton Mifflin Company, Boston, 1965.

Mouat, Lawrence H.: *Reading Literature Aloud*, Oxford University Press, New York, 1962.

Reid, Ronald F., ed.: *Introduction to the Field of Speech*, Scott, Foresman and Company, Chicago, 1965, chap. 3.

Seaberg, Dorothy I.: "Can the Ancient Art of Storytelling Be Revived?" *The Speech Teacher,* September, 1968, pp. 246–249.

Sessions, Virgil D. and Jack B. Holland: *Your Role in Oral Interpretation*, Holbrook Press, Inc., Boston, 1968.

CHAPTER SIXTEEN

TELEPHONE, RADIO, AND TELEVISION

The electronic media—the telephone, public address system, radio, and television—have added new dimensions to the teacher's role as a speaker. Their essential similarities as means for the transmission and reception of sound, and particularly the human voice, audibly and quickly over long distances or in large areas of space, have produced this change. They have enhanced his world of interpersonal communication. They have increased his responsibilities to participate in broadcasting situations outside the school in order to fulfill certain professional or public relations functions. They have further challenged him to know the theory and practice of oral communication, employing his skills over intraschool telephone, sound and radio systems, as well as through closed-circuit television for classroom instruction. In some situations, he also speaks on open-circuit television to student listeners at home, who are taking high school or college courses. Because any of his communication may be recorded on regular magnetic tape or videotape, his potential use of these media and the effects of his oral performance are greatly expanded.

TELEPHONE AND PUBLIC ADDRESS SYSTEM

THE TELEPHONE

Although texts and pamphlets on telephone technique are available to you, certain basic points are not usually covered. These follow. Outside your face-to-face communication, you use the telephone more than any other electronic medium. It is the most personal of all. Most of your calls are on a one-to-one basis—you talk directly with the listener—and like most teachers, you could not survive professionally without the telephone. Used properly, it is probably your most effective communication instrument.

Your principal calls you on the school phone or intercom system to instruct you about a new schedule. You call fellow teachers to arrange social and business meetings. You use long distance to arrange quickly a section program for your state teachers association. You talk with the parents of a child who is ill, or needs special help in his work. You discuss plans for the appearance of students at a luncheon of the Rotary Club. You convince the business manager of the need for a new piece of equipment in your laboratory—by making a phone call. You set up a reserve reading shelf in the library by talking with the reference librarian over the intercom system. You agree to accept a change in arrangements for a field trip you are planning when the bus company dispatcher explains on the phone that his drivers are not available. You call the students involved to make a hurried change of departure time for the trip.

All these situations, and many more, necessitate your using the telephone tactfully and effectively. It is fast; you and your listeners can react immediately to each other's remarks and feelings. You can raise questions, answer them, explain problems—all in a matter of minutes—and arrive at conclusions impossible by other means of communication. In your life as a teacher, the telephone is the core of an extended program of human relations that you must maintain. In using it successfully, you must adapt attitude, knowledge, and oral communication skills to its limitations and particular advantages in extending the scope of your speech activities.

THE PUBLIC ADDRESS SYSTEM

Rarely can an active, competent teacher escape the need of using a public address system at certain times. The situation may vary from your employing an amplifier in a large classroom, the sound system in the school auditorium, or a microphone setup for a talk at a professional conference in a hotel, to using the same type of equipment at an outdoor ceremony such as a commencement.

Of course, there is no reason to use it if you do not need it. You must realize that a microphone demands that you stay close enough and in the proper location for you always to be "on mike." You cannot, therefore, move as much or as freely as you would without it. A microphone also sets up a physical barrier between you and your audience; you may tend to talk *to* it rather than *through* it, especially if you lack training and experience. Thus, some loss of directness and rapport with your audience may develop.

The advantages of using a microphone include these: (1) you can reach a large or diffuse audience in a manner having the intimacy of your delivery to a small group, and (2) you may also override distraction or noise by the sheer power or capacity of the equipment.

Certain suggestions are relevant. Use the same volume and inflection you would use in talking to a smaller group. Keep your speaking direct and conversational. Let the system do the work of projecting your voice. Most systems permit you to have your face about eighteen inches from the microphone. Do not shout; you will inevitably produce vocal distortion if you do.

You may also create undesirable tension in your audience. Talk to the audience as though you were addressing fifteen to twenty persons in a small room. Do not touch the microphone or the standard. Do not kick the base of the stand. Avoid coughing, explosive laughing, heavy breathing, and paper rattling during your talk.

As a precaution, personally check the equipment in advance, and if possible, run through your talk once over the system before giving your actual presentation.

RADIO AND TELEVISION

Fortunately, effective speaking is effective speaking whether it is delivered to an audience face-to-face or over radio or television. The principles of such effectivenes in conference, interview, discussion, classroom or public speech, discussed in earlier chapters, also apply to radio and television. Each speaker needs a significant subject governed by a definite purpose, with clear organization and good content, adapted to his student or community audience and occasion. He requires sufficient practice to develop oral language that is clear and convincing, and a suitable delivery adapted to the circumstances. In support of these observations, Dr. Harold Nelson, Head of Radio and Television at Pennsylvania State University, makes this statement:

> *Too many speakers think they should be doing something quite different when speaking on the radio than when speaking with a live audience. Actually, this is not so! The same qualities of direct, informal, conversational communication are needed, while making the necessary adjustments to the mechanics of the radio medium.*[1]

Some of these basic principles, however, necessitate particular consideration and adaptation to radio and television.

There are certain principles important in the presenting of a speech in face-to-face situations that also apply to radio and television. These include novelty and contrast, careful preparation, exact timing, broad appeal, strong personal communication, and effective voice and diction.

[1] Harold E. Nelson, "Broadcast Training in Speech Departments," *The Speech Teacher*, vol. 13, no. 4, November, 1964.

NOVELTY AND CONTRAST

The ordinary speech or lecture should be avoided on radio and television. Audiences on these media have come to expect more than the individual, personal presentation unless the speaker has distinctiveness or a certain impact such as that of a Martin Luther King or a Fulton Sheen. It is better to plan something with more novelty and contrast—a discussion, an interview, a symposium, or a question-answer situation.

CAREFUL PREPARATION

To ensure against distraction in the radio or television audience, the preparation of the talk is most vital. The organization should be simple and easy to follow. Relationships between points must be clear; transitions should aid the listener to move easily from point to point.

The speaker should make his specific purpose clear early in the talk and should restate and reemphasize it at appropriate times as the talk proceeds, using internal summaries to point up his development of ideas.

In radio or television discussion, the leader has a similar role. He must point up relationships for the listeners between contributions as they are made, connecting them to the key ideas and purposes presented throughout the discussion. Such devices clarify the progress of the deliberation of the speakers as it occurs.

EXACT TIMING

In broadcasting, "time is money," and therefore studio employees, as well as speakers, must observe split-second schedules. Any speech, discussion, or interview that does not use its assigned time requires the station to fill the gap with some kind of "standby" material. Any performance that runs overtime is routinely cut off the air. Both of these situations can be avoided by careful preparation and exact timing of the manuscript, realistic practice in delivering it, and by conscientious cooperation with station personnel.

BROAD APPEAL

By their very nature, open-circuit television and radio reach audiences of wide interests. A speaker must remember to serve this wide appeal in the choice, planning, and presentation of his talk. Unless a selected group such as a class is indicated as a listening group over closed-circuit television, he must have universality in his choice of basic content, illustrations, and examples in order to hold the interest of a widely heterogeneous audience. His language, also, should be selected for its immediate understanding by his listeners, many of whom may not be giving him their undivided attention.

STRONG PERSONAL COMMUNICATION

Radio and television audiences differ from those that confront a speaker before a class or a community group. Instead of their being assembled in a classroom or auditorium, where the speaker sees them and addresses them somewhat formally as a large group, they are in their homes, in cars, in business places—alone or in very small, intimate groups. The message to them must be very personal and very direct. Composition and delivery suitable for a large crowd will be inappropriate for the family group in the living room.

The personal, communicative, conversational style needed for radio and television speaking can be developed. The speaker uses familiar expressions, a conversational manner, direct address using "I," "you," "we," "us," etc., and personal appeals. He usually achieves intimate techniques of delivery more successfully by broadcasting from a studio in which methods can readily be adapted to the home listening groups to be reached.

EFFECTIVE USE OF VOICE AND DICTION

Broadcasting requires more skillful use of the speaker's voice and diction than ordinary speaking. In radio, exclusively an audio medium, voice is 100 percent of delivery. In television, it is at least 50 percent of the job. Effective control of all of the elements of voice is essential to successful radio and television speaking—pleasant, serviceable vocal quality; pitch and melody with suitable contrasts; intelligent use of rate, phrasing, and pause; ability to use force and emphasis meaningfully; clear-cut articulation and diction. Conversely, lack of these attributes is a distinct liability in broadcasting. An unpleasant quality, ineffective vocal control, or careless diction can ruin the presentation of the message, no matter how carefully it has been prepared.

USABLE SCRIPT FORMS AND PROGRAMS—
RADIO AND TELEVISION[2]

The general principles for speaking over radio and television developed essential guides for you in adapting your individual speaking skills to broadcasting media. Further use of these media in your teaching rests upon your knowing considerably more about radio and television. *Extensive* use requires that you become an expert in these fields so that you have high proficiency in them.

This section attempts to give elementary information and initial direction to your use of radio and television in teaching. One of the first essentials is that you know something about basic script and program forms available to you and become aware of some of their possibilities. This knowledge should help you in choosing and preparing those types that you and your students may develop.

START WITH A PURPOSE. In preparing a script or program for educational broadcasting, decide first upon your *purpose*, not upon the script *form*. Many purposes exist. Ask yourself these questions as guides. Do I desire primarily to create appreciations and stress attitudes? Am I especially concerned with broadening pupil interests? Shall I try to motivate student reading and investigation? Is my basic goal the development of critical thinking? Do I wish to establish certain basic principles?

GENERAL SUGGESTIONS. Classroom scripts often lack variety and new material. Try to avoid stereotyping and "standardizing" your pattern, simply because the first script succeeds. If the same writer does a *series*, be sure that he is aware of the students' needs for a change of pace and a fresh approach as means of holding interest.

Avoid the booby trap of using available material simply because it is available. Preplanned teacher guides in the file often may tempt you unwisely as the primary basis for your content. *Think of your listeners*, also. Revise script forms after each use to provide a shift of emphasis, new personalities, new examples and illustrations, and current data.

Try to escape the pedagogical style so common in educational writing. Concentrate on language appealing to the pupil rather than the acceptable or

---

[2] Adapted from William Levenson and Edward Stasheff, *Teaching through Radio and Television*, Holt, Rinehart and Winston, Inc., New York, 1952, pp. 66–115, 130–166.

approved jargon of fellow educators. You are trying to get messages through to the students, not showing off your erudition to your colleagues.

Know your material thoroughly. Research your areas for content completely. Write from a basis of plenty, not from scarcity or superficiality of material.

Know the types of scripts and programs that have been used successfully in educational broadcasting. These are the straight talk; the interview; the panel or round table; the forum or debate; the actuality broadcast; the quiz; the demonstration; the simulated classroom or classroom demonstration; the dramatization and musical drama; the public relations program; and the musical program. A discussion of the first nine of the above types follows.

THE STRAIGHT TALK. As we have already noted, this form may often be used on radio but rarely on television unless the speaker is distinctive or a striking personality. For a radio program it has certain advantages—it takes only one person, requires a minimum of rehearsal, and is simple to produce. From an educational point of view, a well-developed talk can include a great deal of information in a short time. The form is direct and the responsibility is fixed. If the speaker's personality is attractive and holds interest, a talk can be a valuable program. For small children, it is easy to listen to, because only one voice presents the message to them. The limitations of the straight talk are those mentioned earlier in the section on basic principles— ineffective communication can ruin it. For classroom use, teachers should be careful of the controversial subject when given a one-sided treatment by a speaker. They should also avoid using speakers not having animated delivery.

In addition to earlier general suggestions, these specific guides may help. Write for the *ear* not for the *eye*—the way a script *sounds* is more important than the way it *looks* or *reads* silently. Establish attention at once; then introduce the basic material. Use the experience of the pupil-listener on which to build and *add* new concepts. Avoid long and complex sentences; employ concrete, familiar words. Draw illustrations and examples from the pupils' experience. Employ humor. Children like to hear about people; write about people. Use human interest materials, references to experience, lively illustrations and descriptions. As a teacher-speaker, "sell" yourself to the student listeners; they will then also want to hear and see *you*. Keep your language conversational, using the "you" form to help establish a common bond; however—beware of "talking down" to children. Be sincere, without affectation in manner and voice. Talk the child's language, but make it genuine. Present only a few *new* concepts at a time. Assume little or no recall in radio talks. Perhaps the pupils were not listening! Employ a brief summary to "set" and recheck *key* ideas.

THE INTERVIEW. A common type of educational program, the interview can be very valuable. It allows you to bring outstanding personalities and well-known experts to your students. By raising questions "problem" situations can be created in an interview; thus, interest can be created and maintained. Prominent people become humanized in such a program. You, as a teacher, can guide the discussion to greatly benefit pupils. With two voices coming through monotony is avoided. However, the choice of interviewees is vital. You need informed persons with a certain style, for best appeal. Develop meaningful questions; avoid stilted, artificial ones. Try to stay away from technical, adult vocabulary.

In preparing, remember that a great interview personality for adults may not be considered so by children. Develop a well-rounded interview, presented with ease and facility. Tie points together with an appropriate summary conclusion.

Procedures in preparing the content of the interview vary: (1) in a preliminary meeting of the interviewer and the guest, the interviewer notes the most productive questions plus related points made by the expert, and uses these as the questions on the program; (2) a transcript is prepared of the informal conference, from which the final script is made; (3) questions are sent in advance to the expert; his answers are edited and from them questions are prepared for the program.

THE PANEL OR ROUND TABLE. This is a common but good type. In it conflicting points of view build an atmosphere of interest and dramatic quality. Listeners, especially students, get the point that dogmatic positions must be avoided, and that conclusions must be supported. Spontaneous exchanges are followed with interest.

A better program results if participants do not read scripts, but rather extemporize effectively as the discussion develops. Selection of expert, competent discussants of differing viewpoints is essential to a vital program. A provocative, current subject is also a fundamental need.

Even without a script, a preliminary meeting and rehearsal are necessary. The preliminary session establishes issues and lines of participation. A basic, guiding participant's outline can be developed from this meeting. Common grounds of agreement and conflict can also be noted. In general, it is better to have a designated leader or moderator. Much time can thus be saved, and "dead air" avoided during broadcasting. A recorded rehearsal and playback session help to ensure smoother air procedure and aid elimination of irrelevancies and digression. The leader can also develop a brief, specific summary to help the listeners.

THE FORUM OR DEBATE. This form resembles the panel in its purpose and development, but is usually more definitely structured. It can be a lively program that stimulates thinking, presents various points of view on a subject of interest, suitably worded for debate. Good speakers carry the ball in the first part of the period, and can handle questions in the second part, following all of the speakers' presentation.

In the Junior Town Meeting type, the program ran one-half hour. Two or three student speakers, each presenting a fundamental and differing viewpoint, gave initial speeches on the subject. A subject of local interest was the usual choice. After the prepared speeches, a question period, open to the studio audience, was held in which each speaker was "put on the spot" regarding his talk and ideas related to it. Best practice used a moderator to tie the talks together and channel questions, as well as audience question period with questions written out and submitted on cards, and some free-lancing if time permitted. The chairman introduced the speakers, summarized their original comments, handled and directed questions, made appropriate transitional comments, and summarized the product of the debate.

It is also possible to broadcast a standard school debate with slight modifications in time and format to obtain a similar type of program.

THE ACTUALITY BROADCAST. This "on-the-spot" broadcast of an event actually happening (live) can be very exciting. It also has the possibilities of vivid, emotional appeal, reality, and unexpected happenings. It rarely lacks interest. One possible limitation is that of loss of time because of delays in the event or the wrong emphasis, which might dominate air time. In listening to a Congressional debate, it could be suicide to be "stuck" with a monotonous roll call, intruding on air time before the actual debate. Sometimes the pickup and need to "fill in" are a challenge even to an experienced announcer. In preparation, the chief focus is on the event, not on a script. This means careful selection of the occasion is exceedingly important. A skillful narrator as announcer is a "must." To help, a supply in depth of facts of history, biographical material, a list of guests present, description and color, with possible questions for interviews are extremely useful.

THE QUIZ. This form is effective, stimulating, and interesting. It has a "game" format with questions used to develop worthwhile information. In some cases, it may have been overworked commercially with information *unrelated* to school use. Competition may have been overdone. In such situations, learning is incidental.

Careful planning can remove any such disadvantages. The rules must be clear, and stated briefly early in the program. Participants need to be identified and kept involved. Do not let the show drag. Avoid pauses, especially at the beginning. Easy questions are usually asked first, but build up in difficulty as the program proceeds. Questions should not all come from the same category or field successively; get variety, but relate all items to the common core. Timing must be done carefully. A quiz master who does not embarrass children is essential. Also, you must have the correct answers to all questions.

THE DEMONSTRATION. This is one of television's great contributions to education because of its ability to teach skills. The most successful programs have been in art and science because of their fundamentally *visual* nature. Music demonstrations have been vivid because of the possibility of reinforcing individual demonstration with symphonic work, and the accompanying audio product that commands interest. In each case, whatever subject is used, the problem is to build upon the student's existing knowledge, which is often difficult to determine. Therefore, most demonstration programs "begin at scratch" and review, briefly but interestingly, the basic principles to be used in the program.

The benefits of demonstration on television are obvious. In preparing, be aware that the camera places each viewer in the very center of the demonstration. He can see things on the screen that he could not possibly view, even if he were crowded around a table on which the demonstration is taking place. The camera work in many presentations is almost miraculous. Added to this, a skillful demonstrator whose comments are relevant, fluent and not too fast, whose hands operate almost independently of his speech, and whose material is interesting, is the key to a stimulating experience for young people who view him. When he also enlists the help of some of his interested students, he adds an additional element of audience satisfaction.

THE SIMULATED CLASSROOM OR CLASSROOM DEMONSTRATION. Used over radio, this program attempts to maintain the natural atmosphere of the classroom while the teacher and pupils go about their regular business in the lesson for the day. On radio, the experience for the listener limits the program to one dimension—that of sound. Such an effort may retain many of the regular features of classroom teaching, but obviously eliminates the chalkboard and other visual stimuli.

Because of the difficulty and expense of taking mobile equipment into schools, other versions have been tried with some success. The first, over *radio*, moves the teacher and the class to the studio where they try to present their day's lesson in a much easier situation for production. As microphones and various technical necessities are introduced, the natural atmosphere is gradually lost. If rehearsals are required, the loss is more evident as formalism takes over.

On *television*, the simulated classroom is often employed, clearly as a means of saving time and expense by having all participants come to a broadcasting studio, prepared to represent as many of the familiar classroom details as possible. Under these conditions, *audible* and *visible* aspects are present in the viewing situation. However, because certain added necessary adjustments must be made for television—lighting, color of materials, location of the chalkboard and classroom furniture in relation to cameras and microphones and others—the natural atmosphere of a classroom also disappears. Essential rehearsals for television further remove certain aspects of spontaneous participation.

However, after the teacher and pupils have learned the demands and limitations of the studio, they become more sophisticated and do very effective work. As a teacher faced with the responsibility of planning or appearing in such a program, you will need both professional assistance, training, and experience before you gain maximum results.

DRAMATIZATION. This form of program, using a well-developed script, can present ideas very effectively. It can result in a powerful emotional appeal. A great many subjects can be handled via the dramatic program. It can afford opportunity for expression to many individuals with memorable impressions. Successful commercial dramatic programs have made great use of the juvenile interests in adventure and humor. The radio educator of course cannot use Hollywood principles and give the children what they want. Mature judgment, intelligent planning, and high standards must be maintained. However, the adventure appeal is present in the writings they study in English in the works of Stevenson, Irving, Mark Twain, and others. Properly handled, the same interests can be utilized if you attempt to write and produce a dramatization for radio or television. In so doing you face a more difficult task than that of preparing the other program forms.   However, it is worth the effort to work with the dramatization, using simple situations and plots in which children play children's parts.   Sometimes music may be introduced as an integral part of such a program.   Care should always be taken to clear copyrighted selections before they are used, however. Examples of such simple forms are the fiesta of a foreign land, often the favorite in a school-assembly program, and certain kinds of story dramatization.

Original scripts can serve as an excellent means of integrating creative work in writing, speaking, and acting.   Care should be taken to keep technical details of setting, costume, lighting, and properties on the simple side, also.

Usable successful dramatic scripts may be procured from educational, radio, and television stations such as those in New York City, Chicago, Rochester, Toledo, and Cleveland, as well as libraries of college or university stations. The U.S. Office of Education and many organizations also are sources of similar script materials.

It is also helpful to consider types of programs as they relate to equipment, since many schools operate on very restricted budgets and facilities.   The lists which follow attempt to indicate such possibilities.

TYPES OF PROGRAMS RELATED TO EQUIPMENT

1   Limited Equipment
   a   Radio or television talks
   b   Readings and storytelling
   c   Newscasts and announcements
   d   Comedy routine (one person)
   e   Comedy program (two persons)
   f   Interviews
   g   Commentary
   h   Book review
   i   Simple quiz program
   j   Sportscast
   k   Special event: on-the-spot commentary
   l   Disc jockey
   m   Music: solo instrumental; solo vocal
   n   Poetry program: lecture recital

o   Readers' theater: poetry or drama
p   Choric interpretation
q   Round table: three or four people
r   Variety program—with individual numbers

2   More Extensive Equipment.   All the above are possible, plus these as suggestions:

a   Dramatic shows
b   Chorus: vocal music; quartets—instrumental or vocal
c   Dramatizations and adaptations of short stories, novels, travel
d   Women's programs through demonstrations: styles, food, furnishings
e   Agricultural programs
f   Special occasion shows
g   Public service programs: school and community
h   Town Meeting of the Air; larger round tables
i   Audience participation shows
j   Assembly programs

Some teachers develop interest and helpful programs through the organization of clubs or through radio or television workshops in their schools. Others find the FM or ETV station in a school a valuable means of developing a wider, more stable total program of activities.

It is impossible in this chapter to cover all the services needed to train teachers who would desire to utilize fully and expertly their proficiencies in radio and television.   It is hoped that the directions indicated may stimulate you, if you have such interest, to enroll in summer programs and workshops, and in numerous in-service institutes, many of which are subsidized by the federal government and by colleges, universities, and school systems cooperating in such enterprises.

FOR FURTHER READING

Dale, Edgar: *Audio-Visual Methods of Teaching*, rev. ed., Holt, Rinehart and Winston, Inc., New York, 1954, chaps. 14 and 17.

Levenson, William and Edward Stasheff: *Teaching Through Radio and Television*, Holt, Rinehart and Winston, Inc., New York, 1952.

McBurney, James H. and Ernest J. Wrage: *Guide to Good Speech*, 3d ed., Prentice-Hall, Inc., Englewood Cliffs, N.J., 1965, chap. 22.

Wood, K. P.: "The Voice on the Telephone," *Journal of Communication*, November, 1951, pp. 12–15.

Zelko, Harold P. and Frank E. X. Dance: *Business and Professional Speech Communication*, Holt, Rinehart and Winston, Inc., New York, 1965, chap. 11.

INDEX

This book was set in Intertype Garamond by Monotype Composition Company, Inc., and printed on permanent paper and bound by The Maple Press Company. The designer was J. Paul Kirouac; the drawings were done by B. Handleman Associates, Inc. The editors were Robert Fry and David Dunham. Les Kaplan supervised the production.